April 2002

For dear Isabelle —
 and her wonderful family with love from our family.
 Shalom,
  Lillian Siskin

American Jews:
What Next?

EDGAR E. SISKIN

The Jerusalem Publishing House

For Our Children

JONATHAN, JOSHUA, SHARONE

And Their Children

Copyright ©1998 Edgar E. Siskin

All rights reserved. No part of this publication may be reproduced in any manner without permission in writing from the publisher, except brief extracts quoted in articles or reviews.

Published by The Jerusalem Publishing House
39 Tchernichovsky St
POB 7147
Jerusalem, Israel 91071

Printed and bound by Keterpress, Jerusalem
Designed and typeset by In-House Services, Jerusalem

Contents

Preface   v

1 When Cultures Interact   1
Cultures in Collision / Death of A Culture / American Cultural Colossus

2 Lost Tribes & Living Relics   11
Historic Tides of Acculturation — Egyptian, Babylonian, Persian, Greco-Roman / Jews Defect in Muslim World / Professed Descendants of the Ten Lost Tribes / The Goal of Aliya — Beta Israel, Bene Yisrael and Others / Pilgrim Fathers, American Indians, Crypto-Jews / Deep in the Heart of Texas — Lost in the Multitude

3 Jewish Acculturation & Assimilation in America   24
Major Jewish Migrations to America / Faith and Vision of Jewish Immigrants and American Pilgrims / Jews Accommodate to Surrounding Culture — Hanukah and Christmas / From Extant to Extinct — Jews in Small-Town America

4 The Varieties of Jewish Religious Experience   37
Three forms of Observance — and Non-Observance / The Sabbath (Shabbat) / High Holidays / Judaism in Mid-Twentieth Century America / Reform Judaism / Jewish Homes with no Mezzuzah / The Marketing of Holiness / God in the Twilight / Civil Religion / Nails in the Coffin / "Guidance not Governance" / Conservative Judaism: Resisting Reform Respectably / Growth, Malaise, Liberal Ferment / Statement of Principles / Bar/Bat Mitzvah American Style / Cultural Winds of Change

5 The Acculturation of Orthodox Judaism   61

Orthodoxy Turns Right / Reasons for Revival / Ultra-Orthodoxy and Acculturation / Feminism / Law (Halacha) and Custom (Minhag) / The Orthodox and Change / Orthodoxy and Sexuality / The World's Slow Stain

6 Modern Behavior of An Ancient People   77

Family in Transition / Marriage / Divorce / Zero Population Growth / Domestic Violence / Addiction / Suicide / Cults / Spirituality / Homosexuality / Crime

7 Walking Down the Aisle .... Where To?   98

Then and Now / Why Jews Intermarry / Interdating / Rabbis Who Officiate / The Synagogue Confronts Intermarriage / Optimists and Realists / Conversion, Outreach, Inreach

8 Incurable Virus   112

Jews on Approval / Virus at Large / Abandonment of the Jews / American Christians and Antisemitism / Anti-Zionism / Roman Catholics and Jews / Pope John Paul II / Protestants and Jews / Evangelical Protestants and the Jews / Blacks and Antisemitism / The College Campus / Media / Myths, Distortions, Falsehoods / Spreading Islamic Terror / Fade-Out of Objective Truth / Jewish Troublers of Israel / English Literature on the Jews / American Authors on Jews / The Culture of Antisemitism / Eliminationist Antisemitism

9 American Jews & Israel   146

Seduction by the Liberal-Left / Anti-Israel American Jews / The Avoidance of Aliya / Hopes and Fears / Religious Conflict: Eternal Contradiction / Orthodox and Non-Orthodox Today / An American Non-Orthodox View of Israeli Judaism / An Israeli View of American Non-Orthodox Judaism / Reluctant Non-Orthodox Leaders / Zionist Euphoria Wanes

Epilogue   175

Glossary   182

Preface

Today a growing number of Jews are expressing concern about the condition of Jewish life in America. In particular, findings of the 1990 National Jewish Population Survey have caused apprehension about the continued viability of the American Jewish community. Prior to the Survey's appearance, there had been a general complacency about the future of Jews and Judaism in America. Sociologists and rabbis had written roseate descriptions of the Jewish condition, and their predictions about the future of American Jewish life were optimistic when not euphoric. This was the received wisdom of the uncritical Jewish consensus from which there was little dissent. But since the publication of the 1990 Survey, doubts have been voiced on the prospects for untroubled, crisis-free Jewish continuity.

My interest in the condition of the American Jew has grown out of an intimate association since childhood with Jews and their collective life. My own life began as the son of an Orthodox cantor and rabbi in Edinburgh, Scotland. Not long after the family moved to the United States, I became a student at the Hebrew Union College, the Reform Jewish rabbinical seminary in Cincinnati, Ohio. Since ordination, I have been rabbi of two congregations — in New Haven, Connecticut, with an old-line, classical Reform congregation, and in Glencoe, Illinois, with a proliferating suburban congregation which grew to number approximately two thousand families. I, like all rabbis, was active in the plethoric organizational life of the local and national Jewish communities and gained a minute knowledge of American Jews in all their religious, social, and cultural diversity. The personal and vocational pattern of my life thus enabled me to be a participant-observer in the full range of Jewish practice, belief, and culture from the strict observance of Orthodoxy to the liberal extreme of Reform.

A second perspective from which I have been able to view the American Jewish scene is that of an anthropologist. My first rabbinical position in New Haven gave me the opportunity to pursue graduate study at Yale. As a student in the Department of Anthropology, it was my singular good fortune to come under the influence of Edward Sapir, one of the great anthropologists and linguists of our time. Son of a cantor himself, Sapir was thoroughly conversant with the world of Jewish knowledge, mediated through his own upbringing, his familiarity with

Hebrew, and his emotional ties with Yiddish. Sapir was an inspiring teacher who, through his person and the insights he imparted, changed the course of my intellectual life.

Through my studies in anthropology and my experiences as a rabbi, it became clear to me that the history of the Jews and their culture could be fully understood only by considering the influences exerted upon them by the peoples among whom they have lived. For 2000 years, rabbis and Talmudic scholars have paid scant attention to the secular factors that have inevitably shaped the practice of Judaism and molded much of Jewish life. Based on the conviction that there is an authentic, unique "essence" in Judaism, they believed that whatever does not exemplify that essence is "profane" and therefore irrelevant. This "internal censorship" (Gershom Scholem's term)[1] rules out any objective approach to Jewish historical and religious phenomena. From the standpoint of the dispassionate student of human societies, however, no valid understanding of the Jewish historic experience can be reached without assessing the influence of dominant alien cultures. Such an assessment reveals the inevitability of Jewish acculturation, whether in ancient Alexandria, Kaifeng (China), or present day America.

The distinguished anthropologist Alfred L. Kroeber, stressed the role of acculturation in the unfolding of history. "A large part of history the world over," he has written, "possibly more than half of it, deals ultimately with the results of intercultural influencing — that is, acculturation."[2] The crucial role of acculturation is apparent in any attempt to understand the development of American Jewish life. For it is the culture of the general society which has decisively influenced the Jewish experience of American Jews. That culture, at odds in many ways with inherited Jewish values and traditions, has won the devotion and adherence of the overwhelming majority of American Jews.

Even among the Orthodox minority, committed to the canons of ancestral practice and belief, forces in the dominant culture are insinuating themselves into the traditional patterns of Judaism. Some of the age-old constraints which governed Jewish life are being relaxed. From the high profile media campaigns of the Lubavitcher Hasidim, which feature mitzvah-mobiles[3], billboard advertising, and glossy periodicals of worldwide circulation, to the growing pressure for fuller participation by women in the program of the synagogue, their donning of elegant wigs, hats and dresses for *shul*, the Klezmer bands blasting their rock and roll at weddings, the increase in divorce, and the "gradual disappearance of the ascetic ideal,"[4] it would appear that the limits of the permissible in traditional Judaism are being stretched.

At the same time, we cannot discount the rise in recent years among the younger generation of Orthodox Jews of a counterreformation emphasizing the meticulous observance of stringencies (*humras*) long neglected.

Two contrary influences thus are seen to be operating in the Orthodox community: on one hand, the tide of American modernity pulls it toward what Haym Soloveitchik calls the "embourgoisement of the religious community," and, on the other, the pressure toward the more stringent observance of mitzvot, based upon the enshrinement of texts as the final authority. The course of this conflict may help determine the future of Orthodoxy. Meanwhile, according to Soloveitchik, God is no longer felt as a daily, natural force and presence in the lives of contemporary Jews, which thus distances them from the Jews and Judaism of past generations.[5]

In an earlier age, Jewish exiles lamented, "By the rivers of Babylon, there we sat, [and] wept when we remembered Zion" (*Psalms 137,1*). Today most of their distant descendants in America rejoice, "By the rivers of Babylon, there we sat, and had the time of our lives." There may be ripples of disenchantment and murmurs of discontent, but no religious or ethnic group has been more enamored of America than the Jews. For America with its attainable rewards has sung a siren song which Jews have found irresistible. Moreover, the moral vision of the Founding Fathers, embodying the ideals of freedom and justice and echoing the voices of their own Prophets, resonated with a powerful appeal to a people schooled in suffering and perennially victimized by discrimination and oppression. At the same time, Jews are worried by signs that antisemitism is gaining strength. It is apparent among Blacks, in the media, and among certain Christian religious groups. No one knows what the outcome might be. It already may have diminished the readiness of some Jews to identify as Jews themselves. One of the "dismal findings" of the 1990 National Jewish Population Survey was that 625,000 Jews (approximately 10 percent of American Jews) are "currently practicing another religion."[6]

What is beyond dispute is the creeping eclipse of the traditional value system of Jewish life in the American milieu of recent decades. Family, home, and faith, once bulwarks of that life, have suffered destabilization and erosion. The pace of assimilation, with intermarriage its bellwether, is accelerating. The question is being asked whether, save among the Orthodox, Jewish survival in America may be in doubt. Joyce once wrote of a "sparrow under the wheels of Juggernaut."[7]

The question of Jewish survival in America has interested me since I first became a rabbi. In those early years, I was soon made aware of the impoverishment of Jews in the knowledge of their religious and historical tradition. I vividly remember the first session with my Bible class when no single member of the more than fifty present could identify Joshua, Moses' successor. Soon enough I realized that most of my congregation were Jewishly illiterate.

Studying anthropology at Yale led me to understand the crucial cultural forces at work in the drama of Jewish continuity and survival. Powerful currents in the secular world were determining the religious fate of Jews in New Haven as well as in the larger arena of America. As it had with societies in other times and places, acculturation leading to assimilation seemed the inevitable outcome of interaction between a weaker and a stronger culture.

I had observed the process of cultural breakdown during several seasons of field study among the Washo Indians of Nevada-California. I saw a native Indian culture with all its spirit-world sanctities crumble under the impact of Euro-American culture, its religious universe evanesce, its language abandoned. It was no different for American Jews. I have been a personal witness to cultural assimilation among both native Americans and American Jews.

Documenting my interest and concern for the viability of American Judaism, I gave two papers at annual conventions of the Central Conference of American Rabbis. In 1952, speaking on the subject, The Impact of American Culture Upon the Jew, I said, "The question of survival in an alien world has always concerned the Jew but never more insistently than today." I cited two scholars who were then troubled by the question of American Jewish viability: Professor Harry A. Wolfson of Harvard, who had somberly observed, "The law that is Judaism is something alien in the world in which we live, and to obey it is all sacrifice and no awards," and Professor Eli Ginzberg of Columbia, who had written, "[Despite the Holocaust], the vast majority of American Jews feel little compulsion to adopt a positive attitude (and behavior) to Judaism."[8]

In 1964, the 75th anniversary of the Central Conference of American Rabbis, I presented a paper in which I contrasted the "exuberant optimism" of the C.C.A.R. founders on the quality of American Jewish life in the years ahead with the "uncertainty and skepticism [which in 1964] stalk discussions of the Jewish future." I quoted the demographer who, noting that Jews were not reproducing themselves, foresaw that "in another generation" the Jewish percentage of the national population would decline from 2.9 to 1.6 per cent. I wondered whether the "high tragedy of Jewish persistence in the midst of persecution is to find its counterpoint in the low comedy of Jewish dissolution in the midst of prosperity. It is [ironic] that having flourished in a free society, Jews may be threatened, not by anti-Semitism, but by the inertia and indifference which are the consequences of [acculturation]."[9]

Over the decades I have pursued a personal pilgrimage as a participant-observer intimately associated with the religious and communal life of the American Jew, as well as an anthropologist involved in the theory and field experience of cultural dynamics. This background, different from that of other writers on the American Jewish experience, has provided a singular perspective for evaluating the present and future of Jews, Judaism, and Jewish life in America.

I have sometimes been asked how I, son of an Orthodox rabbi, raised in an Orthodox family, could have become a Reform rabbi. The story is of a boy who left England with his parents to come to America. We arrived in Joliet, Illinois, a small industrial town west of Chicago, where my father became rabbi of the first of a string of small congregations. Born in Lithuania, he attended the Shavel Yeshiva. As a small boy, I began studying with my father, a daily discipline which eventually gave me a familiarity with Biblical Hebrew.

Joliet observed a community interfaith service on Thanksgiving. For one such service my father, as rabbi of the city, was asked to offer the opening prayer. A Reform rabbi from Chicago, Samuel Cohon, had been invited to preach the sermon. After the service the men talked and soon discovered that they had a good deal in common, from origins in Eastern Europe to a fund of Talmudic knowledge exchanged in rapid quotations. They respected and liked each other.

The next time my father went to Chicago, he took me in tow. Once in his book-lined study, Rabbi Cohon took down a Hebrew Pentateuch with Rashi (famous Biblical commentator) and asked me to read. As soon as I was done, Cohon, who had proselyte genes, began talking to my father about registering me for admission at the Hebrew Union College (H.U.C.).

Upon arriving in Joliet, I entered high school. The superior curriculum of my English school, including Latin and Greek, made it obvious that their school had little to "teach" me. I became something of a celebrity, graduating at the age of 14.

The following semester, at age 15, I entered the H.U.C. which would prepare me for a career as a Reform rabbi. I had nothing to do with the decision, just a willingness to do whatever my parents suggested. The fact that I entered H.U.C. with a scholarship and that my family was poor facilitated this decision. Neither my father nor I knew anything about Reform Judaism or that the rabbinical training I would get at their seminary was a far cry from that of the Shavel Yeshivah.

Notes

1. Gershom Scholem, *Sabbatai Sevi: The Mystical Messiah* (Princeton, N.J.: Princeton University Press, 1973), p. 11
2. Alfred L. Kroeber, *Anthropology*, rev. ed. (New York: Harcourt Brace and Company, 1948), p. 425
3. Caravans containing the accessories for ritual observance, such as *tallit* (prayer shawl), *tefilin* (phylacteries), and prayer books
4. Haym Soloveitchik, "Rupture and Reconstruction: The Transformation of Contemporary Orthodoxy," in *Tradition*, Summer 1994
5. *Ibid.*
6. Goldberg, "Statistics War," in *Jerusalem Post*, December 12, 1991
7. Richard Ellman, *James Joyce* (New York: Oxford University Press, 1959), p. 355

8. Edgar E. Siskin, "The Impact of American Culture Upon the Jew," in *Central Conference of American Rabbis Yearbook*, (New York: C.C.A.R., 1952), vol. 62, p. 377
9. Edgar E. Siskin, "Jewish Survival and Jewish Identity," in *Central Conference of American Rabbis Yearbook*, (New York: C.C.A.R., 1964), vol. 74, pp. 139, 131

CHAPTER 1

WHEN CULTURES INTERACT

In the 1930's the American Anthropological Association, responding to the increasing interest among anthropologists in the interaction between cultures, delegated three leading anthropologists, Robert Redfield, Ralph Linton, and Melville Herskovits, to define the concept of acculturation. In 1935 they published a memorandum delineating acculturation as "those phenomena which result when groups of individuals having different cultures come into continuous firsthand contact, with subsequent changes in the original culture patterns of either or both groups."[1] The term "acculturation" has since entered the language as a recognized concept in the study of human societies and as a familiar term in literate discourse.

Cultures interact in a variety of modes. The influence of one culture upon another can be charted along a continuum of change from casual to overwhelming. In our own century, all societies have in some degree become acculturated to Euro-American civilization. Sometimes the encounter has been benign, sometimes disorienting, sometimes shattering. There are tribal societies which have managed to preserve some of their native institutions virtually intact. Others have seen their cultures slowly erode, still others have been "pervasively swamped." Kroeber records how acculturation may lead to the "extinction of one culture by absorption in the other."[2]

Cultures in Collision

In Bethlehem, birthplace of Jesus of Nazareth, at a news conference held just before Christmas in 1993, the town fathers, led by Mayor Elias Freij, spoke unanimously and fervently: "Let's start Christmas a month early the way they do in America." The mayor was euphoric about Bethlehem's future. Peace, he predicted, would bring five million tourists to Israel annually, two million to Bethlehem. His town would need three thousand additional hotel rooms. (Let it not be said that a stranger was turned away because there was no room at the hotel.) Mayor and townsfolk were apparently visualizing their Bethlehem as being less a shrine in the hills of Judea than a religious Disneyland.

Meanwhile, Manger Square, site of the Church of the Nativity, reverberated with carols blaring from loudspeakers and the relentless voices of shopkeepers badgering tourists to buy ritual objects and local gimcracks. A sentimental American mused, Whatever happened to the Bethlehem we invoked when we sang,

> O little town of Bethlehem
> How still we see thee lie.

The difference between the Bethlehem of the New Testament and the Disneyland version is the product of acculturation.

Christmas eve and New Year's eve fell on successive Friday evenings in 1993. Friday evening is the Jewish Sabbath eve, the onset of the holiest day of the week.[3] In most synagogues, the major religious service of the week takes place on Friday night. In 1993 in the United States because of the coincidence of Christmas and New Year's eves with the eve of the Jewish Sabbath, many congregations abandoned their major Sabbath service and substituted a brief early service, thus leaving the evening free. The following day, no Bar/Bat Mitzvahs were scheduled. In a textbook example of acculturation, the Jewish Sabbath had bowed to the constraints of the Christian calendar.

A company in Japan which for generations has made family altars is now manufacturing a model which incorporates a video monitor and cassette recorder. "The center of the household," announced the manufacturer, "has changed from the family altar to the TV set. To keep up with the times, we've arranged that people can pray while watching videos."[4] In another example of acculturation, a sacred Japanese artifact and its ritual use have undergone radical change thanks to the impact of Western technology.

North American Indian tribes exemplify all different modes and degrees of acculturation. The Sioux of the Great Plains have watched their buffalo-hunting culture disintegrate, but the Shawnee of Oklahoma have maintained their aboriginal kinship system practically unchanged. The Menominee of Wisconsin exhibit a variety of acculturation patterns in a single tribe. While "elite" Menominee all but deny their identity as Indians, "native-oriented" members are bent on reviving the aboriginal life. There are Navaho who have moved easily into the Anglo-Saxon world of money and status; at the same time their kinsmen in New Mexico continue to enact their elaborate tribal ceremonies in every compulsive detail.

A frequent fate of the aboriginal culture after contact with Western culture has been "pervasive swamping." Among certain Eskimo tribes, porcupine quill work, which had always been both a basic utilitarian craft and an art form with sacred overtones, quickly disappeared with the advent of the Singer sewing machine. Amazonian tribes have abandoned their native medications derived largely from plants, because the people now insist on cures which come in pillboxes and bottles. All over the world primordial belief and ritual systems have been discarded and forgotten as a result of the collision with an irresistible invading culture.

The outcome of culture conflict will not necessarily be determined by physical coercion. Threats, intimidation, and persecution have not infrequently compelled cultural submission when the forms and institutions of one culture have been forcibly interdicted and supplanted by another. But more often, acculturation has been a consequence of the voluntary assumption by a society of the patterns of another culture. Even superior military power is not the decisive factor. It is the power inherent in a particular culture which determines which of two cultures will prevail in the drama of encounter.

China is a paradigm of the inner power of a culture to prevail over the external might of an enemy. Successively invaded by aggressive conqueror peoples, Tungus, Manchus, and Mongols, China emerged from each invasion culturally unshaken. On the contrary, each of the invaders saw its own culture decline as it became acculturated to the dynamic indigenous Chinese culture. Adoption of the alien culture was in each case an autonomous process. The Aztecs, backward nomads, invaded the Valley of Mexico at the end of the twelfth century, conquered the Toltecs, and in time absorbed their culture. As with the ancient Chinese, the culture of this conquered people, the Toltecs, submerged that of the victorious Aztecs. Within three centuries the Aztecs had established a powerful civilization, which Cortes was able to subdue only with astounding guile and luck.

Hellenism spread over all of Asia Minor between the fourth century before and the fourth century after the Common Era (300 B.C.E.-300 C.E.).[5] Earlier cultural entities were swept away as Greco-Roman culture came to dominate not only the realms of literature, science, art, and architecture, but also the fabric of daily living. Greek and Roman rulers did not impose their institutions upon reluctant or resisting subjects. States which fell under their hegemony embraced the forms and modes of Hellenistic culture with little if any protest.

In the tenth century, the Normans of Northern France were conquered by invading Vikings from Scandinavia. Domiciled on French soil, the victorious Norsemen began to absorb the culture of their recent enemies. A century and a half later, in 1066, the Norman army crossed the English channel, defeated the Saxons at Hastings, and became rulers of England. During the next four centuries the whole cast of Saxon culture changed. Such was the dynamism of Norman culture that the cultural life of both victorious Vikings and vanquished Saxons was in time radically altered. In neither case did *force majeure* play a role. Both the victorious Vikings in tenth-century Northern France and the vanquished Saxons in medieval England were drawn ineluctably to the Norman culture which they proceeded freely and happily to absorb and adopt.

When Japan unlocked the gates of its self-imposed isolation after Perry's visit in 1865, no external pressure forced it to adopt the ways of the West. What followed was one of the most dramatic instances of acculturation in history. Few facets of Japanese life, in both its material and nonmaterial aspects (including family altars), have remained immune from Euro-American influence. Within three generations Japan had become a commercial and industrial giant, a dominant power in the very world of trade and technology founded and fashioned by the West. This development was influenced by no single nudge of outside pressure. It came about as the result of unforced, voluntary choice.

Death of a Culture

Living with the Washo Indians as an anthropologist taught me how easily and quickly a native way of life can break down as the result of contact with a surrounding culture. The Washo are a Great Basin tribe of traditional hunters-gatherers who aboriginally ranged across the High Sierras on the Nevada-California border. Through the decades they came into frequent contact with white settlers. The second Fremont expedition (1843-44) passed through Washo territory, and the Donner Party (1846-47) came to grief there. The Sierra Nevada passes favored by the California-bound pioneers were accessible only through Washo territory.[6] In the course of time, these contacts with the whites proved devastating. No elements in the indigenous life, however venerated, proved immune to the dislocation which followed in the wake of cultural interaction.

Language is a primary datum of cultural identity and cohesion. "A common speech" wrote Sapir, "serves as a peculiarly potent symbol of the social solidarity of those who speak the language."[7] In the 1930's virtually every Washo spoke the native tongue; today only a handful of oldsters still do. Young Washo no longer speak it. Periodic attempts to keep the language alive have met with little success. When I last visited the Washo, the instructor who traveled from Reno to Dresslerville Indian Colony to conduct the weekly class in the language was not a Washo but Professor William H. Jacobsen, Jr., of the Department of Linguistics at the University of Nevada. A tribal leader explained the approaching demise of his language:

> Our language is too much. There's not enough time [to learn it] when you want to be like Americans. We want to preserve

the native language, but it's not easy. My folks didn't care if I
learned the language. They told me, 'It won't help you earn a
living.'"

In little more than a generation, the Washo language, the most "potent symbol" of Washo solidarity, had all but died out.[8]

Today the demise of native languages is no unusual phenomenon. Of the 5,000 languages estimated to exist in the world, one-half are reported to be moribund. Since children are no longer learning to speak them, 90 percent of the languages will probably die out in the next century. Languages began to die out five hundred years ago when Europeans discovered the New World, and the process of acculturation set in.[9]

Basket-making was a highly elaborated art form among the Washo. They were proud of the reputation of their baskets. Datsolalee was a famous Washo basket maker, whose baskets are exhibited by leading American museums and prized by collectors. When I was with the tribe a half-century ago, all the women made baskets. Little girls would sit beside their mothers outside their huts weaving them. Today no one makes baskets. Cradleboards are handed down through the generations, but basket-making is a forgotten craft.

But it is the religious world of the Washo which has experienced the greatest upheaval. Shamanism, structured on the belief in a spirit world, was the aboriginal religious way which dominated the life of the people. The shamans, who were believed capable of manipulating and controlling the spirits, were at once healers ("doctors") and witches, able to both cure and kill. They thus wielded unchallenged authority and power, and almost all were feared and hated. Today shamanism is no longer a functioning institution among the Washo, and the shamans have vanished from the scene. The last Washo shaman died twenty years ago. Now on the rare occasions when an elderly Washo wants a shaman's "doctoring," a shaman from a neighboring tribe will be called in. Washo shamans have disappeared unlamented.

Among the forces contributing to the disintegration of this seminal institution in the people's culture, the crucial factor was the magnetic pull of the dominant society. More than any other Great Basin tribe, the Washo had come into close contact with the Whites. After World War II Whites began spilling into the valleys of the High Sierras around Lake Tahoe, traditional Washo territory, and the old religion could not function or survive in the new, acculturated world. As an official of the Stewart Indian Agency, himself a Washo, put it:

> The Washo became more rapidly acculturated than other
> Indian tribes. The old culture is gone and no one cares about
> reviving it. Our young people no longer make baskets or even
> speak Washo. That's what happened to the old religion. The
> young people adopt white ways.[10]

The rising tide of acculturation cut the people adrift from the ancestral anchorage. What remains of the aboriginal life is a whimper of the tribal past: the old people still play a native card game, do not mention Washo individuals by name, and will recall to others memories of the dead with great reluctance. A girl's puberty rite is occasionally held, and some Washo meet in the fall to gather pine nuts ceremonially. But the Washo way of life lived fully two generations ago survives today almost wholly in memory.

American Cultural Colossus

Professor Raymond Kennedy taught anthropology at Yale before the second World War. After graduating from Yale, he took a trip around the world, and upon reaching Sumatra, in the former Dutch East Indies, got a job working for Standard Oil. He learned Dutch, became interested in the native peoples, and upon returning to the U.S., took a Ph.D. in anthropology and began teaching at Yale. His classes were among the most popular on the campus, attracting hundreds of students.[11]

Kennedy's colorful accounts of native life fascinated his students, who called him Jungle Jim. He would tell of the excitement that simmered on Saturday nights in the small town in Sumatra where he was living whenever a "Buckajonas" film was scheduled to be shown. Hundreds of natives would swarm to the ramshackle tinroofed shed that served as the local cinema. Mystified initially at what the attraction might be, he soon learned that "Buckajonas" was none other than the star of many westerns, Buck Jones. In that remote corner of the world half a century ago, an American cowboy had become enshrined as a Sumatran culture hero. "Buckajonas" was the prototype of the Marlboro Man, who in a later generation became an American global icon. (Shortly after World War II, Kennedy returned to Indonesia to do ethnographic field work. One day when he was on a jeep trip into the interior with a *Time* correspondent, unknown assailants attacked and killed them.)

During one of the summers when Kennedy was working for Standard Oil and observing Indonesian tribesman, I was traveling in central Europe with a rabbinical classmate looking for his father's native village in the Carpathian Mountains. One night we stopped for the night in a seedy provincial town in Hungary, and after dinner wandered down the main street. We were struck by a poster outside the dingy movie theater announcing the feature then playing, *The Cohens and the Kellys*. We bought tickets and got what must have been the last seats in the house. The packed audience sat silent as the film unreeled its Hollywood version of ethnic humor. It was hard to tell how much the onlookers understood of what was transpiring on the screen. To us the interfaith high jinks could be intelligible only to an American audience. But no one spoke and no one left the theater. We concluded that the film was assured a packed and raptly attentive audience simply because it was American.

All countries have felt the impact and sweep of United States influence. America has become the world's uncontested cultural superpower. It is not only America's industrial, financial, and military might that has exerted its sway over the world polity of this century. America has also projected an overwhelming cultural influence wherever there has been contact with other peoples. The products of American material culture cover the world: Singer sewing machines in Greenland, Westinghouse washing machines in Riyadh, IBM computers in Malaysia, McDonald's in Israel, blue jeans universally. American artifacts, or those copied from American models — automobiles, telephones, faxes, televisions, videos, planes, and on and on — may be on the way to becoming global everyday essentials.

American technology, taste, and fashion have been called global icons. Much of the nonmaterial culture of America has become sovereign in the world. Culture patterns which derive from American movies and television — family values, lifestyles, moral standards — have transformed the life and outlook of peoples on the world's far and near horizons. The violence in "Buckajonas" movies, the glittering fashion in "Dynasty," and the casual sexuality in practically all films, are shaping the ethical and moral norms of societies around the world. In Paris recently the ten most popular films being shown were produced in the U. S., a preference the French press called a "cultural Chernobyl." Euro-Disneyland has been called a "huge American base in Europe." It is ironic that as Europe gropes toward unification, the only denominators shared by all Europeans may be American. The cultural capital of the new Europe may not be Paris or London or Rome, but Hollywood.[12]

Symbolic of this influence is the preeminence of English as a spoken and written tongue. English is now the *lingua franca* of humankind. A recent BBC program mentioned the consensus among Third World countries that a knowledge of English is a "prerequisite to progress," and predicted, with a tinge of regret, that of all the varieties of English now spoken, American English is emerging as preferred. Already in the diction of British radio and television announcers the broad English "a" has been displaced by the flat American "a." It may be no exaggeration to say that just as Hellenism permeated the Greco-Roman world two thousand years ago, and Islam the Mediterranean world a thousand years ago, American culture is progressively pervading the unbounded world we know. If societies geographically remote from the United States have been strongly influenced by its culture, those less remote have been transformed by it. Canada, sharing a common border and the same language, imports 75 percent of the cultural products it consumes — TV programs, movies, music, books, magazines—from the "cultural and economic colossus to the south." Many Canadians feel deluged by the cultural Niagara from across the border, and are said to be "exceedingly touchy .... about the stifling cultural embrace of their friendliest neighbor." But the northward tide of American cultural exports does not abate. Demand by Canadians themselves makes it swell the more.[13]

Canadians may feel testy about being swamped by the cultural flood from across the border, but ethnic groups with their own cultural traditions living inside the American border, for the most part, do not. German- Americans, Irish-Americans, Italian-Americans, Japanese-Americans, and other hyphenated Americans feel little urge to rail against the TV shows, films, books, and magazines that inundate their lives. There may be murmurs of discontent, but they are a random protest, not a collective, ethnic outcry.

A generation and more ago, minority groups, through their "protective" associations, would sometimes object to the casting of an obvious ethnic kinsman in an unflattering role in some film or play. Italian-Americans objected to gangster films heavily populated by identifiable Italians. But as the memory of the old world fades and ethnic groups interlace into the texture of the American scene, such objections lose relevance. It is doubtful if Governor Mario Cuomo, or Jack Valenti, president of the Motion Picture Association of America, or Don Marino, Miami Dolphin quarterback, are plagued by anxiety when they watch a rerun of *Scarface* or *The Godfather*. They no longer feel hyphenated. The immigrant culture has fused into the amalgam of American life. The children of the immigrants have become acculturated.

Two ethnic minorities, Blacks and Jews, long the victims of prejudice and discrimination, formed "protective" associations generations ago for combating the disabilities and answering the calumnies to which they were subjected. In 1910 the NAACP, National Association for the Advancement of Colored People, was organized to fight Black racial discrimination and segregation. In 1915 it initiated a national boycott of a racist film, *The Birth of a Nation*, and it has since grown in membership to become the largest institutional advocate for civil rights in the United States.[14] The ADL, the Anti-Defamation League, a division of the B'nai Brith, is the best known of several Jewish agencies combating antisemitism. However, neither the NAACP nor the ADL have voiced opposition to the values of the prevailing culture except as these might rouse bias against Blacks or Jews.

Social historians have differed on the meaning of the melting pot as a metaphor for the immigrant experience. Many who lived in the era of mass immigration (1880-1920) believed it to be a valid image for what was happening and would continue to happen to the newcomers. Later observers held that the marks of distinctive group identification persisted and that even in the fourth generation after arrival, Italians, Irish, Blacks, and Jews continued to live as differentiated communities in a city like New York.[15] The American historian Marcus Hansen believed that the grandchildren of immigrants wanted to revive the ethnic patterns which their parents were doing their best to jettison. These seem to have been romantic fantasies, for even to the casual observer it appeared plain to what extent the old ways, traditional values, and ethnic distinctiveness had eroded. Some of the emanations of difference may remain but the dissolution of the old patterns has not diminished. On the contrary, the wave of erosion gathered momentum with each passing decade.

Much has been written about the pride discovered by American minorities in their cultural antecedents. Alex Haley's *Roots*[16] is the paradigm testimonial of an American ethnic, who in probing his past, experiences a rebirth of pride leading to self-acceptance and self-esteem. Haley's book achieved an astonishing popularity and sent thousands scurrying to dusty attics and wizened patriarchs in search of family pedigrees. Recent books by Native Americans (American Indians) sound a clarion call for the resuscitation of aboriginal cultures. Those who take it up are articulate and picturesque, good copy for press and magazines, sufficiently charismatic to attract both native and non-native followers.

It is ultimately a futile cry. Relatively few Indians are interested in participating in a rain dance in New Mexico or a potlatch in Oregon, or in reliving the glory of the Sioux at Little Big Horn. Not many Blacks hanker for the life pattern of a Yoruba tribesman before his abduction as a slave. Blacks are ineluctably committed to the life of mainstream America. Native Americans are preoccupied with economic goals, in climbing out of the poverty of the pariah. Not many are shaken when their kinship organization or ceremonial system or native language is neglected, even threatened with extinction.

When you are living in a social and cultural milieu so powerful that it tends to break down any coexisting cultural system, your own ancestral ways will have difficulty surviving. The preponderance of latter-day descendants of ethnic Americans do not worry about this. Only if you are a romantic enticed into bouts of nostalgia by the "roots" phenomenon, or angered by perceived ethnic or racial slurs, will you have twinges of regret. Most third- and fourth- generation descendants of immigrants, only dimly aware of the old world traditions, will blissfully identify with the enveloping American ethos. In a word, they are on the way to being assimilated by the American cultural colossus.

Notes

1. Robert Redfield, Ralph Linton, Melville J. Herskovits, "A Memorandum for the Study of Acculturation," in *American Anthropologist*, v. 38, pp. 149-152
2. Alfred L. Kroeber, *Anthropology*, revised edition. (New York: Harcourt Brace, 1948) pp. 425, 430

3. "There is no Judaism without the Sabbath," declared Rabbi Leo Baeck, the heroic German rabbi who survived the Holocaust.
4. *Newsweek*, February 8, 1988
5. B.C.E. (Before the Common Era) and C.E. (Common Era) are used throughout instead of B.C. and A.D.
6. Edgar E. Siskin, *Washo Shamans and Peyotists: Religious Conflict in an American Indian Tribe* (Salt Lake City, UT: University of Utah Press, 1985) pp. 172f., 214
7. Edward Sapir, *Language: An Introduction to the Study of Speech* (New York: Harcourt Brace Jovanovich, 1921) pp. 15f.
8. Edgar E. Siskin, *ibid*. p. 171
9. Robert H. Robins and Eugenis M. Uhlenback, eds., *Endangered Languages* (New York, St. Martin's Press, 1991)
10. Edgar E. Siskin, *ibid*. p. 173
11. William F. Buckley, Jr., the editor and political commentator, was a student at Yale at the time, and was sharply critical of what he considered Kennedy's irreverent treatment in class of Roman Catholicism. His opinion of Kennedy is found in his first book, *Man and God at Yale* (1951)
12. *Newsweek*, April 13, 1992
13. Jeffrey Simpson, "Living Beside a Cultural and Economic Colossus." *New York Times*: August 24, 1986, Sec. 4, p. 3
14. Membership in the NAACP is not limited to Blacks. Jews have in fact, been prominent in its leadership. Joel Spingarn (1875-1939) was a founder and became president, 1913-1919
15. Nathan Glazer and Patrick Moynihan, *Beyond the Melting Pot* (Cambridge: M.I.T. Press, 1963)
16. Alex Haley, *Roots* (New York: Doubleday, 1976)

CHAPTER 2

LOST TRIBES AND LIVING RELICS

Historic Tides of Acculturation — Egyptian, Babylonian, Persian, Greco-Roman

Examples of Jewish acculturation go back as far as the fifteenth century before the Common Era. Clay tablets of the second millennium unearthed in Ros Shamra, northern Syria, site of ancient Ugarit, reveal a culture which in the opinion of scholars, had a marked influence on the language and literature of the contiguous Hebrews. The Bible is replete with cognates from ancient Egyptian and Mesopotamian texts. A wave of Persian influence spread over Judaism in the wake of the Babylonian exile (586 B.C.E.), demonstrated by the sudden prominence of such Zoroastrian emblems as angels, demons, the Messiah, Satan, and concern with the afterlife.

Like other Mediterranean peoples, Jews were profoundly affected by the irresistible tide of Hellenistic culture which swept through Asia Minor between 300 B.C.E. and 300 C.E. The Maccabees may have taken up arms against the Greeks in the second century B.C.E. to halt their advance into Palestine, but the march of Hellenization went on remorselessly. Judah Maccabee, champion of the pure monotheism of Yahweh worship, found pagan figurines concealed in the cloaks of his soldiers slain in battle. In time, Greco-Roman artifacts saturated Jewish life. Pagan symbols were mounted over synagogues and displayed on Jewish graves. The evil spirits lying in wait were appeased by devices of the pagan world — eagles, lions, fishes, wreaths, winged victories. Saul Lieberman and Erwin Goodenough have documented the extent to which Hellenism interpenetrated rabbinic Judaism and the degree to which the Greek language was adopted by all classes of Jews in Palestine.[1]

To say that Jewish communities have sometimes been absorbed and their distinctive identity lost in the surrounding cultural milieus, provokes reactions running from surprise to disbelief. For it contravenes a widespread assumption — the indestructibility of the Jew. In fact, to speak of the Jews as an eternal people has become a cliché. And with good reason. Through the centuries, every means for inflicting suffering and death upon Jews has been devised, culminating in the deliberate attempt to exterminate them. Yet they survive.

Tolstoy called the Jew "the emblem of eternity, he whom neither slaughter nor torture .... could destroy .... [He] is as everlasting as eternity itself."[2] Mark Twain rhapsodized, "All things are mortal but the Jew; all other forces pass, but he remains. What is the secret of his immortality?"[3] Jews looked upon their indestructibility as a theological absolute. "We are in possession of divine assurance," wrote Maimonides to the Jews of Yemen in the twelfth century, "that Israel is imperishable and eternal."[4]

Yet Jews have assimilated. The historical truth is that while Judaism has survived during the thirty centuries of Jewish history, whole communities which once flourished as centers of Jewish life have disappeared through assimilation. Cecil Roth, the Anglo-Jewish historian, has called Jewish history "one constant procession of communities which have sprung up and withered away."[5] He rejects the popular image of the Jew as unassimilable. That Jews have assimilated in wholesale numbers at different times in different places is a documented reality of the Jewish past.

The gateway to assimilation is acculturation. Jewish history is a chronicle of continuous cultural interaction between Jews and the diverse peoples among whom they lived over a period of three thousand years. Alien cultures have inevitably influenced Jewish life, sometimes cursorily, sometimes radically. Polish Jews in the *shtetl* were little affected by the life of rural Poland, but first-century Jews in Alexandria were "pervasively swamped" by the culture of the Greco-Roman world.

A survey of Jewish population trends over the centuries since Roman times reveals how significant a role assimilation has played in the course of Jewish history. More than eight million Jews are believed to have lived in the Roman Empire at the height of its power in the third century of the Common Era. Salo Baron tells us that every tenth Roman was a Jew.[6] Yet by the beginning of the thirteenth century, the number of Jews in the world had dwindled to one million. With the Chmielnicki pogroms in the Ukraine in 1648, the world Jewish population dipped to its lowest point in history — less than one million. This marked a drop of 66-85 percent over a period of fourteen centuries. Such a decline borders on the catastrophic. If Jews had enjoyed what demographers call natural population increase after Roman times, their number today would be at least ten times what it is. Much of the population loss can be attributed to persecution in its many forms — threats, intimidation, violence, forced conversions, killings. But the principal cause, according to Roth, was assimilation into the surrounding non-Jewish world.

Jewish history does not validate the popular assumption that persecution assures Jewish survival. "Antisemitism is the best guarantee for Jewish survival" is an adage which Jewish experience disputes. The darkest centuries of the Jewish past, which were marked by relentless persecution, did not strengthen the Jewish community, but led to its near fatal exhaustion. Persecution nerved many Jews to resist but many more formed the queues leading to the baptismal font.

Roth has described some of the Jewish communities which withered and vanished. Perhaps the most notable was the Alexandrian community of the early pre- and post- Christian centuries. Alexandria was the most powerful Jewish community of the Greco-Roman world. It had become the great center of Hellenism with a population of 500,000 to 1,000,000, two fifths of whom were Jews. At that time, more Jews lived in Alexandria than in Jerusalem. The German historian Mommsen called it "almost as much a city of the Jews as of the Greeks."[7] There were huge synagogues, strong communal institutions, and Jewish families of great wealth. Jews were leading playwrights, historians, and philosophers. Philo, a Jew, was one of the greatest philosophers of the age. The closest ties bound the Jews of Alexandria to those of nearby Palestine and virtually every Alexandrian Jew contributed to the maintenance of the Temple.

Then in the first century, growing repression brought on two mass uprisings by the Jews, which were violently crushed. The Jewish community never recovered. At the end of the Greco-Roman period, Alexandria itself went into eclipse as an intellectual and commercial center. The decline of the Jewish community anticipated the general breakdown. "The whole culture simply melted into nothingness."[8] When Benjamin of Tudela visited Alexandria in 1170, he reported finding three thousand Jews.

An ancient historian reports a meeting in the city-state of Ionia between Aristotle and an Ionian Jew "who spoke Greek and had the soul of a Greek." This suggests that by the mid-fourth century B.C.E., even before the spread of Hellenism, Jews were not only settled in the far borders of Greece but were being assimilated into Greek culture.

By the early years of the Common Era, an estimated one million Jews lived in Ionia. Although disdained by the Greeks, they had imbibed much of the prevalent culture with a consequent erosion of their Jewishness. When the Greeks were converted to Christianity, the Hellenized Jews followed. The few who remained Jewish were later forcibly converted by the Byzantine emperors. When the Ottoman Turks became rulers of the region in the 13th century, there were few left of the once numerous but by then almost totally assimilated Jewish population.

A classic instance of the passage from acculturation to assimilation is furnished by the Jewish community of Kaifeng, China. Jews came to east central China from Persia (some say India) in the 12th century, establishing in time a fully functioning Jewish community. An impressive synagogue complex was built in the seventeenth century. But within two hundred years there was little to distinguish the Jew from his neighbor in name, dress, or physical features. Circumcision was no longer practiced, Hebrew virtually forgotten. Having also become poor, they could no longer maintain their synagogue, and in the middle of the nineteenth century, it was torn down. Today there are individuals who retain the memory of Jewish descent, but aside from some parchment scrolls and some place names of uncertain identity, few vestiges of the Kaifeng Jewish community remain.

After the expulsion of the Jews from France in 1394, tolerant Popes permitted a small community to remain in Avignon and the Provence. Never numbering more than three thousand souls, this Provencal community evolved a distinctive cultural and religious life which preserved the scholarly legacy of the great French rabbis, Rashi, and the Kimhis. The Jews of this insular community developed a unique liturgy, folklore, dialect, synagogue architectural style, and musical idiom.[9] If any community held the promise of continuing its identity and traditions, it was the Jewish community of Provence.

Yet with the coming of the French Revolution and the first breath of political and social change, Provencal Jewry's distinctive life and culture ebbed away. Save for a few synagogues, a body of liturgical manuscripts, and a colorful tradition, little remains. When France withdrew from North Africa after World War II, Jews from the Maghreb came to settle in the Provence, but they have no connection with the pristine Jewish community.

In the sixteenth century Venice was a center of world commerce where Jews from Germany, the Levant, Spain, and Portugal had established a flourishing community. Jewish Venice became the focus for an intensive intellectual and artistic life over a period of a century and a half. Some of the foremost Jewish personalities of the age lived there — figures like Don Isaac Abrabanel, David Reubeni, and Donna Gracia, rabbis like Leone da Modena, scholars like Simone Luzzatto, physicians like Jacob Mantino. Exquisitely designed and decorated synagogues were built, Hebrew printing presses prospered, scholars immersed themselves in kabbalistic studies. Wealthy ghetto dwellers decked in brocades, velvet, and silk lived in the luxury which commerce with Asia made possible. Jews mingling with the outside community showed a growing inclination to adopt the ways of their neighbors.

The Jewish community reached the apex of its grandeur in the seventeenth century. But less than a century later Venetian Jewry was financially bankrupt and culturally spent. Napoleon's troops entered Venice in 1797, and, as a symbol of the emancipation they brought, burned its ghetto gates. But the City of Lagoons had already become a Jewish backwater, lost to assimilation.

It is interesting to record the observation of Simone Luzzatto, a luminary of the Venetian community. "Peoples and nations have their days numbered," he wrote, "no less than other sublunary things. Once they have reached the very apogee of their grandeur, their plunge into the abyss of oblivion is not far."[10] It was as though Luzzatto was describing the fate of his own community.

Jews Defect in Muslim World

In the Muslim world, too, there were heavy defections from Judaism. Before the appearance of Muhammad in Mecca in 622 C.E., Jews had settled in oasis colonies throughout the Arabian peninsula. Organized into tribes, they spoke Arabic, and adopted much of the indigenous desert culture. As Jews, they rejected the new faith of the Prophet and for their resistance were attacked in a series of military encounters. No match for Muhammad's fierce partisans, they suffered the customary fate of his vanquished foes — death, exile, forced conversions. But many more Jews took on the practices of Islam of their own volition. The once powerful Jewish enclaves in the urban cultures of southern Arabia, and of oasis communities like Medinah, fade into the mists of a dimly remembered past. Little is heard after 630 C.E. of Jews living in the Arabian peninsula.

Many Sunni Muslims living in Kashmir trace their origin to the ancient Israelites. They have a tradition that Moses is buried in Kashmir and that Jesus came there looking for the Ten Lost Tribes. The Chung-Min, a population of a quarter of a million ethnic Chinese living on the Chinese-Tibetan border, are converted Christians who call themselves "Sons of Abraham" and encircle their sacrificial altars with twelve flags to remind them of their ancestor's twelve sons. An Ibo tribesman from Nigeria living in Tel Aviv describes some of the rites practiced by his kinsmen, formally Christian, which are similar to Jewish rituals, from circumcising boys at eight days to abstaining from forbidden foods. "Ask any Ibo man," he says, "where his tribe is from and he will tell you, 'Israel.'" Shalva Weil mentions the "literally thousands of" Israelite "groups and Zionist Churches" in Africa, "many of which claim to be Lost Tribes …. Countries like Senegal, Dahomey, and Sierra Leone …. are filled with tribes claiming Israelite descent whose religious practices are an amalgam of Christianity and Biblical Judaism."

Jews first settled in the Maghreb on the coast of North Africa in ancient times, and by the Hellenistic period had established themselves in large and prosperous communities. But during the revolt against Rome in the second century C.E. and later under Byzantine emperors, they were cruelly persecuted and forced to seek refuge inland with the Judaeo-Berber tribes whose progenitors had in many cases adopted Judaism. With the Arab conquest in the seventh century, the Jews suffered mass executions and conversions. Some fled south into the fastnesses of the Atlas

Mountains, where they long maintained both their independence and their religious faith. The rest were assimilated into the surrounding Muslim population.

There are enclaves of people in many parts of the world who, while not professing to be Jews, claim to be descended from Jews. The signs of their Jewishness may vary from the possession of Jewish artifacts and the performance of rituals which bear some close or remote resemblance to Jewish religious rituals, to the memory or inherited legend of Jewish kinship. They may have no notion at all of what the Jewish artifacts signify or what the mysterious ceremonies mean. Yet their sense of difference from the people around them is clearly perceived and stubbornly preserved. At the same time, numerous clues verify the disposition of Jews to enter into the life and culture of dominant neighbors who were not Jews. They demonstrate that assimilation was a not infrequent counterpoint to the Jew's stiff-necked resistance to persecution and conversion.

Professed Descendants of the Ten Lost Tribes

Many groups in the world who claim affinity with the Jewish people profess to be descendants of the Ten Lost Tribes. According to the Biblical account, in 722 B.C.E. the Assyrian Emperor Shalmaneser IV invaded and conquered the Northern Kingdom, Israel, consisting of ten of the twelve Hebrew tribes, and carried its inhabitants into captivity.

> King Shalmaneser marched against him, and Hoshea became his vassal and paid him tribute. But the King of Assyria caught Hoshea in an act of treachery: he had sent envoys to King So of Egypt, and he had not paid the tribute to the King of Assyria, as in previous years. And the King of Assyria arrested him and put him in prison. Then the King of Assyria marched against the whole land; he came to Samaria and besieged it for three years. In the ninth year of Hoshea, the King of Assyria captured Samaria. He deported the Israelites to Assyria and settled them in Halah, at the [River] Habor, at the River Gozan, and in the towns of Media. (*2 Kings 17: 3-6*)

Speculation on the subsequent fate of the Ten Lost Tribes has been spinning its conjectural web for three millennia and has produced one of the great treasure-troves of myths and legends, some with a residuum of historic credibility, others wholly fanciful. The reality is that the Ten Tribes were in all likelihood scattered through the Assyrian empire and beyond, absorbed by the ancient peoples among whom they were exiled, never again to be united. "In almost every country in the world," writes Dr. Shalva Weil, Hebrew University anthropologist and authority on the Ten Lost Tribes," are groups which either claim to be Lost Israelites or are claimed by others to belong to the Ten Lost Tribes."[11]

Some of these native groups, whose habitat is largely in the Third World, number in the millions, and among them are those who today seek to convert fully to Judaism, to establish contact with Israel, and to prepare for the eventual possibility of migrating. Israelis differ on the question of encouraging the settlement of exotic peoples from the Third World on their small land. Pietists whose views are fashioned by *Halachic* tradition would facilitate their coming, for that would be fulfilling the eschatological vision of ingathering the dispersed Jews to the sacred soil of Israel, and so speeding the coming of the Messiah.[12] But secular Israelis are fearful lest the advent of groups widely different culturally from the mainstream of Israelis, followed by possible mass conversion, precipitate a witches-brew of demographic, social, and religious problems.

The Goal of Aliya — Beta Israel, Bene Yisrael and Others

Two tribal groups which decades ago emerged from the aboriginal twilight eventually to join the generality of Jews in Israel are the Beta Israel (Falashas) of Ethiopia and the Bene Israel of India.

The Falashas, now known as the Beta Israel (House of Israel), have lived in Ethiopia for centuries. Legends about them have come down from the early Middle Ages. In physical appearance and general culture they differ little from their Ethiopian neighbors, and were long referred to as the "Black Jews of Abyssinia." Their religion is a peripheral Judaism literally obedient to Biblical precept. Like other "lost" Jews, the Falashas may be the descendants of converts to Judaism. It was the orientalist, Jacques Faitlovich, a Polish Jew living in France, who early in the twentieth century, brought the Falashas to the attention of the Jewish world. Their welfare and reunion with *k'lal yisrael* became a mission which he pursued with indefatigable zeal.[13] In 1948 the Jewish Agency became a source of funding for the Falashas. Despite fearsome difficulties, a continuing exodus of Falashas has been making its way to Israel, culminating in the heroic Operation Moses of November 1984 – January 1985. Their identity as authentic Jews has finally received rabbinic validation. A landmark was reached in 1995 when twelve Beta Israel were ordained as rabbis by the Israeli rabbinate. 44,000 Beta Israel now live in Israel.[14]

Similarly the origin of the Bene Israel of India is unknown, although they are said to have left their home in the Galilee near the beginning of the Common Era because of the harsh exactions of the Syrian Greek ruler Antiochus Epiphanes. Settled on the west coast of the Indian peninsula, they were for centuries isolated from other Jews, and their religion became deviant from traditional Judaism. In the eighteenth and nineteenth centuries Jews from Cochin and Baghdad effected a renewal of ties between the Bene Israel with other Jewish communities. With the coming of the British, the Bene Israel moved north to Bombay, where they have since participated actively in national and civic life. In 1993, Bene Israel in Bombay numbered 4,500. Since l948, 18,000 Bene Israel have made *aliya*.[15]

Prominent among Third World groups claiming ancestry from the Ten Lost Tribes are the Pathans living on the Afghanistan-Pakistan border. Legendary warriors, they trace their lineage to King Saul. (In modern times, they are said to have fought fiercely against the Soviet invaders of Afghanistan.) They may have had contact with Saadia Gaon, the renowned tenth-century rabbinic authority, philosopher, and prime leader of Babylonian Jewry. Their elderly women light Sabbath candles, the men wear a four-cornered prayer garment, they treasure amulets with Hebrew writing, and call themselves Banei Israel. The Pathans were of special interest to Itzhak Ben-Zvi, the second President of Israel, who had a long association with groups of lost and scattered Jews, visiting and conducting research among them. He wrote about them in his well-known *The Exiled and the Redeemed*.[16]

The Shinlung are a numerous tribe who live on the border of northwest India and Burma. Some of them, claiming descent from one of Jacob's sons, Menashe, seem bent on becoming Jews and migrating to Israel. Several thousand now practice circumcision, observe *kashrut*, and have built a number of synagogues in the states of Mizoram and Manipur where the Shinlung are concentrated. Some dozens of young Shinlung have come to Israel and been formally converted in a program sanctioned by the rabbinate.

The Shinlung have been brought to Israel and to conversion as Jews by an organization, *Amishav* ("My People Returns"), which is dedicated to finding descendants of the Ten Lost Tribes and other "lost Jews" and reuniting them with the Jews of Israel. *Amishav* was founded in 1975 by Rabbi Eliyahu Avichayil, a Jerusalem teacher, with the support of the prestigious Rabbi Zvi Yehudah Kook. Avichayil has personally shepherded the Shinlung from their native habitat to Israel and through the conversion process to Judaism. He is motivated by the guiding belief of pietists that the ingathering of Jews will hasten the coming of the Messiah. His life is dedicated to the fulfillment of this mission.

While the ingathering of descendants of lost tribes may rouse the eschatological hopes of pious Jews, it stirs uneasy apprehensions in Israel government bureaus. The Immigrant Absorption Minister fears that the migration of native population groups, now a trickle, might in time become a tidal flood. After all, the overriding hope of many rural tribesmen today is to emigrate from the Third World to the industrial world. Conversion to Judaism and the move to Israel offer such an avenue of escape. Once in Israel, there is no telling how many relatives of the newly converted would want to join their kinsmen, and under the Law of Return, with its humanitarian provision for family reunification, Israel might be obliged to receive and shelter them. The Minister of Absorption is suggesting restrictive changes in the Law of Return. Meanwhile, the hard-working Rabbi Avichayil is criticized as an obscurantist busybody.

Pilgrim Fathers, American Indians, Crypto-Jews

The Pilgrim Fathers thought that the American Indians were descendants of the Ten Lost Tribes. The Puritans were immersed in the Old Testament as much, perhaps more than, in the New. They believed that in sailing in search of refuge from religious oppression, they were replicating the experience of the ancient Hebrews in their Exodus from the land of their serfdom, escape from a tyrannical monarch, and safe passage through the seas. Avid Bible readers, they must often have wondered what happened to the ten tribes carried into captivity. It was, therefore, not farfetched to believe that the strange people encountered in their new home were descendants of the Ten Lost Tribes. The identification of the American Indians with the Ten Lost Tribes has persisted since the landing of the Pilgrims. When the Mormons arrived in Missouri in 1831, they spoke of the Indians in Kansas territory as their "fellow tribes of Israel."[17] Among the Mormons themselves there is the belief that they are descended from the Ten Lost Tribes.

When the Jews in Spain were forced to choose between conversion and exile in 1492, it is estimated that 200,000 chose to leave. But an equal number elected to undergo baptism and stay. Of these many began to practice Judaism secretly, hence the designation, Crypto-Jews, or *conversos*. When suspected of "Judaizing" by the Inquisition, the *conversos* were apprehended, interrogated under torture, and burned in an auto-da-fé. Some of the *conversos* left Spain for Spanish colonies abroad where they continued their secret practice of Judaism. But wherever they went, the Inquisition had preceded them.

Pockets of the descendants of Crypto-Jews are today found wherever Spain had established its sovereignty, from India to Peru. There has been a remarkable discovery of these hidden Jews in our time. In remote parts where they had lived as Christians for hundred of years, individuals have come forward to disclose the tightly held secret of their derivation. They tell a similar story. Warned never to divulge their Jewish origin, they clandestinely performed certain random rituals clearly associated with Judaism — lighting candles on Sabbath eve, circumcision, *shehita* (ritual animal slaughtering) — and marking certain days — Passover, Hanukah — as holy. At the same time, they comported themselves as observant Christians, attending Mass, taking communion, receiving the ministry of priests at baptism, marriage, last rites, and burial. Most of the *conversos* lived in small towns where it was easier to escape detection by the harsh and ubiquitous Inquisition. They had taken their place in the towns as merchants, traders, craftsmen, and in surprising number, ecclesiastics.

In the last century it was thought that the *conversos* had been lost in the general population and it is only in comparatively recent years that their existence has been revealed. Living in remote places, it was only with the building of roads and improvement of transportation that they came to light. Today in the hilly fastnesses of Portugal near the Spanish border live many Crypto-Jews. "Some villages," reports Roth, "appear to be full of them."[18] George Borrow, the nineteenth-century English writer and traveler, had a fascinating encounter with Portuguese *conversos* which he recorded in his *The Bible in Spain (1834).*[19]

In the New World, settlements of Crypto-Jews were established both in its cities and in its distant borders. Today communities of Mexican and American Indians enact rituals with obvious Jewish resemblances. In the once remote New Spain of the present states of New Mexico, Arizona, and Texas, young secret Jews have emerged to describe their hidden Christian-Jewish lives. A few have been reconverted to Judaism.

Deep in the Heart of Texas — Lost in the Multitude

When I was a student at the Hebrew Union College, I came to know a Jewish community on the Texas Mexican border, some of whose members claimed descent from Crypto-Jews who had come to New Spain following the expulsion from Spain in the 16th century. Now communicants of the Roman Catholic church, they had over the generations drifted far from the moorings of Jewish life. Yet they still clung to the wreckage of Jewish ancestry and ritual observance.

It was the practice of the Hebrew Union College to send students to small communities to officiate at High Holiday (Rosh Hashanah and Yom Kippur) services. Too small or impecunious to support a full-time rabbi, they were glad to avail themselves of the College's willingness to provide student rabbis who would fill a need for isolated Jewish communities and would at the same time receive their earliest pulpit experiences. That summer I had been taking courses at the University of Chicago with little else to do but wait for word of my Holiday assignment. A week before Rosh Hashanah it came — Brownsville, Texas. Never having heard of Brownsville, I went to the library, consulted a map, and discovered that it was a Mexican border town on the Rio Grande River near the Gulf of Mexico in the extreme south-east corner of the country on the same latitude as Key West, Florida.

I first met the congregation on Rosh Hashanah eve. Our "synagogue" was the Masonic Temple, a rectangular box of a building dating back to Civil War times. Tall French windows stretching from floor to ceiling lined the walls. Large ceiling fans which droned throughout the service did little to cool the suffocatingly hot night. Looking out at the rows of people who filled the hall, I was struck by the number of dark Hispanic looking individuals among them. They were eyeing me intently, their movements measured and deliberate, seeming to hang on to every word I said. Most had never seen a rabbi before. I later learned that I was the first "rabbi" to officiate at a service in the lower Rio Grande valley since Civil War days, when Brownsville was an important port for the Confederacy.

I led the service, read the prayers, gave the sermon. Two singers borrowed from a church choir, accompanied by a wheezing harmonium, intoned the responses in uncertain Hebrew. The congregation read their prayers and responses with an uncommon unity and solemnity. In the sermon I drew moral conclusions from some dramatic events in Jewish history. The service over, people crowded forward to greet me and I felt the surge of goodwill.

During the next ten days, the length of my stay, many phone calls came from families inviting me for dinner in their homes or for outings across the border. Some of the calls came from the handsome "Hispanic" men and women whose rapt participation in the Rosh Hashanah service had so impressed me. I then began to understand why the services had proved so absorbing an experience for them. Not professing Jews, they had yet felt some mystic, if remote, connection with Judaism. Some suspected it, some had traced it genealogically. In any case, it was not easy to relinquish the ghostly memories.

I was told of grandmothers and mothers who lit candles on Friday evening, of the avoidance of forbidden food, of slaughtering animals ritually. On Friday nights the Bible was read (the Old Testament, not the New). There was the strict warning to tell nothing about these practices and traditions to anyone; they were to remain within the family. Grandmothers were the repositories of Jewish knowledge, guardians of such vestigial Jewish practice and memories as were dimly honored. A father interrupted his daughter while she related an experience with secret Jews at the University of Texas by suddenly exclaiming, "We are the *Judios Disparramodas* ("Dispersed Jews"). A few of these descendants of the Crypto-Jews of New Spain were interested in studying Judaism and thereafter possibly re-converting, but most considered themselves Roman Catholics and lived according to the rites and disciplines of the Church.[20]

Before taking my leave of Brownsville, a committee met with me to say they hoped I would return the following year, and that perhaps when ordained in four years, I would consider moving to Brownsville to make it my first rabbinical post. I left by the night train to San Antonio 250 miles north, the first lap of my return journey. There must have been seventy-five people at the station to see me off, each with a gift of remembrance. A few of these souvenirs are to be found on a shelf in my study in Jerusalem, reminders of my encounter with the posterity of some of the hidden Jews of Texas.

There is no question of the preponderant recognition of Christian identity by these descendants of *conversos*. Only in rarest cases will they return to Judaism. They are lost to the Jewish people. The "Jewish" component in their lives is a faint gallery of icons, interesting but peripheral. While their adherence to the husks of an ancestral faith may elicit wonder, their full integration into the world of Christendom is evident.

Floyd Fierman traced recent descendants of the Crypto-Jewish pioneers of New Spain and found among them a spectacularly rapid assimilation, with virtually no grandchildren or great-grandchildren remaining Jewish.[21] As Fishberg, one of the early anthropologists of the Jews, has written, "It is evident that the .... Crypto-Jews .... are lost in the multitude."[22] And Roth comments that as prejudice against the *conversos* declined, "the forces of assimilation [made] themselves felt to a degree hardly paralleled even in the age of persecution."[23] Heschel said that the twentieth century Jew "is a messenger who has forgotten the message." Adapting Heschel, Fierman observed that the nineteenth century Southwest Jew "was a messenger who didn't deliver the message."[24] It seems a strange irony that Jews risked the auto-da-fé to practice Judaism during the Inquisition, but gave it up when they could practice it freely as United States citizens.

Notes

1. Saul Lieberman, *Greek in Jewish Palestine* (New York: Jewish Theological Seminary of America, 1942); Edward R. Goodenough, *Jewish Symbols in the Greco-Roman Period*, (New York: Pantheon Books, c. 1053-68)
2. Joseph L. Baron, *Stars and Sand: Jewish Notes by Non-Jewish Notables* (Philadelphia: The Jewish Publication Society, 1943)
3. Mark Twain, "Concerning the Jews." *Harper's Magazine*, 1898
4. Isaac Husik, *An Anonymous Medieval Christian Critic of Maimonidies* (Philadelphia: Dropsie College, 1911)
5. Cecil Roth, *Personalities and Events in Jewish History* (Philadelphia: Jewish Publication Society, 1953), p. 13
6. Salo W. Baron, *A Social and Religious History of the Jews*, second edition (Philadelphia, Jewish Publication Society, 1952), vol. 1, p. 171
7. *Ibid.*
8. Roth, *ibid.*, p.10
9. Darius Milhaud (1892-1974), the modern French composer, born in Aix-en-Provence, is thought to have been the descendant of an old Provence Jewish family.
10. Simone Luzzatto, "The Hebrews among the Nations," in *The Judaic Tradition*, ed. Nahum N. Glatzer, (Boston: Beacon Press, 1969), p. 406
11. Shalva Weil, *Beyond the Sambatyon: The Myth of the Ten Lost Tribes* (Tel Aviv: Bet Hatefusot, 1991), pp. 77-94
12. "Thus they shall remain in the land which I gave to my servant Jacob and in which your fathers dwelt; they and their children and their children's children shall dwell there forever, with my servant David as their prince for all time." (*Ezekiel 37:25*)
13. Faitlovich maintained close contact with the American Jewish community. A great many religious schools apportioned a part of their weekly tsedaka collection to the Falashas. On one of his visits to America he came to our religious school in New

Haven and spoke to the assembled children on the Falashas. It was a day long remembered by the fascinated audience.

14. *Statistical Abstract of Israel*, 1994. Central Bureau of Statistics, Israel 1994. p. 97
15. *American Jewish Yearbook* (Philadelphia: Jewish Publication Society, 1994), p. 484; *Statistical Abstract of Israel, ibid.*
16. Itzhak Ben-Zvi, *The Exiled and the Redeemed* (Philadelphia: Jewish Publication Society, 1957)
17. David McCullough, *Truman* (New York: Simon and Schuster, 1992) p. 22
18. Cecil Roth, *A History of the Marranos* (Philadelphia: Jewish Publication Society, 1932), p. 369
19. *The Bible in Spain* (London: Oxford University Press, 1925)
20. Professor Stanley Hordes of the University of New Mexico, an authority on the Jews of New Spain, has encountered Crypto-Jews and their descendants not only in New Mexico but also in a broad swath of territory extending from Texas to California and as far north as Colorado. (Arlynn Nellhaus, " Unveiling the Secrets of the Crypto-Jews, " in *Jerusalem Post Magazine*, May 29, 1992, p. 12)
21. Floyd S. Fierman, *Roots and Boots: From Crypto-Jews in New Spain to Community Leader in the American Southwest* (Hoboken, Ktav, 1987)
22. Maurice Fishberg, *The Jews: A Study of Race and Environment* (New York: Scott Publishing Company, 1911)
23. Cecil Roth, *ibid.*, p. 375
24. Fierman, *ibid.*, p. 142

CHAPTER 3

JEWISH ACCULTURATION AND ASSIMILATION IN AMERICA

Major Jewish Migrations to America

Three major migrations have brought Jews to North America during the past three hundred years. The first immigrants who came in the seventeenth century (1654) were Sephardic (Spanish-Portuguese) Jews who sailed from Brazil, Holland, and the Caribbean islands, and settled along the eastern seaboard. The next two centuries saw their number augmented by Ashkenazim, Jews from Eastern and Central Europe, although together Sephardim and Ashkenazim counted no more than 3,000. The second migration, which began arriving toward the middle of the nineteenth century, was made up primarily of German Jews, who soon became dominant in the Jewish community. By 1880 they numbered 300,000. The third wave began to come in the 1880's and consisted of masses of Eastern European Jews seeking escape from Czarist oppression and pogroms. Soon they outnumbered the German Jews.

Between the years 1880 and 1920, two million east European Jews poured into North America, most of them crowding into New York City and the eastern states where they lived in poverty and squalor. A fourth migration may be said to have come in the aftermath of the Holocaust and included many ultra-Orthodox Jews and Hasidim who had escaped extermination. Once in America, they settled in metropolitan ghettos like Williamsburg in Brooklyn, Lakewood, N.J., and Fairfax in Los Angeles.

The customary view of the Jewish settlement in America over a period of three hundred years is that its three major migrations represent a continuum, a sequential historic development wherein successive generations of immigrants, building upon the foundations laid by forebears, progressively improved and enhanced the fabric and structure of American Jewish life. However, as some historians have pointed out, the truer picture might be that while there was some sense of continuity and inter-relatedness between one migration and the next, settling in America consisted of a series of discrete migrations, three beginnings, in which many descendants of each migration were, over time, lost through intermarriage and assimilation.

First generation immigrants might be strong and venturesome. Asser Levy, who landed with the first Sephardim in 1654, demanded from the hostile Dutch authorities his burgher rights of performing guard duty and bearing arms. Their children built institutions, founded congregations, erected synagogues, met the needs of fellow-Jews. But their children and grandchildren cared less about Jewish enterprises, and their interest in Jewish welfare and survival waned and dribbled away. They were heirs, not creators or builders. Intermarriage became a destabilizing force, and many children of the second and third generation had, at most, a tenuous Jewish identity.

The decrease in Jewish commitment from the first to later immigrant generations is confirmed by Malcolm Stern's genealogical study of the Jews in colonial America. Stern validates the view that the first migrants in Colonial times went through a communal life cycle which began with vigorous collective assertion and ended with desuetude and disappearance. Most of the families were absorbed by marriage with non-Jews. Stern's analysis of approximately one thousand marriages before 1840 reveals that while 23 percent have some Jewish descendants, ten percent have Christian descendants and 72 percent have died out.[1]

A Jew has been defined as a Jew who has Jewish grandchildren. Such Jews are a diminishing breed today. One sociologist has observed that it is the Jew of the fourth generation [the third to be born in America] who is the key to Jewish survival. If the fourth generation Jew believes so firmly in Jewish survival that he has taken the steps to strengthen its chances for continuity, incorporating them into the ways of his/her family life, the likelihood for corporate Jewish survival is thereby enhanced. Otherwise the future will witness the growing attenuation of the Jewish ties that bind, a debilitation which has happened in the history of American Jewry with each successive migration.

The encounter of Jews with life in America may at first have been profoundly disorienting. They had come for the most part from squalid ghettos and impoverished rural villages where life was a bitter round of humiliation and want, often attended by violence. Now they found themselves in a land where equality and liberty were proclaimed in national charters and guaranteed by law, and where fear and hatred no longer festered in the air they breathed. This new life was, moreover, replete with economic opportunity; material rewards were within the reach of even poor peddlers. In all of Jewish history this had never been so true as it was now. After the first shock of strangeness, the vast majority of migrants were irresistibly drawn to the new land. They proceeded fervently to identify with it.

Students of society have noted that acculturation advances apace when the donor culture possesses prestige value and when it is compatible with the culture of the recipients. American culture embodied enormous prestige for Jews newly released from the old world. To immigrants whose aspirations for centuries were spun from dreams of freedom, America was a very paradigm of prestige, a land to be admired and cherished above ordinary praise. America — its life, values, culture — must have seemed to many the intimation of Utopian, even Messianic, hopes realized.

Faith and Vision of Jewish Immigrants and American Pilgrims

The forms and symbols of American culture were not only laden with prestige; its values bore a striking compatibility with the faith and vision of Judaism. The Old Testament had been the sacred guidebook for America's founders. The first book printed in the new world was the Book of Psalms. The settling of New England was conceived as a replication of the Exodus from Egypt. George III was Pharaoh, the Atlantic Ocean the Red Sea, the Pilgrim Fathers the children of Israel. These similarities were dramatic confirmation of God's redemptive power for His children. Nothing could have woven Jewish immigrants more closely into the life and ethos of their new home. Tapping the same roots of faith and history, Pilgrims and immigrant Jews disclosed a singular comparability. "The twentieth century ideals of America," wrote Justice Brandeis, "have been the ideals of the Jew for more than twenty centuries."[2]

Not all Jews were intoxicated with the vision of opportunity and freedom held to be synonymous with America. Rhetoric and reality sometimes diverged. Life in America was hard, employers could be harsh and grasping, the pace and tumult of urban living were frightening. Moreover, the reassuring spiritual landmarks, which had been their constant monitors, were losing significance. Some Jews, seeing how difficult it was to lead a life of piety and strict ritual observance, hankered after the undeviating religious mandates of East European ghettos and the "inner decorums" of the *shtetl*. "I am overcome with longing," wrote one, "....for my Jewish world, which I have lost."[3] An eminent rabbi from Vilna, Jacob Joseph, brought to New York to be its chief rabbi, could not cope with the savage infighting of commercial powerbrokers, and after suffering a train of indignities, fell ill and died.

But these were rare cases. The vast majority chose to strive and struggle in the new milieu. Among all imm+igrant groups, Jews ranked next to last in the number returning to their countries of origin.[4] With all of its coarseness and imperfections, America was infinitely better than czarist repression and Cossack pogroms.

Until modern times, Jewish writers and scholars paid scant attention to the influence of alien cultures on the Jews. They spent far more time cataloguing the contribution of Jews to the non-Jewish world. This is perhaps the expected attitude of people who feel constantly threatened. In their defensive, apologetic posture, they must perpetually burnish the merit badges which attest their good citizenship, unswerving patriotism, and contributions to the commonweal. The implied warning is that to persecute Jews is to risk grave cost to the nation.[5] When the Nazis were overrunning Europe in the 1930's, triggering a worldwide wave of antisemitism, a flurry of books documenting the Jewish contribution to humankind in every conceivable sphere appeared in the book shops. Two books in this library of apologetics by esteemed scholars, Joseph Jacobs and Cecil Roth, bore the identical title, *Jewish Contributions to Civilization*.[6]

But a truer portrayal of the role of alien cultural influence on Judaism and Jews is reflected in the old Jewish saw, *Wie es christelt sich, so yudelt es sich*, "As it occurs among Christians, so will it occur among Jews." This became a nugget of folk wisdom. The traditional scholar may have been reluctant to acknowledge or write about it, but the folk philosopher and the plain folk knew that Jewish life was in no small part an historic accretion of extrinsic cultural ingredients. This was most vividly illustrated in America. Out of my experiences over decades as a participant-observer of American Jewish life, I have gained insights which have made me aware of the extent and pace of the American Jew's accommodation to the patterns of the surrounding culture. I offer here observations of this process in America.

Jews Accommodate to Surrounding Culture — Hanukah and Christmas

Christian forms and symbols which are woven into the fabric of American life affect the behavior and attitude, indeed, the very psyche, of many Jews. This is conspicuously true of Christmas, which annually immerses the whole country in its hype and affects all who partake of the culture. Orthodox Jews are an exception, since, not surprisingly, they do not recognize occasions associated historically with Jesus of Nazareth.

Hanukah, the Jewish holiday whose occurrence in December often coincides with Christmas, has in recent times undergone a quantum leap in importance among Jewish holidays. Observed for two millennia as a minor festival, it has now become a major celebration of the Jewish year. Christmas is widely held to be the cause for this transformation. Every year Christmas weaves its magic spell, especially for children. Jewish parents wanted to counter the allurement of a holiday with Christological roots with something Jewish. Hanukah with its resemblances to Christmas — candles, calendar concurrence, gifts — was a ready answer. But Hanukah lacked the enchantment of Christmas (could anything match it?). Hence, the attempt to expand Hanukah into a "rival" of Christmas. There was no deliberate decision, no systematic plan or program, just the burgeoning of an answer to a felt need. The answer, naturally, was couched in the values of the prevailing culture — synagogue and communal celebrations, public displays of menorahs (counterpart to the omnipresent Christmas trees), greeting cards, and above all, gift giving. Hanukah has become an orgy of gift giving, with children often receiving gifts on each of the eight nights of the holiday. Hanukah, refashioned and amplified, is as compelling an example of acculturation as American Jewish life affords.

When our children were young, a new public school was built in our neighborhood, which had become almost wholly Jewish. During the first year, the non-Jewish principal met with the class mothers a month before Christmas in order to discuss the school Christmas program. All but one of the mothers were Jews; the one non-Jew was married to a Jew. The principal told them that since 95 percent of the children were Jewish, it had been decided to leave the content of the Christmas program to the discretion of the parents. They could have as much or as little Christmas observance in the school as they wished. The principal then left the room. The minute he closed the door, one mother jumped up to say how un-American it would be not to have Christmas in the school. She couldn't believe there was a public school in America that didn't observe Christmas. Another mother asserted, "Christmas is a national, not a religious holiday." One of the women told how as a child, playing Mary in the school Christmas play had been one of the most inspiring experiences of her life, and she would never forget it. The mothers voted to request a full Christmas school program — carols, decorations, trees in every room, a Christmas assembly for children and parents. The vote would have been unanimous but for one dissenter — my wife. (Our next-door neighbor raised her hand halfway in ambivalent dissent.)

In his memoir, *An Orphan of History*, Paul Cowan, three generations removed from immigrant grandparents, who grew up in our community, tells of his pilgrimage from assimilation to Orthodoxy, reversing the customary process. He recalls Christmas eves as a boy when the family would gather for the Christmas dinner, unwrap the mountain of gifts under the Christmas tree, and listen to his father's ritual reading of *A Christmas Carol*.[7]

Many Jews feel the pangs of marginality with the coming of Christmas. A writer records how her Jewish family would enact a private Christmas ritual during Christmas week, "but never on the day." Parents and children would pile into the family car at night, cruise through the hushed, decorated streets, and hum the melodies of carols, "but never the words." On returning home, there was always a feeling of guilt, for it was the Hanukah season, and the writer wonders whether this "crude emulation" of Christmas, with Jews humming Christmas melodies, decorating a "Hanukah bush," and welcoming "Hanukah Joe" (Saint Nick's cousin) bringing presents, doesn't mock and demean their own heritage. Christmas, after all, is "our neighbor's Christmas." Yet, she sighs, who can remain blind to the splendor of the season? Those poor little Hanukah candles, even the Maccabees — how can they stand up to Christmas?" The yearning, envy, loneliness, and isolation revealed in this memoir evoke the marginality many Jews feel when Christmas comes. The writer goes on to venture that only a strong sense of security and pride will overcome the "seasonal identity crisis" which Jews feel at Christmas. (It is interesting to note that the author of this reminiscence was the executive editor of a national Jewish periodical.)[8]

During Christmas week, I once took a Christian colleague in our community to lunch at the nearby Jewish country club. As we walked through the main door, there stood a Christmas tree, its top touching the ceiling, thickly festooned with glittering lights and tinsel. My friend stopped, looked up and stared, his jaw gradually falling slack. "Ed, that is the biggest Christmas tree I've ever seen."

Paradoxically the very Jews who will condone or support observance of Christmas in the public schools will insist on keeping the wall of separation between church and state high and impermeable. They seem untroubled by the contradiction. In communities where Christian nerves on church-state issues might be grated, Jewish leaders will caution prudence. "Don't make waves," is the strongly implied, if not explicit, counsel. It is a warning familiar to Jewish ears. History has taught Jews to yield on principle when acting on conscience might ignite an explosion. It is the moral cost exacted by marginality.

It may be that the acquiescence of Jews in school and communal Christmas celebrations is a recognition, conscious or unconscious, of the inescapable realities of American life. Since Christmas is woven into the substance of American culture, as it is into the culture of every predominantly Christian society, Jews, unless totally committed to Halacha, are willy-nilly hostage to this overwhelming cultural actuality. Those who want to get along had better go along, whether it is working on Saturday, taking college exams on Yom Kippur, or voting for Christmas decorations in the public school. It is another milestone lining the road to acculturation — and beyond.

Some will wonder how this can in fact be the American reality. America, after all, guarantees equality to all, irrespective of religion, race, or nation. Presumably the rights and sensibilities of Jews merit consideration and demand safeguarding as much as those of other religious communities. Or is America a Christian nation? The truth is that while America is not a Christian nation legally or constitutionally, it may be a Christian country culturally. In ways obvious and subtle, Christianity is interdigitated in American life. Prayers offered by Christian clergy on public occasions will more often than not be invoked in the name of Jesus Christ. Jews who cherish America and partake fully and enthusiastically of its cultural life will obviously be affected by its Christian elements.

It may be that in recent years the attitude of Jews toward Christian norms and traditions has changed. Perhaps the appeal of Christmas for Jews has waned. North Shore public schools of the 1990's may no longer see Jewish mothers clamoring for full dress Christmas programs. Perhaps fewer Christmas wreaths decorate Jewish front doors, fewer Christmas trees adorn Jewish front rooms.[9] But the demographic facts make this unlikely.

With intermarriage continuously increasing, and with the majority of intermarried partners women of Christian origin, one would hazard that their homes would be more, not less, susceptible to the influence of the predominant Christian culture, one of the centerpieces of which is Christmas. When the children of intermarried parents visit their Christian grandparents and families over Christmas, what could be more natural or expected than that usages treasured by Christians be followed? What better ambiance for solidifying family ties? We have seen how captivating the Christmas spirit can be for Jewish families with none of the religious and psychological complexities of intermarriage. There is no escaping the embrace of the dominant culture.

A more recent example of the adoption of a Christian practice is the custom of sending greeting cards on Hanukah. Christians have been sending Christmas cards to each other for a hundred and fifty years, but Jews had never sent greeting cards on Hanukah. Now many do. Of recent years a new genre of cards has appeared intended primarily for exchange between Jews and Christians, and between Jews and mixed-faith families. Dealing specifically with the relationship between Hanukah and Christmas, these cards communicate telltale messages between Christians and Jews. Their popularity is obviously due to the great increase in interfaith families and to the swelling tide of intermarriage in which one's family, friends, and neighbors are involved.

Jews who live in self-enclosed enclaves like Williamsburg, N.Y., Crown Heights, Brooklyn, or Lakewood, N.J., may have little awareness of Christmas or Easter or other Christian elements in the surrounding culture, for they have deliberately sealed themselves off from the life around them. But Jews who have left Orthodoxy behind and become part of the civic community — and these are the large majority — have been influenced and infused by ways and forms once considered alien, even profane. Rabbi Stephen S. Wise, the leonine leader of American Jewry in the first half of the century, used to heap scorn on the wealthy, renegade Jews who had risen "from Poland to polo in three generations." "Polo" is shorthand for the secular-Christian culture embraced in an ambiance of material surfeit with little concern for anything Jewish.

Upward mobility has been the customary pattern of social movement by Jews. At way stations on the upward ascent, the trend is progressively toward assimilation. In a prior generation, Jews at the social summit on the Chicago North Shore belonged to the Reform temple, which they rarely attended, and to the Jewish country club, which they frequented faithfully, some would say religiously. A morbid sense of linkage with their Jewish identity came with the experience and fear of antisemitism. Paul Cowan's mother, who became a Christian Scientist, was so certain of the coming of a catastrophic antisemitism that she kept pressing her son to learn a trade so that he could survive economically when the curtain fell.[10]

Paul Cowan has described life at the social zenith of Chicago Jewry when he was growing up. Its epicenter was Lake Shore Country Club, of which his parents were members. Here on the shores of Lake Michigan, third generation American Jews walked the lush fairways and manicured greens, took their ease in the amplitude of the comfortable club house. Here they found a "safe haven," a "womb," where they could "act out the fantasies America had imbued in them." In the world out there they had all experienced antisemitism and therefore felt the compulsion always to be "respectable" and "dignified." But at Lake Shore it was different. The club was "the only place they could behave as they pleased." They played golf, symbol of affluent leisure, played poker for extravagant stakes, told dirty jokes in loud voices, and wrote bawdy doggerel to be recited at club parties. They drank too much and generated "so much erotic energy that Lake Shore became known for spouse swapping."[11] They were at once indulging their American day dreams and discarding the millennial moral baggage of the Jew.

Lake Shore bestowed honorary membership upon the senior rabbi of our congregation — myself — but our family seldom went there. Our son played tennis on the club courts and became captain of the Lake Shore team. He struck a modest blow for Jewish pride by refusing to play the teams of neighboring Gentile country clubs which excluded Jews. Jewish converts to Christianity and their near descendants were also barred from membership in the *judenrein* clubs. A deacon in a local church, whose grandfather had been born a Jew, would meet me in the Post Office or drug store, call me aside and fulminate against this show of discrimination.

All four North Shore Jewish country clubs served food forbidden by Jewish dietary laws. Some of the invitations to club events, which I have kept, are a documentary of acculturation. For an "annual children's Christmas party," we were urged to "bring the children and grandchildren .... to visit with Santa Claus." An "Easter Dinner" featured "Gulf Stream Jumbo Shrimp Cocktail" and "Breast of Chicken, Eugenia, with Virginia Ham." Clam bakes occurred regularly. The acculturation of *kashrut* reached an apogee with a Luncheon Specialty, "Frank-Cheezie on a bun: American Cheese and Crisp Bacon inserted into Kosher Frank."[12] A series of post cards informed us that Lake Shore will be closed on Thanksgiving,

Christmas, and the secular New Year. It was open on Rosh Hashanah and Yom Kippur.

Underplaying, when not masking, their Jewish identity was one of the most seductive fantasies. Not a few members were Christian Scientists. While Christmas and Easter were sedulously observed at the club, Jewish holidays passed unmentioned. Save for the hovering shadow of antisemitism, Lake Shore Country Club was a microcosm of the assimilated Jew's nirvana, the penultimate stage of the upwardly mobile Jew's hegira.

Two generations have passed since the days, described by Paul Cowan, when Lake Shore ruled the Jewish social roost. But there has been little change in the attitude toward anything Jewish. A slight shift in membership policy has been ordained. The door, once open only to Jews of German origin, has been left ajar for a few of East European descent. But there is little evidence that this has had a leavening influence Jewishly. The Holocaust, the founding of the State of Israel, the dire need and lethal danger of Jews in many parts of the world, has left many of the insulated Lake Shore Jews unmoved.

When the two hundredth anniversary of Congregation Mikveh Israel of Philadelphia was being planned in the 1940's, it was decided to invite descendants of the founding families to participate in a commemorative service. But these plans were frustrated when, search as they might, the synagogue leaders could find no living Jewish descendants of the founders. In the end, descendants who were no longer Jews were invited to participate. Some of these bore the names of well-known Pennsylvania colonial families.[13]

The first of the Jewish pioneers had come from New Amsterdam in the 1650's to trade in the Delaware Valley long before William Penn founded the colony of Pennsylvania. Most of the Jews became partisans of the Revolutionary cause, two rising to the rank of lieutenant-colonel. At the Constitutional Convention in 1787, Jonas Phillips urged the bestowal of full legal equality upon members of "all religious societies." When Congregation Mikveh Israel made a public appeal for funds to help in their mortgage crisis, one of the contributors was Benjamin Franklin. These forebears had defied the threats of the Inquisition, braved the tortures of fanatical priests, suffered the fires of autos-da-fé, triumphed over tempestuous oceans, outfaced hostile bigots in demanding their burgher rights to bear arms. All to end in the whimper of extinction.

From Extant to Extinct — Jews in Small-Town America

"A Synagogue Is a Hardware Store," "Eternal Lights are Museum Pieces," were captions in a *New York Times* account of what is happening to Judaism and Jewish life in the small towns of the American South. Until recent years, throughout the South, Jews lived in many of its small towns. Their presence is attested by the names of some of the communities: Berger, Felsenthal, Goldman, Marks, Kahnville,

Geismar, Kaplan. The Jews had come to settle as early as the eighteenth century, taking their place as industrious public-spirited citizens, raising their families, and prospering. In time the young people went away to college, found work in the big cities — Atlanta, Memphis, New Orleans — and married. As the older generation of parents and grandparents died out, the children and grandchildren gradually lost touch with the small towns of their birth. Empty synagogues were sold, weed-choked cemeteries were abandoned. The relatively few young people who had remained or returned to their towns, intermarried and assimilated. In many towns no Jew survives. It is being said that American Jewry in the rural South will soon be extinct.

A museum in Utica, Mississippi, called the Museum of the Southern Jewish Experience, has been established for gathering the memorabilia and recording the history of the Jews in the small-town South. Macy Hart, founder and director of the museum reports, "We have many communities that are down to one or three or five Jewish people left." In Port Gibson, Mississippi, the synagogue, more than a century old, was scheduled to be demolished and the land used as a parking lot for the adjacent gas station, when Bill and Martha Lum, Christian residents of the town, decided to buy and restore it. "It's part of the heritage of this town and we just couldn't stand to see it destroyed," said Bill.[14]

Hart was disarmingly forthright in describing his museum's function. "We're moved .... to help those communities go from extant to extinct with dignity." His aim was to establish a program which will "help dying congregations plan for their extinction. We'll go in and talk to them about what it's like to close down a culture, phase out an entire ethnic group. Then we'll go back into towns [and] teach them about the Jewish community that once lived in their towns."[15]

The last Jew living in Donaldson, Louisiana, is Gaston Hirsch, who survived a death camp, came to Donaldson, and married a Catholic. In retirement at 79, he now takes care of the Jewish cemetery. Conducting a visitor through the old synagogue, now an Ace Hardware store, he went looking for the "beautiful windows," and not finding them, said, "It's a sad thing to show you what used to be a holy place."[16] Hirsch is collecting funds to maintain the cemetery when he is gone. Two young men, both Catholics, will administer the fund.

What has happened to Jews in the small-town South is not confined to one region of the country. Small towns in other parts of the country are losing or have already lost their Jews. Jews in small communities intermarry in far greater numbers than Jews in cities where there is more opportunity for inmarriage. With the rate of intermarriage in Denver, San Francisco, and New Orleans skyrocketing, one can be sure that the rate in the small towns of Nebraska, Kansas, and Montana is stratospheric.

Jews have lived in St. John, New Brunswick (Canada) for more than one hundred and fifty years. The 1920's to the 1960's were "golden years" for the 300

Jewish families who were proud to be "actively involved in all facets of life in the Jewish and non-Jewish community." Now with the Jews dying out they are gathering artifacts for a museum in order "to preserve our heritage and share it with the larger community." Visitors to the museum are handed a smudged folder printed on an antique copying machine, which acknowledges that "at the present time we are one of the diminishing communities of the diaspora".[17] They are planning for their extinction. Similar museums will dot the hinterland of North America in increasing number. More than museums, they are the mausoleums of small-town Jewish life.

During my years as a rabbi in suburban Chicago, I learned that some of our newer congregants had come from small midwestern towns, motivated by fear that if they did not move, their children would some day intermarry.

In the early 1950's I noticed that there were a group of members in the congregation who had originated in Ligonier, Indiana, a small town in the northern part of the state not too far from Chicago. The story of their experience from immigrant to suburbanite is instructive. In the last half of the nineteenth century, German Jewish immigrants had come to Ligonier, a town of 300 inhabitants, when two railroads announced that Ligonier would become an important stop for their trains. As the immigrants began to settle in, they brought over their families and embarked on a variety of mercantile, manufacturing, and banking enterprises. They became active in the community, two of their number serving as mayor. They also established an elementary and a high school and a public library. They built large homes on Main Street, which came to be called "New Jerusalem," where the third floors were given over to elaborate parties. A beautiful "temple" (synagogue) was also built.

Early in the twentieth century, the college-educated children began to leave Ligonier and settle in larger cities, mainly Chicago. By 1979 only two Jews remained, inmates of a nursing home. The splendid temple still stands, now used by the Trinity Assembly of God Church. The *South Bend Tribune* concluded a story on the vanished Ligonier Jews, "The cemetery is all that is left to remind residents of a wonderful part of the history of their city."[18]

It is noteworthy that in the small-town South, the Methodist-Catholic Lums acquired the Port Gibson synagogue in order to restore it, and Catholic young men will administer the cemetery maintenance fund in Donaldson, Louisiana. One wonders if the Jews who grew up in these towns and now live in the big cities have no interest in saving the synagogues which they attended as children or in maintaining the cemeteries where their parents and grandparents lie buried. The probable answer is that since most have intermarried and raised their children in another faith, they have little interest in salvaging the memorabilia of an abandoned heritage.

To describe Jewish history as a "constant procession of communities which have sprung up and withered away" would not be inaccurate. Throughout most of their history, the Jews, as a persecuted, stateless people have been compelled to wander in search of a secure haven. Many suffered and died because they were Jews. Many more paid the price demanded by the state or the church — conversion to the dominant faith. Other Jews stopped being Jews and assimilated.

During their millennial wanderings, Jews established communities in distant corners of the world. Isolated from the mainstream of Jewish life, these communities in the course of time suffered decimation and absorption. The human relics of these communities are still found, often clinging to fragments of artifacts, rituals, and memories of unmistakable Jewish stamp. Had these communities enjoyed natural population increase, the number of Jews in the world today would be many millions more than recorded in census rolls. But persecution and assimilation interdicted nature's normal patterns and decreed instead extinction.

Jews have disappeared as Jews not only in the hinterlands of Africa and Asia. The American continent has also been the scene of lost communities. Enclaves of Crypto-Jews once lived in the colonies of Central and South America established by Spanish conquistadors. Descendants of the Sephardic immigrants in colonial America were assimilated after two or three generations.

Anthropologists have pointed out that absorption of the weaker culture by the stronger has been a common phenomenon in the history of human societies. Since he began his wanderings two thousand years ago, the Jew has been the cultural odd man out, the perennial minority, a "pariah people."[19] With the onset of the modern age, the pace of acculturation and assimilation has been accelerating. There is reason to wonder when, and if, the pace will slacken.

Notes

1. Malcolm H. Stern, "Function of Geneology in American Jewish History," in ed. Jacob R. Marcus, *Essays in American Jewish History* (Cincinnati, American Jewish Archives, 1958), pp.69 ff.
2. Louis D. Brandeis, "Greetings From Louis D. Brandeis" in *The Menorah Journal*, Vol. 1. January 1915, p. 4
3. Irving Howe, *World of Our Fathers* (New York: Harcourt Brace Jovanovich, 1976), p. 71
4. Ibid., p. 72
5. Antisemites have been obdurately willing to take the risk. No risk was too costly for the attainment of the *judenrein* state.
6. Joseph Jacobs, *Jewish Contributions to Civilization* (Philadelphia: The Conat Press, 1920)
7. Paul Cowan, *An Orphan in History: Retrieving a Jewish Legacy* (New York: Doubleday and Company, 1982), p. 9

8. Carol Kur, "Jews, at Christmas," *New York Times*, December 24, 1984, sec.1, p. 19
9. Sometimes back rooms. Only Jews lived on our block. Their Christmas trees were not visible from the street. We were sometimes tempted to believe that our neighbors, in a spasm of Jewish guilt, or because of their rabbi's propinquity, had given up their trees. The awakening came the day after New Year's when discarded trees lay in many of the driveways waiting for the garbage truck to haul them away. On our street, it was in back rooms that Christmas cheer prevailed.
10. Paul Cowan, *ibid*. pp. 3, 9. "My family celebrated Christmas and always gathered for an Easter dinner of ham and sweet potatoes."
11. *Ibid*. p.76
12. Acculturated kashrut is nationwide. A 1989 menu of the Scottsdale, AZ, New York Kosher Style Restaurant Deli includes "Fresh Shrimp Salad," "Bacon Burger," and "Jumbo Bacon Burger." The menu is headed, "Shalom y'all" in Hebrew and English script.
13. I learned this from Rabbi Abraham A. Neuman, then the rabbi of Mikveh Israel and president of Dropsie College.
14. Peter Applebome, "Small Town South Clings to Jewish History," in *New York Times*, September 29, 1991, p. 28
15. Mary T. Schmich, "Jews are Consigned to History in South," in *Chicago Tribune*, November 2, 1987
16. Applebome, *ibid*.
17. Saint John .... Jewish Historical Museum (Saint John, N.B., Canada) Membership Form
18. Rose Cunningham, "City Proud of Jewish Heritage," in *South Bend Tribune*, April 18, 1979
19. Max Weber, *Ancient Judaism* (New York: Free Press, 1952), p. 364

CHAPTER 4

THE VARIETIES OF JEWISH RELIGIOUS EXPERIENCE

"Judaism is not merely a question of faith," said Franz Kafka. "It is above all a question of the practice of a way of life in a community conditioned by faith."[1] Judaism is a complete way of life, not just a set of rituals or an agenda of beliefs. The observant Jew feels that God is scrutinizing his every deed and gesture, monitoring his every thought and impulse. "Every human action is a means of communion with God."[2] The overarching mandate of Judaism is "You shall be holy, for I, the Lord your God, am holy (*Leviticus 19,1*)." The goal of every observant Jew is a life of holiness.

Edward Sapir (1880-1938), the noted American anthropologist, observing that cultures are dominated by "controlling ideas," designated the idea of holiness the controlling idea of Jewish culture. "Jewish culture is saturated with the idea of holiness," he wrote. "It is like a collective phobia that if you do not behave yourself every minute of the day, you cannot come into the presence of the Almighty."[3] Few religions have so pervaded every aspect of life as Judaism.

Three Forms of Observance — and Non-Observance

There are three major religious denominations in American Jewish life — Orthodox, Conservative, and Reform. Orthodoxy is committed to a faithful observance of traditional Judaism, Conservatism is less committed, Reform least of all. Congregational records reveal the relative numerical strength of each denomination. The

Reform movement now has by general admission the largest number of members. Close behind is the Conservative. Ranked far behind in numbers is the Orthodox, although a large unaffilliated component of American Jews consider themselves Orthodox.

Reconstructionism (Judaism defined as a civilization, founded by Rabbi Mordecai M. Kaplan in 1934) is the youngest of the principal denominations, far smaller than the Reform or Conservative. Reconstructionism today is quite different from the movement founded sixty years ago. It has undergone changes which would have surprised, perhaps bewildered, the founder and his disciples. A decreasing commitment to Zionism is a dramatic change in a movement conceived by Kaplan as "Zionist Judaism." Such a lessening interest replicates the trend in the general American Jewish community. There is also a marked difference in viewing issues in the larger secular world. Always sensitive to the demands of the prophetic message, Reconstructionism has of recent years demonstrated a strong preoccupation with such issues as radical feminism, gay rights, multiculturalism, and other issues which comprise much of the socially activist agenda of the liberal-left. Thus in both its Jewish and general perspectives Reconstructionism has embraced the concerns and trends of the environing culture, a clear illustration of acculturation.

Among the splinter groups which represent maverick interpretations of Judaism are followers of Humanism (Non-theistic Judaism, analogous to Christian Humanism), Polydoxy, and the Havurah movement. Theologically, ritually, and demographically, each of the major denominations is in a state of flux.

The American Jewish Committee Yearbook of 1989 records an "unprecedented revival" of Orthodox Judaism during the past two decades, with an accompanying rise in the self-esteem and prestige of its adherents."[4] There are communities where Jewish law is scrupulously obeyed and Jewish ritual and custom meticulously practiced as prescribed in the traditional codes. In New York, Los Angeles, and Chicago, entire neighborhoods live by the rigorous disciplines of Halacha (Jewish law). Yet these represent a small minority of American Jews.

Due to the energetic enterprise, imaginative entrepreneurship, and aggressive programs of their rabbis and devotees, it is true that the observant Orthodox have been growing in numbers in recent years. The religious and moral values they espouse appeal to young Jews who are dissatisfied with the permissive and undemanding Judaism they have known, and disillusioned with the values of the secular society. Meanwhile, the picturesqueness of certain Orthodox groups has given them high visibility and commended them to media attention. This accentuates their presence, leading to an inflated impression of their number. By the most liberal estimates, however, the Orthodox comprise less than 10 percent of the total population of American Jews.

In truth, Judaism as lived or practiced by the great majority of American Jews is scarcely recognizable as the Judaism of tradition. Perhaps it is inaccurate, some would say fanciful, to use the term "practice" when speaking of the religious behavior of most contemporary Jews. For the great majority of Jews are non-practicing. The intricately detailed network of traditional Jewish religious observance and belief affects their lives only superficially. They have little knowledge of it. The average modern Jew, left alone in the storehouse of Jewish belief, observance, history, and tradition would grope and stumble like a blind man in a maze. The extent of his practice will usually include partial ritualistic observance of Passover and Hanukah, synagogue attendance on the New Year (Rosh Hashanah) and the Day of Atonement (Yom Kippur), and presence at the life-cycle ceremonies of family and friends — a wedding, a funeral, a Bar/Bat Mitzvah. Jewish identification may include membership in a synagogue. But to be a member of a synagogue today may mean no more than a casual involvement in its quasi-religious program.

What has happened to Judaism in America as Jews have become progressively acculturated to the American environment might be called an agenda of religious abandonment. Hard as it may be for some Jews to acknowledge, the religion which for centuries was the axis around which their lives turned, has been neglected and ignored to the point of abandonment by the majority of those who still call themselves Jews.

What follows is a discussion of the impact of acculturation on the Sabbath and High Holidays, traditionally regarded as inviolate occasions of Jewish observance.

The Sabbath (Shabbat)

With one exception there is no occasion in Jewish life held more sacred by tradition than the Sabbath, the seventh day of the week, on which Jews are enjoined to rest and pray. The one exception is the Day of Atonement, which is aptly called the Sabbath of Sabbaths. In the words of Rabbi Leo Baeck (1874-1956), "There is no Judaism without the Sabbath." Ahad Ha'am (1856-1927), the Zionist ideologue, once wrote, "More than Israel has kept the Sabbath, the Sabbath has kept Israel." In the traditional Jewish community, there has always been a recognition of the surpassing importance of the Sabbath, and no Jew could have imagined Judaism without its observance.

Ahad Ha'am's adage has even found its way into the Reform liturgy for Sabbath eve. Not many Reform Jews may be aware of this because few of them attend Sabbath eve services. Congregations of more than a thousand families will muster a meager number on Friday night. Some congregations have built chapels where most of the services are held, so that the sparse gathering of worshipers will not feel lost in a cavernous main sanctuary. Special Sabbath eve services are often scheduled, honoring some occasion or organization, at which the rabbi seldom speaks. Even this fails to boost attendance. A rabbi endowed with eloquence or other personal charms may draw people to services. But by and large, nothing that the synagogue offers is sufficiently tempting to lure Jews from the distractions of home and community.

In his 1985 president's message to the Central Conference of American Rabbis, the national body of Reform rabbis, Rabbi W. Gunther Plaut called Friday night Sabbath eve services a "resounding failure." He had attended Reform services around the world and his mood was unrelieved gloom. Only "six to ten percent of our members" attend them, he said. Plaut advocates a reassessment of Sabbath eve worship and, if required, "its abandonment."[5]

Sabbath morning services fare no better. Of those who do attend, most may be outsiders, a motley gathering of family and friends come from near and far to witness the Bar/Bat Mitzvah of a member's child and to partake of the luncheon which follows. Plaut notes that these Bar/Bat Mitzvah congregations "crowd out our own." How many of "our own" are crowded out is dubious. Without a Bar Mitzvah on Shabbat morning, the Reform synagogue is likely to be empty.

In many Conservative congregations, the Friday night service, once the major religious service of the week, has been dropped from the synagogue calendar, victim of the contending secular culture. Friday night presents too many counter-attractions, from television to the high school basketball game. In Conservative congregations the Saturday morning service has now become the more important, with its commingled congregation of members and Bar/Bat Mitzvah visitors ("drop-ins"). The competing attractions of Saturday morning are apparently not so formidable as those of Friday night.

As Shabbat observance struggles for a place in the Jew's week-end schedule, the question is being asked whether the Jewish Sabbath is compatible with mainstream American life. On Friday night and Saturday morning the secular calendar spreads a net of workaday, recreational, and social activities wide enough to gather virtually all members of the community in its mesh. With doctors' and dentists' appointments, school sports, tennis and golf, and all the other activities which crowd the family weekend, there is precious little time or space for the synagogue.

Along with decreasing synagogue attendance, centuries-old Sabbath home observances have vanished as a part of Jewish life. Fewer and fewer homes will see Sabbath candles lit with the onset of Sabbath, hear the kiddush (blessing for wine) chanted, the hallah (Sabbath bread) blessed. It is not likely that grace after meals will be recited and Sabbath table songs (*zemirot*) sung.

If there is any validity in Ahad Ha'am's apothegm, that it is the Sabbath which has preserved the Jewish people, survival prospects for the American Jew may have to be rated as uncertain.

High Holidays

If synagogues are empty on the Sabbath, they are filled to capacity on two occasions in the year, Rosh Hashana (New Year) and Yom Kippur (Day of Atonement)

— the High Holidays. The High Holidays, which usually fall in September, and the ten days which separate them, comprise the holiest period of the Jewish year. Called the "Days of Awe," or the "Ten Days of Repentance," they are the days when, according to traditional belief, God judges each Jew and decides his mortal fate for the coming year. Every Jew is called to atone for his sins, to mend his ways, and to become reconciled with God and man. Perhaps his penitence will persuade the Divine Arbiter to render a favorable verdict, to "avert the evil decree."

Today far fewer Jews than formerly accept the old theological underpinning of the High Holidays. Children of enlightenment, they are not persuaded, much less intimidated, by age-old supernatural notions. But great numbers of American Jews will repair to the synagogue, if not for "religious" reasons, then out of communal custom and propriety, family memory, lingering loyalty to a tradition, or what Ludwig Lewisohn named "the call of the blood." The motivation could even be the prudent urge to hedge one's bets, to take no chances with the Arbiter of life and death. A growing number, finding the call of the synagogue less compelling than it was to their parents or grandparents, will play truant, staying at home, taking a break from work, even going to work. All of these Jews may be members of a congregation. In 1988, one of the largest congregations in the country reported that ten percent of its members made no request for High Holiday tickets.

How a Jew observes the High Holidays depends on his denominational affiliation. Orthodox Jews will spend all of Yom Kippur day in the synagogue, fasting for twenty-four hours. The most pious will spend the night as well in the synagogue at prayer. Conservative Jews will pray less ardently, partly in English, with considerable emotional restraint. Most will probably fast. Reform Jews will pray decorously, almost wholly in English, going home during the noon prayer-break, often to watch the baseball playoffs, returning to the synagogue for the Memorial Service. Comparatively few will fast. During the High Holidays, Jews exhibit a continuum of observance patterns, extending from complete absorption in the traditional practices to disregard for the least of them.

Judaism in Mid-Twentieth Century America

During World War II and in its aftermath, many young American Jews seemed to undergo a change in their attitude toward Judaism. The casual indifference of an earlier generation appeared to give way to a deeper interest in the synagogue and a readier acceptance of its agenda. I was frequently made aware of this while serving in the Pacific as Jewish chaplain of the First Marine Division during our two-year northward advance from New Caledonia to North China. It was especially remarked in the war veterans returning home, many of whom had "discovered" Judaism for the first time in military life. Whether because of the lacerating disruptions of combat, or the absence of atheists in foxholes, or personal contact with a chaplain, many had found the encounter with Judaism, fragmentary though it may have been, unexpectedly rewarding. The Nazi enemy, bent on the extermination of the Jews and of the moral values Judaism represents, itself may have been largely responsible for the reawakening of faith and the renewal of religious identity. When the men not long discharged from military service came back to civilian life, married, and had children, they found in the synagogue the answer to what had become a continuing Jewish and religious need.

In time, synagogues could be found all over the suburban landscape as Jews moved from the inner city. The synagogue was often the only Jewish institution in the community, and affiliating with it was the handiest vehicle for the affirmation of Jewish identity. Moreover, sending one's children to its religious school gave hope that the Jewish heritage would be preserved. With the home caught up in the secular preoccupations of American suburban life, the synagogue became the principal agent for the Jewish nurture of children, and joining it became part of the expected pattern of Jewish family life. The result was a dramatic growth in the established Jewish religious movements.

Reform Judaism

The first Reform Jews in America arrived in the mid-1800's. They came from Germany, where Reform Judaism had its inception at the end of the eighteenth and beginning of the nineteenth centuries. There were already well-established congregations in America, founded by Sephardic Jews two centuries earlier. Sephardic Jews traced their origins to the Jews of Spain and Portugal who had been banished by King Ferdinand and Queen Isabella in 1492. They had come to North America from Brazil and the Caribbean, and had settled in towns along the eastern seaboard, from Newport, Rhode Island, to New Orleans, Louisiana. They followed the ways of strict Orthodoxy. No attempt had been made to organize their congregations into a central body.

The German Jews, wishing to escape an antisemitic German milieu, in addition to the lure of opportunities in the U.S., began coming in large numbers in the middle decades of the nineteenth century. By 1880 there were a quarter of a million Jews in North America, most of them of German origin. The Judaism they brought with them was in no small part the product of the Age of Enlightenment, whose central Jewish figure was Moses Mendelssohn (1729-1786). Although himself a practitioner of traditional Judaism, Mendelssohn was familiar with current philosophical thought and was on friendly terms with some of the leading intellectual figures of Germany.

These Jewish children of the Enlightenment had two principal objectives in view: the first, to make the ritual and general atmosphere of the synagogue service consonant with "dignified" German Protestant norms; the second, to promote the idea of Judaism as an ethical religion. An ancillary purpose was to de-emphasize the separateness of the Jewish people. Hence, "outdated" ceremonies were discarded from home and synagogue, the vernacular and an organ introduced into the worship service, and references to Jewish nationhood in the prayer book eliminated. The founders of Reform wanted to fashion a Judaism which would be palatable to Jews who had emerged from the ghetto and were becoming acculturated to the "enlightened" world. Perhaps a Judaism adapted to the intellectual and social currents of the modern world would save them from assimilation; they would not have to choose between strict adherence to Jewish law and secular life in the Gentile world.

In 1885 a conference of rabbis meeting in Pittsburgh drew up a manifesto which set forth the guiding principles of the new Judaism. The Pittsburgh Platform became the charter of classical Reform Judaism. Exhorting Jews to live "in accord with the postulates of reason," it rejected all laws incompatible with the "habits of modern civilization and any national definition of Judaism." If this "rational" and "progressive" credo of early Reform seems naive, it is no more than the reflection of an age uninhibited by the constraints of tradition. But while proclaiming allegiance to the imperatives of pure reason, Reform rabbis at the same time strongly avowed rituals of identification with the Jewish people that were not exactly consistent with the untainted rationalism of the Pittsburgh Platform. One such ceremony was circumcision. No rabbi characterized circumcision as "outdated." (Some Reform Jews did abjure the practice; in the 1920's a professor at the Reform rabbinical seminary in Cincinnati did not have his sons circumcised.)

Another symbol of identification was the prohibition against intermarriage. Even the radical universalist, David Einhorn, condemned it, calling intermarriage "a nail driven into the coffin of Judaism." Yet the Reformers had made a critical break with the Jewish past. The Law of Sinai (*torat moshe mi'sinai*) and its elaboration in the Halacha had always been the supreme mandate in Jewish life. Now Reform Judaism promulgated the institution of a regime independent of Biblical and rabbinic authority. It was a break with the past serious enough to raise doubts as to whether it might ever be repaired.

During the decades before World War II, Reform Judaism was becalmed in the Jewish backwater of Cincinnati, where its central institutions — the Hebrew Union College and the Union of American Hebrew Congregations — had been founded. Commonly considered the religion of well-to-do Jews seeking acceptance by the Gentile world, it drifted serenely along its unhurried and unchanging way. But the years following World War II saw a dramatic change. Now under the aggressive leadership of its new president, Maurice N. Eisendrath, the Union of American Hebrew Congregations moved to the Jewish heartland of New York City, and shedding its image of exclusiveness, set out to win the "unaffiliated," proffering a Judaism with a wide appeal for modern American Jews.

Changes had begun to take place in Reform's ritual and ideological system. What had been frozen for half a century began to thaw. Temple services began to hear more Hebrew. More and more, Bar/Bat Mitzvah was celebrated. Skull caps appeared on worshipers' heads. Support for the newly established State of Israel enlisted the help of rabbis and laypersons. These changes were propelled by the catastrophic events of the forties. The Holocaust and the founding of the State of Israel focused the emotions of Jews powerfully on the questions of Jewish identity and survival. The desire symbolically to identify with the martyred millions was a strong incentive to make Reform more traditional.

Not every Reform Jew was persuaded. Some grumbling was heard from the thinning ranks of the classical Reformers. A Hebrew Union College professor deplored the return to a "new Orthodoxy," and complained, "We cannot lead our people forward by stumbling backward." Julian Morgenstern, president of the Hebrew Union College in the 1940's, lamenting that "the very notion of a Jewish state was sad and tragic," described Zionism as being "practically identical with Nazist and Fascist theory."[6] These seemed futile cries in a growingly self-conscious American Jewish milieu. Meanwhile, new congregations were sprouting all over the country.

As Reform Judaism has emerged into the 1990's, it seems to embody two opposite tendencies; on the one hand, a return to tradition, on the other, a rejection of tradition. The return to tradition is the assumption in the catch phrase, "Reform Judaism is becoming more Jewish." "More Jewish" no doubt refers to ritual forms and symbols long discarded, which have been restored to Reform worship — more Hebrew, a cantor, kiddush, skull caps. It refers also to the spate of published prayer books and manuals designed to familiarize Reform Jews with all manner of traditional ceremonial occasions from the Passover Seder to *Tu Bishevat* (New Year of trees). A manual on mitzvot encourages Reform Jews to consider a selective practice of kashrut. Since 1984, *mohalim/ot*, ritual circumcisors, men and women, have been instructed and trained under the auspices of the Hebrew Union College-Jewish Institute of Religion. That one day Reform Judaism might incorporate and promote these practices and programs would have struck its founders as crack-brained fantasy.

While not without significance, the accretion of ritual may have had only a superficial impact upon the lives of Reform congregants. The restoration of ritual has neither induced more members to lead lives disciplined by Judaism, to attend services, or noticeably to replenish the springs of faith. Nor despite all the glossy manuals is the Reform home distinguished by the practice of Jewish ceremonies. Only the Passover Seder and Hanukah are widely observed. It might be remembered that when rituals are not grounded in faith, they are likely to become not sacred symbols but shallow gestures.

Jewish Homes with no Mezzuzah

During my years as a rabbi, I spent hours every week in "pastoral calling."[7] Reform rabbis were expected to make house calls not only on life-crisis occasions — death, illness, anniversaries, celebrations, commemorations — but routinely in order to forge personal ties with members. Nothing in the rabbinic tradition suggested such visitations. The rabbi of old was primarily the authority on Halacha and people came to him to adjudicate personal and communal issues in the light of Halachic teaching. Pastoral calling is a Christian, mainly Protestant, clerical tradition and is indeed a principal duty of the Protestant minister.[8] The late Solomon Freehof, scholarly rabbi of large congregations and a Reform leader, rejected pastoral calling as a legitimate rabbinical function, calling its adoption by rabbis the "Protestantization of the rabbinate."[9] Thus another example of the acculturation of Judaism to the American Christian model.

An artifact of the Jewish home long considered indispensable is the mezzuzah, a small encased parchment scroll nailed to the right doorpost of the house. Inscribed on the scroll are the Biblical verses which command that a mezzuzah be affixed to the doorpost of every Jewish home (*Deuteronomy 6: 4-9; 11:13-21*). These Scriptural verses are part of the *sh'ma*, the central passage of the traditional prayer service recited twice daily, proclaiming God's unity. Through the ages, martyrs under torture died reciting the *sh'ma*. Few ritual injunctions are more compelling than the mitzvah of nailing the mezzuzah to the house doorpost. The usual explanation for the practice is that the mezzuzah is a reminder of God's protective presence.[10]

In a long career of pastoral calling, I seldom saw a mezzuzah on the door of a member's home. The hundreds of doorposts through which I passed very rarely bore this sign of a Jewish presence within. After World War II when people began migrating from the inner city to the suburbs, many Jews built homes in the suburban region served by our congregation. When they became members, I would sometimes suggest that they hold a house dedication ceremony (*hanukat ha'bayit*) to which they might invite family, friends, and neighbors. Nailing a mezzuzah to the doorpost would be the central rite. I pointed out the appropriateness of asking God's blessing, of sounding a Jewish note, when beginning to live in a new home. Although I made the suggestion scores of times, only two such ceremonies were ever held.

Like most Reform congregations, ours had stripped away most of the ritual integuments of Judaism. Many of the first generation members may not have known what a mezzuzah was. But many of our new families had come from a traditional background and, raised as Conservative or Orthodox Jews, might have been thought less resistant to marking the doorpost with a mezzuzah.

There was a growing impression at the time that Reform Judaism was becoming "more Jewish." But looking for evidence of Jewish renewal or discovery was a frustrating quest. I seldom saw a Jewish ritual object in the homes I visited. Judaism is often called a home religion, for Jewish life is marked around the year by home observances. These call for distinctive ritual objects — Shabbat candlesticks, kiddush cups, a spice box, a braided candle, a Hanukah menorah. Such ceremonial items may have been present in the homes I visited but they were seldom in evidence. Rarely did I see a Jewish book. Occasionally there was a Bible bound in silver, studded with turquoise, or an illustrated coffee-table book on Israel. These had probably been acquired in Israel or were a gift from some returning tourist. It led me to reflect on the lack of difference in our community between a Jewish and a non-Jewish home.[11] Many Jews may have preferred the similarity. A mezzuzah on your door is a mark of difference, and one of the reasons, subliminal or acknowledged, for moving to suburbia may have been the wish to distance yourself from the nagging stigma of Jewish difference. Joining a congregation as an emblem of Jewish identification was desirable, even commendable. But displaying a mezzuzah on your front doorpost might be overdoing it.

The Marketing of Holiness

Rabbinical bodies encourage the marketing approach in the pursuit of holiness. Judaica shops, they point out, advance the program of the synagogue not only because they provide a conduit for Jewish books into the homes of members, thus "increasing observance and commitment," but also because they provide income and cash flow for the synagogue. "Tens of thousands of dollars can flow into congregational coffers .... [it is] a joy to see a full service Judaic store chockful of .... good Jewish items, with a constant flow of people, enriching their Jewishness and the assets of the congregation at the same time. It is a felicitous conjoining of the spiritual and material." God and Mammon had seldom been more auspiciously yoked.[13]

Marketing strategies for prayer books and manuals alternate seductive and strident decibels. "Limited de luxe art editions .... stunning beauty and power .... gorgeous .... utterly elegant .... utterly beautiful." The undergirding premise of this liturgical hype has a surface plausibility. In order "to lead consciously Jewish lives [and] to guarantee [the] transmission [of Judaism] to succeeding generations .... congregants must be versed in Jewish principles and practice .... which best flourish in the home and the daily lives of the Jewish people." It is then ventured that this goal will be achieved by "building a Jewish bookshelf of highly acclaimed guides .... in the homes of every one of our congregants." The facilitator of this project will be the rabbi, "the *moher sefarim* (book seller) of every worthy congregation. [He is] the key to reaching this .... goal."[14]

But building Jewish bookshelves may be a dubious prescription for inducing a revival of faith. Mitzvah manuals may plead for a Jewish ritual regimen but without home and communal reinforcement such pleas will fall on barren ground. Prayer books no matter how artistically bedizened are not likely to bring Jews into the synagogue, or once inside, as on the High Holidays, stimulate them to enter into dialogue with God. Most who come will go through the liturgical choreography decorously. They will read the prayers addressed to God but few will be able to pray to Him. Appeals to buy prayer manuals for the three pilgrimage festivals, *Pesach* (Passover), *Shvuot* (Feast of Weeks), and *Sukkot* (Feast of Tabernacles) will meet a feeble response because Jews by and large no longer go to the synagogue on the major festivals. An executive of a major rabbinical body bravely declares that festival observance is the ground upon which the battle for Jewish renewal and continuity must be fought.[15] He may be right. Knowing the extent of home observance and synagogue attendance among American Jews makes this a gloomy prognosis for Jewish survival.

Students of Western society have considered the impact of the marketing ethos of modern life upon its value structure. In his *Escape from Freedom*, Erich Fromm, the psychoanalyst, examined the relationship of the marketing ethos to moral values, and concluded that in a society stamped with the marketing orientation, the ethical regime eventually succumbs to the values of the market.[16] It may not have occurred to the merchandisers of Jewish bookshelves that a burrowing worm might be at work in the books, and that the gain in cash flow might be offset by the loss of ethical purpose. Vigilance is always needed lest the quest for profit muffle the quest for holiness.

It is, of course, from the secular culture, in which Jews and Jewish life are embedded, that the Jewish denominations have acquired the desire and know-how for marketing their religious wares. Advertising is the medium, and its ecclesiastical acolytes are called upon to project the message. When one liturgical work is hailed as a "revolutionary non-sexist Haggadah" and the announcement of a new Rabbi's Manual beckons, "Buy 4, get 1 free," we know we are browsing in the purple pastures of glitz. Nor will it avail to place blame, point fingers, or squirm in embarrassment at the excess of hucksterism. When the air you breathe suppurates a pus which seeps into every crack in the culture, blaming individuals and institutions is irrelevant. For we are dealing with an ineluctable social process, acculturation.

God in the Twilight

It is doubtful whether with all their wiles, new marketing strategists will succeed in advancing the spiritual objectives of Judaism. The formidable, probably insurmountable, obstacle is a surrounding culture alienated from religious faith. At the end of the nineteenth century, Nietzsche described the modern temper as inhospitable to religion, and a hundred years later Kluckhohn called American culture "profoundly irreligious." The public square which once welcomed religious witness, now views with suspicion anyone who talks about God. Many Americans who still hold membership in a church no longer subscribe to its theological postulates. They belong but do not believe. Some sociologists hold that in a few decades religious believers are likely to be found only in small sects huddled together to resist a worldwide secular culture.[17] Evangelical and charismatic Christians constitute a staunch community of believers who adhere zealously to many of the original dogmas of Christian faith. But the mainstream churches, which disparage evangelism, remain the recognized, authoritative voice of Protestantism.

Civil Religion

Robert Bellah has described the Civil Religion, which he believes defines the spiritual domain of a growing number of Americans. This is a pattern of distinctly American loyalties, symbols, rituals, and calendar events, divested of any reference to traditional creeds, which have displaced theological commitment and worship in churches, and on which most Americans can agree. "American religiosity," in Irving Kristol's view, has a "civic dimension that toweringly overshadows the theological."[18]

The debility of the churches and Christianity finds its counterpart in the malaise of the synagogue and Judaism. That religion has lost its spiritual vitality for many Jews is the assessment of thoughtful observers of the current American Jewish scene, and the surveys confirm it. The basic vocabulary of religion has little meaning for the modern Jew. Professor Lawrence Hoffman, Hebrew Union College liturgist, says that American Jews are "uncomfortable with the notion of prayer," that their synagogues are sanctuaries for the "imposters" of prayer — "sensitivity seminars," "interaction of worshipers," dialogues with the rabbi, all by-passing "real dialogue with God." If prayer makes the modern Jew uncomfortable, it may be because God makes him uncomfortable. The leader of a national congregational body reports that congregants and rabbis everywhere avoid talking about God, and a well-known demographer revealed that only a small percentage of Reform rabbis believe in the traditional Jewish God. Hillel Halkin, the astute Israeli critic, claims that the theology of Mordecai Kaplan (1881-1983), for years regarded as one of American Jewry's most influential religious thinkers, can be compressed into this description of God: "God is the supreme being who does not exist but can be invoked to enhance what we wish."[19] Kaplan, he says, spent most of his life "paraphrasing" God. It is no exaggeration to say that no theologian exerted a more profound influence on the Reform and Conservative rabbinate of his time than the Reconstructionist Mordecai Kaplan.

A Jewish counterpart of Bellah's civil religion has been propounded by Jonathan Woocher.[20] In *Sacred Survival*, Woocher declares that the vast majority of American Jews no longer regard the synagogue, the rabbi, or Jewish sancta as a dominant force in their lives. The Federations, with their comprehensive programs of support for Jewish causes and institutions, national and international, particularly for Israel, provide the inspiration, while their executives furnish the leadership for the Jewish community. The synagogue with its program of prayer, study, and ritual is no longer central in the value perspective of most Jews. Not the religious calendar but the Federation calendar now provides the rallying points for spiritual exaltation — the Federation campaign, the annual national conventions, the mission to Israel. "We are one," chanted during the march through the streets of Jerusalem, may excite a higher tide of emotion than the recitation of *adonai ehad* ("God is One") in the synagogue on Yom Kippur.

The formulation of a Jewish civil religion on the heels of the framing of a generalized American civil religion should not occasion surprise, for it is but another instance of acculturation to an American pattern.

Nails in the Coffin

Recent years have witnessed a cumulative scrapping by Reform of long cherished Jewish ideological and Halachic pieties. To discard traditional Jewish beliefs and rituals was no new venture for Reform. It was synonymous with its birthright. But now the tempo and boldness of rejection seem, if anything, to be accelerating. It may have been widely rumored that Reform was becoming "more Jewish," but facts in the Reform constituency tell a different story. Intermarriage, once frowned upon and denounced by Reform spokesmen, is now accepted in Reform circles, rabbinic as well as lay. A constantly increasing number of young Reform Jews are marrying Gentiles, some converted, more unconverted, and a continually increasing number of rabbis are officiating. Some congregations will not engage a rabbi without an assurance of his readiness to officiate at intermarriages. The Reform Jew of the 1990's is far more accommodating toward intermarriage than was his denominational brother of the 1930's. It has been noted that in 1865 David Einhorn described intermarriage as a nail driven into the coffin of Judaism. In 1975 at the annual convention of the Central Conference of American Rabbis, the executive dean of the Hebrew Union College fiercely championed a rabbi's right to officiate at an intermarriage. Although suggesting a preference for inmarriage, the Central Conference supports the right of a rabbi to preside at an intermarriage.

Another instance of the rejection of tradition was the adoption of patrilineal descent as a criterion for Jewish identity. Among Jews the sole criterion for a child's Jewish identity has always been the Jewish identity of its mother — "a Jew is the child of a Jewish mother." When in 1983 the Central Conference voted to count the father's Jewish identity as sufficient warrant for that of the child, it marked a break with a tradition that had been zealously preserved since antiquity. This repudiation of a strictly held safeguard for Jewish social integrity shocked much of the Jewish world. A leading Orthodox rabbi summed up the sentiment of many Jewish leaders when he said, "There has been nothing more divisive in modern Jewish history than this decision to unilaterally change the definition of Jewishness."[21]

The question of patrilineal descent evoked little discussion, much less protest, among most American Jews. Its repercussions were remote from their concerns. A survey showed that 20 percent of American Jews have accepted the legitimacy of patrilineal descent. Some Reform rabbis were troubled by the stand taken by their rabbinical body. Before the Central Conference acted, Maram, the organization for Progressive rabbis in Israel, whose members live in close proximity to strongholds of Orthodoxy, abjured patrilineal descent as an affirmation for Jewish identity and sent an emissary, a widely respected colleague, to the Conference convention to plead with their Diaspora colleagues not to implement it. The Israeli envoy pointed to the damage enactment would do to *k'lal yisrael*, the cherished value of Jewish unity and solidarity. The assembled rabbis listened to their Israeli colleague, gave him a standing ovation at the end, and voted overwhelmingly against the position he advocated. Whatever else it meant, the unilateral repudiation of matrilineal descent as the crucial criterion for Jewish identity demonstrated how indurate Reform could be in its detachment from *k'lal yisrael*.

Another conspicuous break with *k'lal yisrael* came with the proposal put forth in 1993 by Rabbi Alexander Schindler, president of the national body of Reform congregations, that Reform Judaism embark on a program for the active proselytization of non-Jews. A troubled world, reasoned Schindler, desperately needed the ministrations of a Judaism which had bestowed the fruits of its historic wisdom and experience upon its followers. "Outreach" programs designed primarily for intermarried spouses, which he had been urging for years, were no longer enough. "Active pursuit" of non-Jews was now called for. We must "seek them out and invite them in." Schindler recommended that five million dollars be allocated to fund the program.[22]

Condemnation of the Reform leader's call for the conversion of non-Jews came from all branches of Judaism. Orthodox and Conservative leaders pointed out that Judaism had always opposed proselytization, actually discouraging non-Jews in their initial attempts to convert. Money and effort should be spent in "reaching out to Jews to be Jews, instead of to non-Jews to be pseudo-Jews." A few hardy spirits sought to dissociate Reform Judaism from Schindler's program. Far from reflecting a Reform consensus, no one in the entire world movement, they asserted, had ever advocated such a program. Reform's task was to focus its energies on those leaving Judaism through indifference, to keep Jews Jewish through Jewish education and Jewish experiences, emphasizing experiences in Israel.[23]

That *k'lal yisrael* was now on the outer rim of Schindler's back burner was made clear when the president of the Orthodox Union called his summons to conversion "another step by Reform which widens the gap between us."[24]

"Guidance not Governance"

Rabbi Solomon B. Freehof (1892-1990), leading Reform authority on Jewish practice, phrased an overarching principle of Reform Judaism as "guidance, not governance." No ritual or credal demands are made of Reform Jews. There are guidelines, suggestions, exhortations, but no mandates. "Please don't" is substituted for "Thou shalt not." In a manual on mitsvot issued by the Central Conference of American Rabbis in 1979, the editor declared that Reform Judaism was built on the commitment to "personal freedom of choice."[25] In 1973 the executive dean of the Hebrew Union College, Rabbi Eugene Mihaly, told the annual convention of the Central Conference of American Rabbis that the Conference had no right to tell its members what they may or may not do. "I embraced Reform Judaism to reject that."[26] The *New York Times* reporter, after attending the 1989 centenary convention of the Central Conference in Cincinnati, wrote: "The rabbis never decided .... how to determine right from wrong .... They did agree that freedom of choice remained the cornerstone of Reform Judaism; but they could not agree on specific moral standards after having abandoned so many absolutes central to Jewish tradition."[27]

Without the necessity for following any higher authority or discipline, it is not possible to specify the beliefs which unite Reform Jews, or to designate practices deemed unacceptable, except in terms so broad as to make them Jewishly meaningless. Reform has become a sea of diversity, an "amalgam of contradictory tendencies within American Judaism." The Centenary Perspective of the C.C.A.R. asserts, "Reform does more than tolerate diversity; it engenders it."[28] To the prophet's question, "What does the Lord require of you?" the Reform Jew might very well answer, "I'm not sure." Then after a pause for rumination, "Nothing specific."

A religion which makes few doctrinal or ritual demands has its own attraction for Jews, especially for intermarried couples. Many join the Unitarian Universalist Association, the most liberal of Protestant denominations. There is a vogue of Buddhism among mixed couples. Ari Goldman, former religion editor of the *New York Times*, who spent a year on leave at the Harvard Divinity School, describes the Buddhist couples he came to know there. During a campus visit by the Dalai Lama, he met the organizers of the welcome. The men were all Jews, their wives all born Christians. They praised their new religion because it was sufficiently broadminded to allow for the partial practice of their old ones. Anyway, was "lighting the candles before the Buddha all that different from lighting candles to welcome the Sabbath on Friday night?" As for the Dalai Lama, he wanted to learn about Judaism since so many of his followers were Jews.[29]

Reform has been called a permissive Judaism for a permissive age. Certainly Reform Judaism is flourishing in these permissive times. A mood of confidence informs the movement. And there are the numbers, those quantitative counters so beloved in the general culture, to validate the mood. With its bow to ritualism and its jettisoning of traditional sanctities, Reform has exerted its appeal to many of the unaffiliated who were looking for some vestigial anchorage, many of the marginals who felt restless in the mainstream — the intermarried, feminists, gays, Jews impatient with the disciplines of belief and practice, Jews careening headlong down the fast assimilationist track. Reform Jews today outnumber Conservative Jews, with the Orthodox gaining numerically but trailing far behind. Some Reform leaders, savoring the heady wine of success, are calling Reform the "authentic American expression of Judaism."

Conservative Judaism: Resisting Reform Respectably

It is said that Conservative Judaism arose in America as a reaction to the growth and strength of the Reform movement. Orthodox leaders, already disturbed by the radical teachings of the Reformers, were outraged by the Pittsburgh Platform and what was viewed as its wanton and deliberate discarding of Jewish sanctities. In 1882, two years after the Pittsburgh Platform was promulgated, Sabato Morais, rabbi of the pioneer Sephardic Mikveh Israel Congregation in Philadelphia, established a school of higher Jewish learning in New York City for the education of rabbis and teachers committed to the preservation of traditional Jewish doctrine and practice. This marked the inception of the Jewish Theological Seminary, training ground for Conservative rabbis and parent institution of the Conservative movement. A primary purpose of its founding was to resist the rise of Reform.

Four years earlier in 1878, an event had taken place in Cincinnati, home of Reform, which proved an unexpected catalyst for the new movement. The first class of rabbis at the Hebrew Union College had just been ordained and a banquet was to be held in their honor. At the time, neither the Hebrew Union College nor the Union of American Hebrew Congregations bore a definitive denominational stamp, and there was a possibility that these institutions might in future include all persuasions of American Jews. Some of the guests at the dinner observed *kashrut* (dietary laws). When everyone was seated, the first course was served. It was shrimp, a forbidden food. The observant among the guests rose from their tables and stormed out of the hall. When news of the incident spread, shock waves reverberated throughout the Jewish community. Jews everywhere were scandalized by what became known as the *traifa* (forbidden food) banquet. David Philipson, one of the newly ordained rabbis, later wrote that the *traifa* banquet "furnished the opening .... that culminated in the establishment of the Jewish Theological Seminary."[30] Nathan Glazer surmises that the silence of historians on the traifa banquet is due to an understandable reluctance "to trace such great consequences to the serving of shrimp."[31] After the *traifa* banquet, all hope for a united American Jewish religious community vanished.

Since its founding as a denomination of American Judaism, the Conservative movement has been animated by a strong pragmatic impulse. The founders avowed a commitment to the preservation of traditional Judaism within the context of American life. But no more than a decade after its founding, the Jewish Theological Seminary had fallen upon difficult days and was facing bankruptcy. A new president was sought whose views would represent a synthesis of tradition and modernity. Such a man was Solomon Schechter, the noted Genizah scholar, who was brought from Cambridge University in 1902 to become the first president of the resuscitated Seminary.

The Jewish patricians of New York who supported the Seminary financially, had a specific program in mind. They gave large sums to the Seminary expecting it to produce rabbis trained to help the immigrants bridge the gulf between their noisy, chaotic east European religious modes and the more decorous religious ways congenial to "minds influenced by American culture." Almost all of these wealthy patrons were Reform Jews, members of New York's Temple Emanuel, cathedral congregation of Reform Judaism. Their support for the Jewish Theological Seminary was a practical move designed to sanitize culturally and Jewishly the masses huddled in the tenements of New York. Incidentally, Schechter recoiled from the suggestion that he had been brought to America "for the purpose of converting the downtown Jew to a more refined species of religion." Had he suspected that, he would not have come.[32] A similar impulse led wealthy Reform Jews to facilitate the dispersal of these concentrations of New York Jews to the open spaces of the south and west. They no doubt considered the objective of Americanizing the immigrant masses worth the cost.

Growth, Malaise, Liberal Ferment

In the post-World War II decades, the Conservative movement enjoyed a period of vigorous growth. Claiming 800 congregations with 1,200,000 members, it became numerically the largest of the Jewish denominations. In the minds of many Jews it came to represent mainstream American Judaism and was spoken of as the predominant force in American Jewish life. Avoiding extremes, it was a safe half-way house between Orthodoxy and Reform. According to one study, 44 percent of all American Jews designated themselves "Conservative." Many of these were not necessarily affiliated with a congregation.

But during these years when early promise seemed to be reaching fulfillment, a malaise seems to have been at work in the movement. In 1972, Marshall Sklare, author of an authoritative study of the Conservative movement, wrote that "Conservatism .... at the zenith of its influence has sustained a loss of morale." Others described a "graying, numerically stagnant" movement wracked by "severe turmoil, intensified dissent .... demoralization." In 1987, Conservative Judaism's centennial year, its leaders — Seminary officials, rabbis, concerned laypersons — were said to be conceding that " the movement [was] in disarray."[33]

It has been suggested that a primary reason for the demoralization of the movement was the profound gulf which existed between the Judaism propagated by the leaders and the Judaism practiced by the followers. No definitive code of practices or principles for Conservative Judaism had been formulated in all the years since its founding. Widely divergent attitudes on the belief and ritual system existed among the various cohorts of the movement — the Jewish Theological Seminary, the lay people, the rabbis. The Seminary, fountainhead of Conservatism, espoused a Judaism which venerated Halacha, stressed the traditional worship of God, ritual observance, and Torah learning. The lay people were minimally observant, too busy for Torah study, unaware of Conservative ideology, with little if any commitment to the "holy dimension of Jewish life." Rabbis were caught in the crossfire between the didactics of Seminary teaching and the pragmatics of communal living as exemplified by their congregants. They saw themselves as frustrated mediators between the teachings of Seminary schoolmen and the implacable acculturation of their laymen. In 1902 the founders envisioned the Seminary as a citadel where the eternal sanctities, even when moderated, would be sustained. In mid-twentieth century the emergent reality was described in the terse catch phrase, an Orthodox faculty teaching Conservative rabbis to minister to Reform Jews. Rabbi Max Davidson called this, "A fascinating case of theological genetics."[34]

The 1980's saw a new mood, called by some "feisty" and "combative," emerging in the leadership of the Conservative movement. A generation of rabbis nurtured in Conservatism had arisen, who, no longer beholden to Orthodoxy, advocated practices and principles compatible with a more liberal ethos. Driving to services on Sabbaths and holidays and mixed seating in the synagogue were no longer uncommon practice. Now on the wave of the feminist movement, in which Jewish women played so prominent a part, gender egalitarianism was proclaimed a governing principle. Soon women were counted in a *minyan* (quorum for public prayer), given *aliyot* (called to the reading of the Torah), permitted to read from the Torah, and to don *tallit* (prayer shawl) and *tefilin* (phylacteries), and to become eligible for ordination as rabbis. In 1985 the first woman was ordained at the Jewish Theological Seminary. Women were among the chief catalysts of change in the Conservative movement.

Statement of Principles

In 1988, the Rabbinical Assembly was at last emboldened to issue a "Statement of Principles of Conservative Judaism," of which Robert Gordis was the editor. Entitled *Emet Ve-emunah* (Truth and Faith), it sets forth the "state of belief in Conservatism as a whole." It was the first such pronouncement since the inception of the movement almost a century earlier, and with rousing rhetoric it delineates its premises and aspirations. But the ambiguities, timidities, and imprecision which had long troubled Conservative Judaism, and which may have inhibited the formulation of a definitive statement of principles until almost a century after the founding of the movement, still seem to be in evidence.

Thus in his introduction, the editor trusts that the statement "will indicate to all individual Jews what is <u>expected</u> (emphasis added) of them by the movement to which they have given their allegiance." One gains the impression that Conservatism as here described is a religion of expectations; not requirements, least of all, demands. It "encourages" and "urges." The tone is hortatory, not mandatory; not, Thou shalt, but Thou should. There is the declaration, "Halacha [is] the governing framework of Jewish life," but one looks in vain for imperatives that make Halacha the actual standard by which Jews should live. The Conservative Jew is portrayed as a "traveler walking purposefully toward God's holy mountain," but nowhere are the credal and ritual requirements for purposeful walking designated. *Emet Ve-emunah* might be called a valiant proclamation of wishful thinking.[35]

There is a close affinity with Reform in this permissive, wavering posture toward the obligations of Jewish belief and conduct. Reform insists that Judaism function solely as "guidance" for the autonomous, freely choosing individual. Conservatism calls Halacha "a governing framework of Jewish life," but in the absence of specific prescriptions, "governing" is little more than a rhetorical ploy.

Conservative academics have defined Halacha as both "a binding legal system" and a "disciplinary way which is dynamic and evolving," that is, flexible, malleable. A Halacha which is both "binding" and "dynamic" would appear to be a curious theological *sha'atnez* (oxymoron). The verbal contradiction reflects the deeper contradictions of Conservative Judaism. There is especially the sharp dichotomy between an elite ideological leadership committed to religious observance and a mass lay membership ignorant and heedless of it. The leaders see Judaism as a personal commitment to religious belief, study, and conduct. The lay people, if we are to accept the frequent testimony of their rabbis, feel little commitment to any of this — not to learning Torah, nor to the "holy dimension of Jewish life," nor to worshipping God. Howard Singer defines Conservatism as a faith "with no restrictive personal requirements .... with each individual loyal in his fashion."[36] The similarity to Reform is striking.

Bar/Bat Mitzvah American Style

The manner in which Bar/Bat Mitzvah is now celebrated is often cited as a prime example of the banishment of spirituality from American Jewish life. Intended as a sacred rite of passage imbued with celestial purpose, Bar/Bat Mitzvah American style has become a crude and tasteless exhibition of consumerism. Some of the more garish examples of the prevalent fashion in Bar/Bat Mitzvahs have already entered the weirder folklore of American Jewry.

In Miami, Harvey Cohen's father rented the Orange Bowl for his son's Bar Mitzvah, printed invitations in the form of football tickets, dressed the waiters as referees and the waitresses as cheerleaders, hired a 100-piece high school marching band, and had "Happy Birthday, Harvey," flashed on the scoreboard. Jeff Fishman in Los Angeles had a "Star Wars" Bar Mitzvah with laser beams, fog machines, helium filled silver balloons, and a robot showing guests to their seats. In a New York suburb, a trained chimpanzee handed each entering guest a yarmulke. The cruise ship QE2 was the setting for a Bar Mitzvah in New York harbor, and in Miami, aboard another cruise ship, a Fantasy Island was created filled with parrots and other jungle accessories and featuring a cake shaped like a volcano, which at the party's climax erupted. In these affairs one looked in vain for some faint whiff of Judaism. A Bar Mitzvah party planner in Florida claiming to know the ingredients of a good party, asserted, "Religion is not one of them." Rabbi Jeffrey Salkin has written a manual on Bar/Bat Mitzvahs designed to reflect Jewish values. It's title: *Putting God on the Guest List*.

Bar/Bat Mitzvah glitz and the attendant crudities have angered some rabbis and laymen, and in 1992 the Board of the Union of American Hebrew Congregations went on record as deploring the "idolatry and relentless commercial colonization (*sic*) of our sacred events." But the futility of such resolutions is underlined by the negligible impact of similar pronouncements by the same synagogue body in the past (1968,1972). Apparently the laymen weren't listening, for since the sixties Bar/Bat Mitzvah profligacy has increased and its tastelessness honed to an excruciating vulgarity. Commenting on the "themes" chosen by families for the festive luncheon or dinner, one rabbi commented, "I've seen every theme except human sacrifice." Some parents try to introduce a "spiritual" note by linking the Bar/Bat Mitzvah with acts of *tsedaka* — contributing a percentage of the festivity's cost to the needy, asking guests to bring food and clothing for the poor, giving leftover food to a welfare agency. A Florida rabbi doubted whether these gestures would modify the stifling consumerist Bar/Bat Mitzvah patterns. "It's like issuing an edict asking Americans not to overeat."

Historical records disclose that the lavish Bar Mitzvah is not a new phenomenon in Jewish life. Israel Abrahams relates that in the fifteenth century "large parties [marked by] ostentation .... display .... extravagance ...." were not uncommon features of the Bar Mitzvah. Parents were encouraged to "arrange a banquet when their son became Bar Mitzvah just as they do on the day of his wedding." Sumptuary laws enacted throughout the middle ages were aimed at curbing these excesses. "Jewish moralists and preachers shouted themselves hoarse in exhortations toward greater moderation."[37] There are rabbis today who still do, but their entreaties avail as little today as they did in the fifteenth century. For the American Jew is the paradigm modernist wedded to a secular culture steeped in the gewgaws of hedonism. He has little understanding of the transcendental and less need for the supernatural. Spirituality is an orphan wandering alone in a faithless world, and the American Jew can only feel awkward when he tries to take it in hand.

The cause for the latter-day character of Bar/Bat Mitzvah derives from the culture of the surrounding world, which is inhospitable to the spiritual. Not inwardness but outwardness, not internals but externals, count in that world. "Much of Torah life," Emanuel Feldman observes from the Orthodox perspective, "[mirroring] the society around it, has been brought down to the level of externals." If this is true of Orthodoxy, how much more true of the masses of Jews who have discarded or forgotten the essentials of Judaism.

Cultural Winds of Change

The convergence of Conservative and Reform patterns of belief and practice may be viewed as the result of the operation of cultural forces in the general environment which all Americans share. Conservative Jews began to drive to services on Shabbat because they lived too far from the synagogue to walk and were addicted to the automobile. Gender egalitarianism in the synagogue and the ordination of women as rabbis were brought about by resolute women committed to a feminist agenda. That the Reform movement had already begun to ordain women was of incidental significance. In driving to services and in changing the status of women in the synagogue, Conservative and Reform Jews were carried along by the same currents swirling in the general culture. Imperatives in the secular culture are often responsible for shaping the form and content of Judaism in America.

The respective responses of Conservatism and Reform to the issues of intermarriage and patrilineality reveal the influence of the prevailing culture in determining religious attitudes and decisions.

Many Reform rabbis officiate at intermarriages. Conservative rabbis do not. If a Conservative rabbi should, his rabbinical association, the Rabbinical Assembly, might very well expel him. But there are some members of the Rabbinical Assembly who would circumvent this possibility by making conversion to Judaism easier. The present requirements for conversion are often deemed too demanding. Robert Gordis, whose rabbinic and scholarly credentials were immaculate, urged a more liberal approach to conversion in order to reduce the "thousands upon thousands of .... defections from [Jewish] ranks." Apparently "rabbinic accommodation to [intermarriage] is not confined to Reform rabbis." Here the intention is not to copy Reform's open acceptance of intermarriage but rather to tolerate it as a fact of American life.

The well-remembered Halachic decision by the late Professor Louis Ginsberg, in his time doyen of the Jewish Theological Seminary faculty, is revealing in this context. A Baltimore congregation ready to split on the issue of segregated seating appealed to the Seminary for a judgment. Professor Ginsberg advised that while mixed seating was a violation of Jewish law, "breaking up a congregation was a greater evil." Ginsberg was conceding the inevitability of change in Jewish practice caused by acculturation.

The issue of patrilineality also shows how cherished traditions are affected by the winds of change. Since earliest time Judaism, as we have noted, recognized a child's Jewish identity solely by that of its mother. When Reform Judaism broke from this universal Jewish convention in 1983, the traditional Jewish world was dismayed. The Conservative movement criticized the decision as a "misguided departure from the unified approach of the Jewish people." The Rabbinical Assembly threatened to expel any rabbi who failed to support matrilineal descent. Yet over two hundred members of the Assembly urged further study of the question. This has been interpreted as a "movement .... to rethink the resolution" which mandates expulsion for rabbinic transgressors.

There is little question that patrilineal descent as sufficient warrant for Jewish identity will continue to be an issue in Conservative circles. Some say that Conservatism will eventually go the way of Reform and sanction its legitimacy. People remember how the ordination of women was once condemned by the Conservative movement. Now there are women in every class ordained at the Jewish Theological Seminary.

If Conservatism in future sanctions patrilineality, it will not be primarily because Reform has also done it. It will be because it is trying to cope with the perplexing social realities confronting most American Jews. These are the dogged givens of the prevailing culture, specifically, the mounting wave of intermarriage and the shrinking Jewish birth rate. The motivation for endorsing patrilineality lies in the fabric of the general culture, which is the same for both Conservative and Reform Jews. As Singer has observed, both have felt the need to conserve the numerical stability of American Jews. Thus do old Halachic restraints dissolve in the corrosive ambiance of cultural reality.

Notes

1. Irving Howe, *World of Our Fathers* (New York: Harcourt Brace Jovanovich, 1976), p. 641

2. Louis Finkelstein, "The Jewish Religion: Its Beliefs and Practices," in *The Jews: Their History, Culture and Religion*, ed. Louis Finkelstein, (New York: Harper & Bros., 1949) 2:1739

3. Edward Sapir, "The Application of Anthropology to Human Relations," in *The American Way: A Study of Human Relations Among Protestants, Catholics and Jews*, ed. N.D. Baker, C.J.H. Hayes and R.W. Straus (Chicago: Willett Clark, 1936) p. 128

4. Jack Wertheimer, "Recent Trends in American Judaism," *American Jewish Yearbook* (Philadelphia: Jewish Publication Society, 1989) 89:149

5. W. Gunther Plaut, "President's Message," *CCAR Yearbook* 35 (New York: CCAR, 1985) pp. 4-5

6. Michael A. Meyer, "A Centennial History." In Samuel E. Karff, ed., *Hebrew Union College Jewish Institute of Religion at One Hundred Years* (Cincinnati: HUC Press, 1976) pp. 59, 132-3

7. I was one of a generation of rabbis to whom pastoral calling was a rabbinical function of major importance. In my schedule, Saturday and Sunday afternoons were spent making house calls. It was not unusual for eight calls to be made on a single Saturday or Sunday. Hospital calls were made on week-days. To rabbis ordained in recent years, pastoral calling may be less in demand by congregants, although in 1973, Wolfe Kelman, a leading Conservative rabbi, singled out the "pastoral function" as the most important "expectation" of the "contemporary rabbi."

8. It is assumed that the pastor's duty to call will induce a reciprocal duty of the church member to attend church. On the wall behind the desk of a Protestant colleague in Glencoe hung a framed motto which read, "Members visited by the pastor at home on weekdays will visit the pastor in church on Sundays." In our congregation there was no reciprocal obligation for a member to attend religious services after the rabbi called.

9. The following framed motto was once suggested for Freehof's study wall: "The call of duty should not descend into the duty of calling."

10. Folklorists see the mezzuzah as an amulet intended to ward off evil spirits.

11. We were hardly in a position to verify the difference, for during the 24 years that we lived in Glencoe, we were invited to two non-Jewish homes.

12. Clyde Kluckhohn, *Mirror for Man: The Relation of Anthropology to Modern Life* (New York: McGraw Hill, 1949)

13. Often American Jews will liken a congregation to a business or corporate enterprise. In a Yom Kippur message to members, a congregation president quoted approvingly a rabbi who had written, "If we were a business, our product would be making Jews." The president wanted his readers to consider his message a "report to the stockholders," which left him "very optimistic about this year's successful operation."

14. *CCAR Newsletter*, August 1986; CCAR communication, January 1987

15. Joseph Glaser, *CCAR Yearbook*, vol. 94, 1985, pp. 79-81

16. Erich Fromm, *Escape from Freedom* (1941)

17. Kluckholn, ibid., p. 247; Stephen L. Carter, *The Culture of Disbelief: How American Law and Politics Trivialize Religious Devotion* (New York: Basic Books, 1993); Peter L. Berger, "A Bleak Outlook Seen for Religion," in *New York Times*, January 25, 1968

18. Robert N. Bellah, "Civil Religion in America," in *Daedalus*, Winter 1967, pp.1-21; Irving Kristol, "Taking Political Things Personally," in *Times Literary Supplement* (TLS), March 1, 1991, p. 5

19. Lawrence A. Hoffman, "Creative Liturgy," in *Jewish Sentinel*, Winter 1975, p.47; Hillel Halkin, "God Is in the Swimming Pool," in *The Jerusalem Report*, September 9, 1993, p. 46

20. Jonathan Woocher, *Sacred Survival: The Civil Religion of American Jews*, (Bloomington: Indiana University Press, 1987); Wertheimer, ibid., p. 149
21. Wertheimer, *ibid.*, p.149
22. Sue Fishkoff, "U.S. Orthodox, Conservatives Rap Reform Proselytization Plan," in *Jerusalem Post*, October 16, 1993
23. Haim Shapiro, "Reform Leader: Most of Us Don't Support Proselytizing", in *Jerusalem Post*, October 18, 1993, p. 3
24. Sue Fishkoff, *ibid.*
25. Simeon J. Maslin, ed., *Gates of Mitzvah: A Guide to the Jewish Life Cycle* (New York: CCAR, 1979) p. 4
26. Eugene Mihaly, Response to "Report of the Ad Hoc Committee on Mixed Marriage," *CCAR Yearbook* (New York; CCAR, 1973), pp. 85-87
27. "Message from the President: Is Choice the Only Issue?" *CCAR Newsletter*, December 1989, p. 1
28. Centenary Perspective
29. Ari L. Goldman, *The Search for God at Harvard* (New York: Times Books, Random House, 1991) pp. 94-96
30. David Philipson, *The Reform Movement in Judaism* (New York: 1941), p. Press, 1972), p. 57
31. Nathan Glazer, *American Judaism*, 2nd ed. (Chicago: University of Chicago Press, 1972), p.57
32. Norman Bentwich, *Solomon Schechter* (Philadelphia: Jewish Publication Society, 1938), p. 191
33. Wertheimer, *ibid.*, p. 127
34. Marshall Sklare, *Conservative Judaism: An American Religious Movement* (Glencoe, IL: Free Press, 1955), p. 286
35. Robert Gordis, ed., *Emet Ve-emunah*
36. Howard Singer, "The Judaism Born in America," in *Commentary* (December 1986), p. 46
37. Israel Abrahams, *Jewish Life in the Middle Ages* (New York: MacMillan, 1917), pp. 144, 291

CHAPTER 5

THE ACCULTURATION OF ORTHODOX JUDAISM

Orthodox Judaism has experienced a wholly unexpected revival in America in recent years. At the end of World War II, few could have predicted that Orthodoxy would become a vigorous force in American Jewish life. Second- and third-generation descendants of the immigrants who had come to America between 1880 and 1920 had defected from Orthodoxy in such numbers that many were predicting the end of Orthodox Judaism as a viable religious denomination. Moreover, with the extermination of millions of Europe's Jews in the Holocaust, the human reservoirs for traditional Judaism that had always replenished the American Orthodox community, had all but dried up.

Yet today Orthodoxy in America is strong, energetic, growing, confident of the future. "It is no mere fossil," writes Glazer, "as it would have been reasonable to consider a few decades ago."[1] The historical fact is that for the first time in two hundred years, Orthodox Judaism is no longer in decline.

To many observers, Orthodoxy projects the image of a religious movement frozen in time, incapable of change. It is true that the advocates of greater stringency seem to be in the ascendant and that Orthodoxy as a whole seems to be moving to the right, thus appearing to validate the prevailing image. At the same time, there is considerable evidence that Orthodoxy is not impervious to change, that it is, in fact, being affected by the encroachments of the secular culture.

Orthodox Jews can no longer be pictured as living in the impoverished and squalid ghetto where popular fancy had long immured them. They have integrated themselves into American life. There are Orthodox Jews in the universities and on Wall Street. Lubavitch Hasidim send mitzva-mobiles to cruise city streets and buttonhole secular Jews in order to enact rituals of prayer and sanctification on the spot. Orthodox Jews lobby Congress and state legislatures for the passage of laws favorable to causes they support. They appeal to municipalities to erect large Hanukah menorahs (candelabra) on public property whose candles burn during the eight nights of the festival of Hanukah, which often coincides with Christmas.

Sometimes the candelabrum will be placed next to a Christmas creche, which has been built as a result of the importunings of Christians for the public recognition of Christmas. Orthodox Jews have no objection to the exhibit of religious symbols on public property, although their Reform and Conservative coreligionists will have fits about this apparent violation of the principle of the separation of church and state. Orthodox Jews pay little mind to the nervous tics of liberal Jews regarding public acknowledgment of Judaism. The Orthodox have come into their own in religiously pluralistic America. Their mood is summed up in the rallying calls, "We are on the march" .... "The future is ours." Their critics sometimes call this "Orthodox triumphalism."

Orthodoxy Turns Right

With its growth and increased zeal, Orthodoxy has taken a distinct rightward turn in ideology and practice. While generally becoming more devout, Orthodox Jews are by no means united in their belief and behavior patterns. The strictest are exclusivist toward the rest of the Jewish world and dismissive of the secular world. The moderate display a more flexible approach to the tradition and are open to a selective involvement in the secular culture. Between the two there are gradations of zealotry. But few will deny that the general trend in all Orthodoxy seems to be to the right.

The strictest Orthodox are commonly called *Haredim* or ultra-Orthodox. (Charles Liebman calls them "Sectarians.") The more moderate Orthodox are called "Centrists." The stages of strictness may be indicated by the head covering worn by the men. The stricter the wearer, the more elaborate the headgear. *Haredim* wear black fedora hats. On Shabbat and holy days, some will wear a fur hat (*shtreimel*) over the *kipah*. Fur hats are the vogue in Hasidic groups, the style often depending on the particular sect. Centrists wear skull caps (*kipot*), black or colored, cloth or knitted, which cover a small portion of the head. Centrist Jews are sometimes referred to as the "knitted kipot."

What has been called a "major revolution" in the ultra-Orthodox community finds its younger members assiduously seeking out and following a greater stringency in Halachic and ritual practice.[2] Called the world of *humrot* (stringencies) or

Bnai Brakism, it is a movement made up largely of yeshiva students, who, counting themselves an elite, fulfill a religious regimen more punctilious than that of the older generation of *dati'im,* (religious Jews). The term Bnai Brakism derives from Bnai Brak, the predominantly ultra-Orthodox community near Tel Aviv. This stress toward greater stringency is inspired by the influence of Hazon Ish, Rabbi Avraham Yeshayahu Karlitz, the teacher and sage who came to Israel from Lithuania in 1935 and founded a yeshiva in Bnai Brak. In the relatively short span of its existence, Bnai Brakism has become a "foremost phenomenon in shaping the life style of all of Orthodox Jewry."[3]

An intransigent exclusiveness appears to characterize the ultra-Orthodox. They would delegitimate other Jews, from the non-Orthodox to those Orthodox who are in disagreement with them. Rabbi Norman Lamm, the Centrist president of Yeshiva University, has remarked, "Many of our people no longer regard non-Orthodox Jews as part of *k'lal yisrael,* the worldwide fellowship of Jews. They scorn lay people, the *balabatim,* holding that their opinion "is the reverse of the opinion of the Torah."[4] Moreover, strife between ultra-Orthodox *rebbes* is not uncommon, their devotees sometimes resorting to violence. Ultra-Orthodox rabbinic leaders deliberately subvert any move toward cooperation with other groups. They would insulate their followers against Western ways, deeming all secular activities dangerous, including secular education, literature, art, music, radio, television, newspapers, and magazines. This is the yeshiva world of the ultra-Orthodox in which a coterie of rabbinic autocrats reigns supreme.

A sampling of the ultra-Orthodox agenda, both within the larger Orthodox fold and beyond it, discloses how far its devotees will go in pursuing their doctrinaire way. Synagogues without a *mehitza* (the barrier separating men and women), are ruled illegitimate, off limits to the faithful. Social mingling between the sexes is not permitted on synagogue premises whether for adults or youngsters. Strictest observance of religious rites is required generally, but particularly for lay leaders. The added strictness has given rise to the jocular reference to a "*humrah* (stringency)-of-the-month club."

Coeducation in the synagogue school is frowned upon and boys and girls are separated by the time they reach the third grade. Secular Hebrew and its literature are denigrated. In a steady campaign of calumny, Reform and Conservative rabbis are denounced. Marriages performed by them are declared invalid, therefore needing no *get* (religious divorce) for their annulment. Reform Judaism is charged with causing intermarriage, Conservatism with leading to Reform. Rather than attend non-Orthodox services, Jews are urged to stay at home. Before the High Holidays, metropolitan newspapers will carry large advertisements warning Jews who wish to fulfill the sacred precept of hearing the *shofar* (ram's horn) blown on Rosh Hashanah, not to step into a Reform or Conservative synagogue. To hear the *shofar* in such surroundings is *a hillul ha-shem* ("desecration of God's name"), a sacrilege.

The Centrist Orthodox seem models of modernity compared with the Sectarians, but many of their number feel the ground shifting under their feet. They had always believed in harmonizing traditional Judaism with Western culture. The motto of Yeshiva University, long a citadel of Centrism, is *torah u'madah*, Torah and Science. Yet not long ago the student paper featured a symposium which questioned, "Why Do Yeshiva Men Attend College?" The registrar of Yeshiva's rabbinical seminary, the Rabbi Yitzchak Elhanan Theological Seminary, summed up the changes of the past twenty years in the statement, "We have moved way to the right."[5] Young Israel, the stalwart organization of Orthodox youth, was established on a synthesis of tradition and modernity. Now that synthesis is challenged as Orthodox institutions once thought "modern" appear to be intimidated by the relentless pressures of the religiously intractable.

Reasons for Revival

The revitalization of Orthodoxy in America after decades of somnolence has been attributed to a variety of causes. The startling increase in the number of all-day schools is a factor of first importance. Staffed by teachers committed in great part to ultra-Orthodox doctrine, some of these schools encouraged the beliefs and practices of an earlier time. Many of the children became more observant than their parents. Nor did the parents object. Fearing the rising tide of assimilation, they were not averse to exposing their children to a religious mode more rigorous than their own. In the encircling social environment of the all-day school, the children found friends who shared their daily lives, their values, and, in many cases, the years which lay ahead. These schools enjoyed an astonishing growth from the 1940's, when there were 35 Orthodox all-day schools in America, until 1975, when all-day schools numbered 563. Today there are many more.[6]

Another factor contributing to the reinvigoration of Orthodoxy was the greatly improved economic status of Orthodox Jews. Sharing in the general post-World War II prosperity, they and their children were able to go to college, enter the professions, and move steadily up the economic ladder. They could now afford membership in a congregation, all-day schools for the children, Jewish summer camps, trips to Israel.

Above all, Orthodoxy offered important non-material rewards for Jews seeking stability in an unstable world. Making a living was no longer a problem but the world in which one made a living presented many problems. For that world was apparently undergoing a progressive erosion of its moral fiber. Divorce was rampant, juvenile deliquency and crime rising, drug use and alcoholism increasing. The soaring rate of intermarriage was a black cloud on the social horizon. A new permissiveness was abroad, which, combining hedonism with the cult of the individual, lent sanction to ideas and conduct once thought aberrant, anti-social, or immoral.

In contrast to this chaotic order, Orthodoxy stood for the time-tested precepts and institutions of Judaism. Sanctity of marriage, integrity of the home, and purity of family life, were still values of surpassing importance in the constellation of Orthodox practice and belief. Jewish survival was still an unnegotiable premise. Orthodox Judaism did not hesitate to set limits, to define what was acceptable, what deviant; to insist if need be, "Thou shalt not." Hence its appeal for Jews who found secular life devoid of moral purpose. It drew to its fold Jews who wanted to live under the authority of binding religious law interpreted by charismatic masters of the law. It exerted a powerful attraction for Jews, who, unlike those in the Reform and Conservative camps, wanted not only guidance but governance as well. Such Jews are often *ba'alei teshuva*, those who "return" to Judaism. (Some have called them "born again Jews"). Their return came at the end of a quest for some spiritual way. The appeal of Orthodoxy lay precisely in its limitation of personal autonomy in matters of belief and practice. The *ba'al teshuva* welcomes the imposition of authority in his life. He is committed to the declaration on the kitchen wall plaque, "The Ten Commandments are not multiple choice."

American Orthodoxy has also been strengthened by financial support from individual Jews not necessarily Orthodox themselves. Such Jews run the gamut of personal identification with Orthodoxy from those who are devotees of charismatic rebbes to those who have no Jewish denominational affiliation at all. Most have sprung from Orthodox roots and still have strong ties of memory and sentiment with traditional Judaism. The indifference of their children and grandchildren to Judaism may represent to them a personal failure to meet their responsibility as Jews. Giving money to the most zealous guardians of the faith may be the ransom they pay for assuaging guilt and appeasing God. "I have failed. Perhaps I can save the remnant that remains. I may die without Jewish descendants, but before I go, I'll bequeath my treasure to those who will defend and preserve the faith."

Ultra-Orthodoxy and Acculturation

"Non-observant Orthodox" was the term coined by Joseph Lookstein (1903-1979), the prominent American Orthodox rabbi who founded the Ramaz School in New York, to describe Orthodox Jews who violate basic Jewish tenets, yet belong to Orthodox congregations and are adjudged to be in good standing religiously by rabbinic authority. It happens not infrequently that widely esteemed rabbis, after adjudicating individual breaches of Halachic precept, will go on to legitimize the Orthodoxy of backsliders and declare them qualified to be bonafide members of a *minyan* (prayer service). For rabbis who believe that failure to observe a *mitzvah* (commandment) is defiance of the word of God, such decisions exhibit a surprising leniency.

The rabbinic decisions which illustrate this unexpected tolerance of Jews who violate Halachic injunction have been analyzed by Rabbi Solomon B. Freehof. He cites prominent *poskim*, authorities in rabbinic law, who in certain circumstances exculpate Jews who do not observe the Sabbath, fail to put on tefilin, do not fast on prescribed fast days, or are not circumcised. They demonstrate, concludes Freehof, "a patient understanding of the influence of modern western life, which must be lived in constant contact with the non-Jewish environment."[7] There could be no more accurate description of the process of acculturation and no better illustration of its influence.

Recent modifications of prior Halachic decisions reflect an accommodation to the wider Jewish and non-Jewish world. When the Ethiopian Jews succeeded in reaching Israel in 1986, the official Israeli rabbinate, which had hesitated to accept them as authentic Jews, ruled that henceforth marriages among them must be performed by an officially sanctioned rabbi and only after certain initiatory rituals had been performed. There was an immediate and strenuous protest both from the Beta Israel (Ethiopian Jews prefer this designation) and from much of the Jewish world. No response from the rabbis was immediately forthcoming, but in 1989 they announced that in future, Beta Israel could be married by Rabbi David Shloush, chief Hasidic rabbi of Netanya, and a member of the Rabbinic Council, under conditions which would not slight their *amour-propre*. While this marked no revolutionary change in the posture of the religious establishment, it did signal a decision to retreat from a previously declared position. A small gesture, a whiff of compromise, yet telltale in Israel. Equally indicative of the retreat from intransigence was the decision by prominent *Haredi* Israeli rabbis to make allowances in the conversion process for the numerous non-Jewish spouses and children of Soviet Jews who have come to Israel.

The most formidable strongholds of Orthodoxy may be less than impermeable to the influence of the secular culture. As has been noted, ultra-Orthodox leaders prohibit the use of many of the artifacts of the western world regarded as profane. Thus television, that paradigm gadget of secularity, is banned to *Haredim*. Yet not long ago in a Jerusalem mall, several dozen yeshiva youths from a nearby enclosed Hasidic neighborhood, attired in black hats and tunics, were seen packed together outside a TV store viewing a basketball game televised from America. (The New York Knicks were playing the Chicago Bulls.) Standing there for two hours, the yeshiva boys were engaged in an activity expressly forbidden by their rabbis. Children from a Jerusalem *Haredi* neighborhood often gather outside a nearby luxury apartment building and when apartment dwellers approach, ask if they can come up to watch television. The rabbis have worked hard to build a wall against the outside world, but they may not have built it high enough. The question is whether any wall can be high enough to shut out the secular world in the twenty-first century.[8]

Feminism

A formidable challenge to the Orthodox way and its rabbinical leaders is posed by Orthodox women influenced by feminism. The ferment of gender egalitarianism that has affected American culture as a whole has had its impact upon Orthodox women. While it has not made the radical inroads into Orthodoxy that it has into the Reform and Conservative camps, it has led to the creation of new usages and rituals which would have been inconceivable a few years ago. Moreover, it has led to a new mood among many Centrist Orthodox women — a determination to articulate and to demonstrate their claim to a larger role in the religious life of their community. While not defiant of rabbinic authority, they will not refrain from raising questions about Halachic ordinances which, they feel, victimize them.

When Orthodox women, disregarding Jewish tradition, formed *tefila* (prayer) groups for women only, tremors of varying intensity rumbled through the Orthodox world. Even a Centrist institution like Yeshiva University, speaking through five of its Talmudic scholars, issued a peremptory ban on such prayer groups, which they called a "product of the licentiousness of feminism."[9] In Jerusalem, interdenominational women's prayer groups have attempted to pray at the Western Wall, only to be sent scurrying by infuriated ultra-Orthodox men hurling everything at hand, from curses to chairs. Nevertheless, women's *tefila* groups, their determination undiminished, continue to meet in cities from Los Angeles to Jerusalem — with the approval of some Orthodox rabbis.

The movement for gender egalitarianism in the synagogue has been fertile ground for the creation of new ritual occasions. In some Orthodox circles the birth of a girl is attended by festive rites which are an obvious counterpart of the *brit milah* (circumcision) for boys. *Shalom bat* (daughter's welcome) gatherings bring family and friends together in home and synagogue for a *kiddush* accompanied by celebratory singing and speech-making. In some synagogues the mother will recite the *birhat hagomel* (blessing of redemption), delivered traditionally when illness or danger has been overcome. When an Orthodox girl reaches her twelfth birthday, she may become the celebrant in a special *se'udah sh'lishit* (third meal) festivity held on a Shabbat afternoon or Sunday. On this Orthodox equivalent of the Conservative and Reform Bat Mitzva, she will deliver a *d'var torah* (interpretation of Torah) to demonstrate her familiarity with the essentials of Jewish tradition and faith. Recently a teenage girl was allowed to read from the Torah during an Orthodox service in Los Angeles.

The restlessness and dissatisfaction of a growing number of Orthodox women with their role in the traditional synagogue is attributable not only to the feminist movement, but also to the importance which has for some time been assigned to the Jewish education of girls by all branches of Orthodoxy. Until modern times, there was little concern for the education of girls in the traditional community.

When Samson Raphael Hirsch (1808-1888), the renowned nineteenth century Orthodox rabbi of Frankfurt, opened a high school for girls, it signaled a change in the attitude toward women destined inevitably to have wider repercussions in the Orthodox world. Now many Orthodox schools have their programs of intensive Jewish education for girls. Today it is the graduates of the Orthodox schools, well educated, Jewishly literate women, who form the vanguard encouraging change in the status of women in the Orthodox world. These developments have had, and will continue to have, an obvious impact on the hierarchical structure of the traditional Jewish family.

Law (*Halacha*) and Custom (*Minhag*)

The accommodation of Jewish life to external cultural norms is, as we have seen, a leitmotif of Jewish history. Customs (*minhagim*) which often arose as a response to influences in the surrounding culture, became in time an integral part of Judaism and of Jewish life. Despite the misgivings of some rabbinic authorities, the *minhagim* enjoyed the hearty support and participation of the people, becoming part of what has been called Jewish folk religion.[10] It is not surprising, therefore, that Moses Isserles (1520-1572) incorporated the description of many customs into the *shulhan arukh* (1564-5), Joseph Caro's authoritative codification of Halacha. Ashkenazim (Jews of East European origin) consider these to be as binding as law. When *minhag* conflicted with Halacha, it was often Halacha that yielded. "Custom abrogates law," is a rabbinic adage.

When Rabbenu Gershom (960-1028), "Light of the Exile," assembled a synod in 1000 to prohibit polygyny (marriage to multiple wives) among Ashkenazic Jews, he was responding to the pressures of Christendom, which mandated monogamous marriage for its communicants. Although not common among Jews, polygyny was permitted in both Bible and Talmud. But the medieval church, which hovered darkly over Rabbenu Gershom's world, condemned plural marriage. His ordinance (*takkana*) was a prudent concession to the puritanical ethos of Paulinian Christianity. At a time when "episcopal fanaticism" was spreading and the church militant about to embark on the First Crusade, anxious Jewish leaders would naturally strive to eliminate any practice which might give offense to those itching to persecute Jews. That the persecutors were not appeased is a recurring lesson of Jewish history.

The interdiction of polygyny under pain of excommunication extended throughout the lands of Christendom where Ashkenazim lived. It was never operative among Sephardim, who lived mainly in the Muslim world where polygyny was practiced. Monogamy may have been felt as a pragmatic necessity by Ashkenazim, but not by Sephardim. Thus an inherited form of marriage was forbidden to Ashkenazim because of the supervening contiguity of the Christian World.

Halacha forbids a married woman to uncover her hair,[11] but prevailing custom has progressively softened the proscription. Because a woman's hair was considered "nakedness," a man was prohibited from praying within sight of it.[12] The obligation to cover the hair was considered *torah mi'sinai*, that is Pentateuchal, obligatory. But as general fashion exerted its sway in succeeding centuries, Jewish women began to ignore the old prohibition. They took to wearing wigs, and these, despite *heremin* (edicts of excommunication) against their use, spread throughout the European Diaspora.

In the last century, a distinguished rabbinic sage, Rabbi Isaac Hurewitz, heaped scorn on the "despised and miserable wig *(sheitel)* [which] transforms [a woman's] glory into a vile disfigurement," and called to witness the women who "[do] not listen to the calls of the leaders .... and [follow] the *minhag* in almost all cities where Jews are found, [especially] in our home in the new land [America], where all women go out with an uncovered head." Rabbi Hurewitz sums up the issue with a sound sociological conclusion: "The entire matter, what is forbidden and permitted, is not rooted in the Talmud and codes but in the custom of women in the particular time and place."[13] Rabbi Ovadia Yosef, Israel's influential Sephardic former chief rabbi, a strong critic of wigs, favors a woman's right to show her hair.

An example of custom overriding Halacha is seen in a radical change toward the idea of women as teachers. Halacha bars women as teachers. Maimonides and the Shulchan Aruch unconditionally approve the Halachic ban. Today few Orthodox rabbis would support such a pronouncement. Women have for years taught in the full gamut of Orthodox schools — from Beit Ya'akov to Ramaz — without a murmur of Halachic protest. That this injunction is today virtually ignored is further testimony to the power of *minhag*.

An interesting irony is found in the kolels of the yeshiva world. A *kolel* is a group of married men who devote themselves wholly to advanced Talmudic studies. Outside distractions are discouraged, including the distraction of earning a living. A modest stipend is provided for the *kolel* member. The main breadwinner is often the wife. Today, in many *kolels* the husband's status is measured by the earning power of his wife. *Haredim* feel the impact of feminism in oblique ways.

An outer frontier of egalitarianism from the Orthodox perspective was reached in an article by a clarion voice for "emancipated" Orthodox women, Blu Greenberg. Entitled, "Will There Be Orthodox Women Rabbis?", the article projects the possibility that Orthodox women well educated in Torah studies, might one day become leaders in the community, even rabbis. Orthodoxy, Greenberg writes, may be moving toward that "unique moment in history." What then? "When that happens, history will take us where it takes us." The mood is up-beat fatalism.

Reform began to ordain women in 1971. Conservatism, initially expressing grave misgivings at such a flouting of Jewish tradition, followed suit a few years later. While no one could confidently predict that one day Orthodox women will be ordained as rabbis, it would seem reasonable to foresee Orthodox women gaining increasing recognition and autonomy in their own community. Orthodox women, sympathetic with certain aspects of the feminist agenda, pressing for greater egalitarianism, will hasten such a development.

The Orthodox and Change

The landscape of the ultra-Orthodox world reveals interesting evidence of Orthodoxy's adoption of the contrivances and artifacts of the surrounding alien culture. The Lubavitch movement publishes a glossy English language magazine, *Lubavitch International* ("News from the Lubavitch Global Network"), which is obviously produced in consultation with a professional public relations agency. With illustrations in striking color, featuring irresistible Lubavitch moppets and the benevolent Rebbe, the late Rabbi Menachem Schneerson himself, the magazine reports the activities of Lubavitch centers all over the world — from Cairo to Sydney, from Munich to Moscow.

A few years ago the *New York Times* carried large advertisements portraying a mother and daughter lighting Sabbath candles, with the text extolling the woman's role in preserving Judaism. What surprises some Jewish readers is the Lubavitch sponsorship of advertisements picturing women as examplars of religious merit. It is true that the Bible heralds the virtues of individual women — the matriarchs, Deborah, Esther. It is also true that on every Shabbat eve during the kiddush, the husband ceremonially lauds his wife by reciting the *eshet hayil* ("Woman of Valor") passage from Proverbs 31, 10-31. Nevertheless public focus on women as models of religious merit runs counter to a traditional Jewish sensibility, which assumes the subordinate religious status of women. In any case, the newspaper ads carried a strong emotional appeal and could have been devised only by copywriters thoroughly at home on Madison Avenue.

In 1983 the *New Yorker* magazine published a series of articles by Liz Harris, later issued as a book, describing the world of a Lubavitch family living near the movement's world headquarters on Eastern Parkway in Brooklyn.[14] (Other articles on the Lubavitcher have appeared in some of America's most popular publications, such as the *New York Times Magazine* and *National Geographic*.) The very thought of a woman investigative reporter roaming at large in the nerve center of the Lubavitch world would have shocked ultra-Orthodox minds not long ago.

Orthodox Jews cover their heads at all times with either a hat or skullcap. For centuries skullcaps were somber black of staid design. But of recent years there has been an explosion of skullcaps in vivid colors, materials, styles, and symbols. Skullcaps are now made of tartan, paisley, leather, and suede, embroidered with figures ranging from Batman to Ninja Turtles, from Mickey Mouse to Ghostbusters. The logos of the Cubs, Mets, Bulls, and Lakers, professional sports teams, adorn skullcaps worn by small fry.

What strikes observers as a convincing illustration of the ready adaptation of Orthodoxy to a current vogue is the fad of rabbi cards. These are four-by-six-inch colored cards similar to those devoted to professional athletes that are collected, traded, and treasured by American kids of all ages. But instead of athletes, rabbis are the subject of rabbi cards, which in addition to the picture, bear the vital religious statistics of the subject rabbi in Hebrew and English. As to the value of the individual card, it varies according to inscrutable market forces at work in the Orthodox community. In 1990 the *Miami Herald* reported that the card of Rav Yisrael Abu Hatzeira was in great demand. Abu Hatzeira was the Moroccan wonder-working Rebbe known as Baba Sali, who died in 1985 and to whose burial place in the Negev thousands of north African Jews come on pilgrimage annually. The *Herald* called his the Don Mattingly of rabbi cards. (Mattingly was the slugging first baseman of the New York Yankees.)

It is clear that some Orthodox groups, especially the Lubavitcher, are deploying strategies of the secular culture so long anathematized — advertising, PR, hype — for their pragmatic ends. Defenders of the Lubavitcher justify the employment of PR and hype on the grounds that their purpose is promotion of a sacred cause. The means may be tainted but the ends are pure. It is the hoary problem of means and ends. In a radically different context, Henry IV of France, blurted, "Paris is worth a mass." Some would have thought that ultra-Orthodoxy would have but one answer. But it has been suggested that the ultra-Orthodox have a built-in flexibility which allows them to overcome moral scruple even in spiritual strongholds like Crown Heights and Meah She-arim. Meah She-arim is the largest ultra-Orthodox quarter in Jerusalem, whose *Haredi* leaders are often accused of cutting moral and legal corners as they maneuver their pivotal political clout in the Knesset to gain maximum fiduciary and political advantage.

There is also the possibility that the spirit of hype may erode the spirit of pristine Orthodoxy. One should not minimize the awesome power of hucksterism and its satellite agents. American life today with its twin themes of acquisitiveness and consumerism is the realized dream of the huckster. "The manipulative imagery that has traveled from Madison Avenue .... has become an unavoidable part of society's background noise."[15] Will the "background noise" of hucksterism drown out the still small voice of *chasidut* (piety)? The *Haredi* may expect to walk away unchanged from the encounter with the American marketplace but, then again, he may never be the same.

Orthodoxy and Sexuality

A study of the attitude of Orthodox Jews toward pre-marital sex reveals a startling intrusion of the secular culture into the stringent world of traditional Judaism. The survey reported that 40 percent of Centrist Orthodox Jews approve of pre-marital sex among couples dating steadily, and more than 50 percent approve of pre-marital sex among engaged couples. Young Orthodox are apparently more liberal in their sexual attitudes than those of an older generation. This would refute the accepted view that the younger generation of Orthodox Jews is "moving to the right." Perhaps in some ways, but apparently not in the attitude toward pre-marital sex, which the Halacha forbids. Certain practices of the dominant culture may be adopted even in the strongest bastions of Jewish tradition. An Orthodox young unmarried woman and her Orthodox boyfriend used to walk two miles to our home to have dinner with us on *erev shabbat*. They were observing the traditional prohibition against riding or driving on the Sabbath. After dinner they would walk back to her apartment and spend the night together. The *Haredi* community might remain sealed off from the modern world, but this is much less true of the mainstream, Centrist Orthodox.

Haredim take every stringent measure to shield their young from what they consider the corruptions of the secular world, particularly those thought to pertain to sex. The sexes are separated from childhood. Since touching girls before marriage is a sin, dating is prohibited; social dancing, considered "immodest public behavior," is forbidden. Emerging sexuality is ignored, sex education non-existent.

Centrist Orthodoxy tells a different story. Ari L. Goldman, former religion editor of the *New York Times*, is a Centrist Orthodox Jew with a yeshiva background. He relates that when he was going to high school and college, his Orthodox friends mingled quite freely with girls. Social dancing was approved. Five o'clock tea dances sponsored by the Mizrahi were high points in the monthly calendar. Later in the 70's and early 80's, Goldman describes how he and his bachelor friends combined the life of Orthodox tradition with sexual liberation. After spending the night with a girlfriend, the man would "rush off" to the synagogue for prayers. (This is known as a "tefilin date" and has become an in-house witticism of the Orthodox.)

Every Shabbat, the Lincoln Square Orthodox synagogue, one of the largest in New York (1300 members, half unmarried), becomes the bustling venue for pairing off ("the easiest pick-up line in New York") with sex likely in the offing. Rabbi Shlomo Riskin, responsible for the growth and vogue of the synagogue, who now lives in Israel, clearly sees the problems spawned by Orthodoxy's clash with the modern world, but his rejection of the attempt to make Orthodoxy compatible with pre-marital sex is dismissed by Goldman as "old, tired ways." The way chosen by Goldman and his generation prevails at Lincoln Square.

There is no lack of rationalization for the sexual activity of the young mainstream Orthodox. It is, after all, a "healthy gift from God." Cited in justification is the Talmudic counsel that when sexual desire become acute, one should "put on dark clothes, go to another town, find a woman, and satisfy one's lust." Appended is the caution to be discreet.[16]

If the 70's and early 80's showed some relaxation in the austerities of Orthodoxy, the late 80's as we have seen, witnessed a sharp turn to the right, yielding to the hegemony of *Humrot*. Now zealotry and intolerance would threaten, perhaps banish, possibilities for flexibility and diversity. With no thought for co-existence with the modern world, the focus was on sanctions from within, the regime of an exclusionist pietism. A wave of prohibitions swept the Orthodox community, from social dancing and showing one's hair by married women to the banning of foods like M and M's, tuna fish sandwiches in non-kosher restaurants, and Coca-Cola, whose "secret ingredient" is allegedly *traif*.

But the persistent realities and lures of the secular world are not so easily blocked out. After Goldman was prevented from leading his congregation in prayer on Yom Kippur because of his religious derelictions as a newspaper reporter, an officer of the congregation phoned to confess his embarrassment. "This is a modern *shul*," he expostulated. "Most everyone here 'eats out' (i.e. *traif*). We just don't talk about it." Later another member called to admit that on Fridays after sundown, exhausted at the end of the week, he takes a taxi home. In America the modern world can breach the stoutest ramparts of faith.

The World's Slow Stain

Even a casual review of the history of Judaism leaves no doubt that change in its practice and doctrine has been a continuing process through the centuries. Famous rabbis such as Rabbenu Gershom and Moses Maimonides were able to effect change in traditional practice and outlook. Influences exerted by the dominant culture, whether Hellenistic, Muslim, Christian or Euro-American, could actuate change in institutions and doctrines once held inviolate.

There is a widespread impression that Orthodox Judaism opposes Halachic change, that the Halacha is a fixed body of laws impervious to revision or innovation. Orthodox authorities deny this. They claim that if the attitude of the Orthodox rabbinate seems resistant to change, it is only because the conditions which would necessitate it are not yet present. Should such conditions come into being, there would be no obstacle to modification.

To Americans living in an age where change is rapid and frequent, the Halachic way seems willfully stubborn. To non-Orthodox Jews, the Orthodox rabbis appear like troglodytes into whose caves the needs and cares of ordinary people never enter. Most American Jews, like most Americans, are used to speed in all things, including theology. In a span of two brief decades Reform Judaism has initiated and implemented radical change in some of the strongest bulwarks of Jewish tradition: ordaining women as rabbis (1971), deciding that patrilineal descent was enough to validate a child's Jewish identity (1983), declaring homosexuality no bar to rabbinic ordination (1990), and embarking on an aggressive program for converting non-Jews to Judaism (1993). Conservative Judaism, maintaining a somewhat slower pace, appears to be moving in the same direction. Meanwhile, Orthodox Talmudic authorities wrestle for years over the Halachic legitimacy of women's prayer groups without reaching a decision. To the Orthodox there is good reason for moving cautiously. To others this makes little sense in the twenty-first century.

The rejection of the outside world by *Haredim* may mask their fear of it. They see the secular world as posing a serious threat to the substance of Judaism, and they believe that there is but one effective prophylaxis against its contagion: no contact with it. The result is a condition of virtual quarantine where Jews may not venture beyond their own exclusive domain. But this withdrawal into isolation may be a symptom of insecurity arising from the fear that without Draconian preventives the secular culture will overwhelm them.

Current belief would persuade us that Orthodoxy is growing in numbers and strength, and that the younger Orthodox are stricter in observance than the older. We have seen, however, that there are not a few signs that the secular culture is seeping into the Orthodox world. This will not surprise the student of human societies, which have long demonstrated how the majority culture works its eroding will on the world around it.

We hear little of defections from strict Orthodoxy. The *Haredi* community is closely knit and tightly controlled, and the children are zealously trained and strictly supervised. But there are some who leave the fold. During the nineteenth century, there were the yeshivah students of Eastern Europe who would come to their study sessions with Haskalah pamphlets concealed between the pages of their Talmud tractates. Not a few broke away from ancient moorings, became ardent Zionists, made their way to Palestine, and founded the settlements which eventually became the national Jewish homeland. During her sojourn in Crown Heights among the Lubavitcher, Liz Harris was told that *Village Voice*, the widely read New York counterculture weekly, circulates among Lubavitch yeshiva students. "They smuggle copies of it into the dormitories. It's sort of the *Playboy* of the New York Hasidic community." Crown Heights and Williamsburg are not immune to the world's slow stain.

The external world will continue to make its impact on the observant Jewish community. Perhaps the ultra-Orthodox will change little. But the modern Orthodox, caught up increasingly in the tide of acculturation, living their synthesis of tradition and modernity, may produce interesting mutations of American Judaism.

What of the future of non-Orthodox Judaism? Both the Reform and Conservative movements seem to be moving toward an increasingly permissive, autonomous practice of Judaism. With "guidance, not governance" at its masthead, Reform rejects the imposition of discipline in its agenda of Jewish belief and practice. The late accretion of some rituals in Reform is a smattering of superficial glosses, delusory gestures, not commitments to faith.

Conservatism is following in the wake of Reform, with much of its laity no less autonomous in their attitude to Judaism. The acceptance by Conservatism of women and homosexuals as rabbis dramatically illustrates the movement's radical break from its founding principles. Conservative and Reform Jews thrashing in the same sea of Jewish ignorance, differ little in their attitude toward Judaism.

With so little difference between the Reform and Conservative movements, why, it is being asked, don't they merge? The question has been asked before, but never with more cogency or timeliness than now. The advantages are obvious — the consolidation of similar, sometimes identical, programs of education, social action, patterns of worship, the easing of budgetary burdens, the greater impact on life in Israel of a larger constituency. Some form of merger or union would appear to be the counsel of commonsense, but it is a rare and fearless voice which openly advocates it.

Opposition comes from those who have a vested or emotional interest in maintaining existing institutional structures. We can understand the motivations — sentimental attachment to historic and family tradition, disinclination to yield personal prestige and influence in sectarian fiefdoms of power, reluctance to change. But as the differences between Reform and Conservatism continue to narrow, and the competition for souls and funds intensifies, union may commend itself persuasively to the leaders as the rational and prudent course. Other groups may join in a non-Orthodox amalgamation — the Reconstructionists are the most likely candidates. New religious alignments promise to become the reality in the uncertain American Jewish future.

Notes

1. Nathan Glazer, "New Sociological Perspectives," *American Jewish Yearbook* (Philadelphia: Jewish Publication Society, 1987), p. 18
2. Menachem Friedman, "Life Tradition and Book Tradition in the Development of Ultra-Orthodox Judiasm," in *Judaism Viewed from Within and from Without*, ed. With introduction by Harvey L. Goldberg (Albany, N.Y.: State University of New York, 1987), p. 235
3. *Ibid.*, p. 236
4. *Ibid.*, p. 242
5. Jack Wertheimer, "Present Trends in American Judaism," in *American Jewish Yearbook* 1989, p. 118
6. *Ibid.*, p. 115
7. Solomon B. Freehof, "The Non-Observant Orthodox," in *Journal of Reform Judaism*, Spring 1987, p. 47
8. In 1992, during Rosh Hashana and Yom Kippur services in The Great Synagogue (Heichal Shlomo) in Jerusalem, usherettes in the women's balcony wore uniforms consisting of a white blouse and black slacks. One had thought that Orthodoxy

considers slacks forbidden for women because it violates the ordinance prohibiting women from wearing men's attire. Women wearing slacks on the holiest days of the year in the synagogue building which houses the headquarters of the Chief Rabbinate, is a mark of the ability of an artifact of Western culture to invade the most sacred precincts of Orthodoxy.

9. Sylvia Barack Fishman, "The Impact of Feminism on American Jewish Life," in *American Jewish Yearbook*, vol. 89 (Philadelphia: Jewish Publication Society, 1989), p. 47
10. Edgar E. Siskin, "Transcendental and Folk Aspects of Judaism," in Judaism, summer 1987, passim; Charles S. Friedman, *The Ambivalent American Jew: Politics, Religion, and Family in American Jewish Life* (Philadelphia: Jewish Publication Society, 1973)
11. *Sofrim* 14:18
12. *Ketubot* 71a
13. *Shulhan Arukh*: Orah Hayim 75, 2
14. Lis Harris, *Holy Days: The World of a Hasidic Family* (New York: Collier Books, MacMillan, 1985)
15. Randall Rothenberg, "Politics on TV: Too Fast, Too Loose?" in *New York Times*, 15 July 1990, News of the Week Review, p. 1
16. Ari L. Goldman, *The Search for God at Harvard* (New York: Times Books, Random House, 1991)

CHAPTER 6

MODERN BEHAVIOR OF AN ANCIENT PEOPLE

Family in Transition

The nineteenth-century German Jewish artist, Moritz David Oppenheimer (1799-1882), painted scenes of Jewish home life depicting religious occasions in the warm ambiance of the family. He was one of a coterie of nineteenth-century Jewish painters and writers whose works delineated the spiritual aura of observant Jewish home life. These portrayals of the tranquil beauty and piety of the traditional Jewish home conjure up cherished images of family cohesiveness. A nineteenth-century French annalist wrote of the "conjugal and parental love" that characterized the Jewish family. "One never hears of a depraved father, of a mother who has antipathy for her children, of a son who refuses assistance to his elderly parents. Nowhere is family sentiment more profound than among Jews."[1] The Talmud tells us that "God dwells in the pure and loving home."[2] Through all the centuries of Jewish wandering, expulsion, and martyrdom, the home was the main bulwark of community moral, social, and religious strength.

Home life was interdigitated with religious observance and it was in the bosom of the family that most Jewish ceremonies were enacted — the Seder, Sukkot, Hanukah, and, most important of all, Shabbat, greeted and terminated each week in the glow of holy candlelight. Jews cited the probity and piety of the Jewish family as proof of the moral worth, even superiority, of Judaism and the Jewish way of life.

The home was known as the *mikdash me'at*, "the small sanctuary." Heschel called it the "real sanctuary" and the synagogue its "auxiliary."[3]

When the great migrations from Eastern Europe began a century ago, the families who arrived in America were little different from the traditional Jewish families of prior times. But this quickly changed as the newcomers felt the shattering impact of their new world. Irving Howe, chronicler of immigrant life, has written that, "Every recollection of Jewish immigrant life .... notes that as soon as the Jews moved from Eastern Europe to America, there followed a serious dislocation of the family."[4] Thirty years ago, Nathan Glazer wrote of the threat to Jewish values in the Americanization of the Jewish family, and predicted that the trend would become more pronounced.[5]

The world of twentieth-century America was disruptive of the life and outlook of the world Jews had always known. Faced with the economic, social, and cultural hazards of their new life, they had little energy left to safeguard the pillars of the Jewish home and preserve the hierarchy of pristine family relationships. In the frantic melee of trying to keep afloat, putting bread on the table, providing a roof for the family, bringing some order into the chaos of daily life, long-established patterns of the ghetto or *shtetl* home, and of family roles and relationships were radically altered. The father's authority, formerly unchallenged, became more attenuated; the mother became more than ever the dominant force in the family's practical affairs; the children became more independent, less submissive. Meanwhile, the springs of faith in synagogue and studyhouse were drying up. Some of the old traditions lingered. The Sabbath retained intimations of its sanctity in the stony landscape of tenement existence; the Passover Seder brought the family together to celebrate the liberation of Israel from Egyptian slavery, an event which had a familiar and stirring resonance for Jews living in freedom after centuries of oppression. But there was no slowing the drift from the old pieties.

As the Jewish family grows more and more alienated from the sources of its heritage, we again see how the social and cultural character of Jewish institutions comes to mirror that of the societies of which they are a part. Some of the changes being predicted as possibilities for the Jewish family of the future will strike Jews with some memory of tradition as bizarre. In its Annual Report of 1990-91, the Reform Union of American Hebrew Congregations announced that "the transformation of the Jewish family is under way." With the increasing adoption by Jewish parents of non-Caucasian children, it is suggested that there may emerge indications of a multi-ethnic, multi-racial Jewish community that will be normative in the twenty-first century. It will then be more accurate to speak of "Jewish families" than of "the Jewish family."

Marriage

An Israeli journalist traveling in the United States on a lecture tour was surprised at how often his female hosts launched into a lamentation of their daughters' refusal to marry. "My daughter, who's thirty (something), refuses to get married," was the plaint he heard dozens of times.[6] Anyone with only a slight familiarity with the present American Jewish scene will be aware of the vast difference between the traditional and modern Jewish attitudes toward marriage. Unlike traditional Christianity, which considers celibacy an ideal, Judaism has always extolled marriage, considering it a religious duty.

In the Bible, marriage is the metaphor repeatedly used for God's linkage with Israel (*Hosea 2:21,22: Song of Songs*). Akiba warned, "He who remains unmarried impairs the divine image," and went on, "He who has no wife lives without joy, blessing and without goodness."[7]

Recent population studies reveal that an increasing number of Jews never marry. When they do, it is likely to be at a later age. In the 1960's, 97 percent of all Jews over the age of 65 had been married at least once; in 1975 the number had fallen to 86 percent. It is a trend that now prevails in Jewish life.

There has been a pronounced rise in the number of "alternative" Jewish households — households consisting of unmarried individuals, single parents, homosexual couples — from 15 percent in 1970 to 38 percent in 1980. Such households may exceed in number those of traditional Jewish families. Less "Jewish" than conventional households, the "alternative" household places less emphasis on Jewish religious observance, education, and organizational activity, including synagogue affiliation. The increasing number of "alternative" households points to an accelerating breakdown of the Jewish family, with its corollary consequences — an undermining of Jewish identity and a diminution in the number of Jews.

A revealing ray of light on the transformed Jewish attitude toward marriage is cast by the disclosure of a president of the Central Conference of American Rabbis that in the last 15 or 20 years radical changes had taken place in the pre-nuptial meeting between the rabbi and the couple. Whereas a decade or two ago, the couple looked upon the meeting with the rabbi as "their rite of passage to the marriage bed," they no longer do, "for they had already shared that bed for some period of time." Now they had begun "to concentrate on the *spiritual* significance of the wedding ceremony. They even want to know what the Hebrew means."[8]

Divorce

The frequency of divorce in the Jewish community has disrupted the integrity of the Jewish home and family. In Jewish tradition one encounters the phenomenon of divorce which is easy to obtain but rarely resorted to. But Jews can no longer pride themselves on the stability of the family. Today the extent of divorce may be as great, even greater, among Jews than non-Jews.[9] In America the Jewish divorce rate doubled between 1959 and 1968, and since 1968 has doubled again.[10] Even among the Orthodox, divorce is making its inroads. More than a decade ago, the supreme judge of the Rabbinical Alliance of America *Beth Din* deplored the "embarrassing amount of divorces among even the very Orthodox and Hasidim, a phenomenon unprecedented in Jewish history."[11]

Within the last decade or two, divorce has intruded itself as a factor in determining aspects of congregational life. Now religious school schedules must make allowance for the attendance of children who alternate weekends between their divorced parents. A large West Coast congregation hires guards to make sure that when day-school classes are dismissed, the children will be able to make their way to waiting buses without being waylaid by an irate or vengeful divorced parent. The guards are Israeli ex-soldiers, an ironic commentary on the common claim that the American Jew is Israel's indispensable protector. In Conservative synagogues, the old Halachic question of whether two brothers can in turn be called up to the reading of the Torah has been pre-empted by the question as to whether at a Bar/Bat mitzvah, the father or stepfather has priority of ascent to the Torah. In some congregations, the honor of being called to the reading of the Torah is no longer given to the parents and grandparents of the bar/bat mitzvah but to the siblings and cousins. This avoids the "trap of trouble that comes from divorced parents with remarriages, which are causing rabbis such agony around the country."

Divorce has been called a "normative life crisis" and this perhaps expresses the view of Reform Judaism as illustrated by its "Ritual of Release" (*seder pereida*). The ritual is included in the latest edition of the official *Rabbi's Manual* published by the Central Conference of American Rabbis.[12] The Ritual of Release finds the rabbi officiating as facilitator in "the final act of separation" between a formerly married couple. It suggests that children, family, and close friends be invited to the ceremony.

The rabbi explains that Judaism has "provided for divorce when a woman and a man, who have been joined together in *kiddushin* (sacred marriage), no longer experience the sacred in their relationship." The climax of the ceremony is reached when the rabbi takes the "Document of Separation" (*te'udat pereida*) and tears it in two, giving one half to each party as symbol of separation. (An alternative service is available if only one of the couple is present.) The rabbi reads: "This is your Document of Separation .... It marks the dissolution of your marriage. I separate it now as you have separated, giving each of you a part." The participants in turn read: "I release my former wife/husband from the sacred bonds that held us together. She/he is responsible for her/his life just as I am free and responsible for my life. This is her/his Document of Separation from me."

When first sent to the CCAR, the Document of Separation was accompanied by a letter which expressed the hope that "it won't have to be used often." If it will not be used often, it will primarily be because divorced Reform Jews, indifferent to a Ritual of Release, will have recourse to the ordinary procedures of the civil divorce court. Divorce, after all, has become a "normative life crisis" for Americans, and Jews are no exception.

Zero Population Growth

The opening chapter of the Bible records God's first command to the newly created human couple, "Be fruitful and multiply" (*Genesis 1:28*). In Judaism it is a religious duty not only to marry but also to have children. This is indeed the purpose of marriage. Childlessness was one of the greatest misfortunes that could befall a Jewish woman (*Genesis 30:23; Samuel 1*). In fact, after ten years of barren marriage, a man was permitted, even enjoined, to divorce his wife.[13] Many children were the norm in Jewish families. After the Chmielnicki massacres in 1648, it is estimated that there were less than one million Jews in the world; a century and a half later there were seven million. In that era, almost all Jewish women married and 30 percent of them had ten or more children. The average was seven.

No contrast between the Jewish family of former centuries and that of today is more dramatic than that seen in their comparative levels of fertility. Paula Hyman has called the early reduction of its fertility the "most striking feature of the Jewish family of modern times."[14] From having been one of the most prolific of peoples, the Jews have become one of the least, at present unable to reproduce themselves.

Zero population growth (ZPG) is the reality in Jewish communities throughout the Diaspora. While the minimum number of children per family required to prevent population decline is 2.1, the average number of children in the Diaspora Jewish family is 1.5. (In Israel it is 2.8.) Consequently there is a steady population recession among Jews everywhere, except in Israel. In 1937, 3.7 percent of the American population were Jewish; in 1968, one generation later, 2.9 percent were. The present birthrate for Jews in the U.S. is approximately 20 percent less than for all other white American groups. Marc Holzer summarizes the demographic course of the Diaspora Jew as a "tragic self-inflicted mode of genocide for all Jews in terms of a communal and cultural religious life."[15]

In considering the factors which have made Jews such committed models of infertility, it is worth noting how many derive from values and movements enshrined in the liberal secular culture. The campaign against overpopulation, high on the ecologist's agenda, where children have been termed "ecological pollution" and pregnancy "antisocial behavior," has found uncritical recruits among Jewish women. Young Jewish matrons living in Westchester County read of overpopulation in India and decide to have no children. Abortion on demand enlists some of its most enthusiastic supporters among Jewish women, married and unmarried. A poll of 33,000 physicians disclosed that 92 percent of Jewish doctors favor it, 69 percent of Protestant.

The typical feminist outlook determines the attitude of many Jewish women toward children, home, and family. The "liberated" woman does not seem to find child rearing, homemaking, or organizational and philanthropic activity — their mothers' and grandmothers' pattern — fulfilling. Their ambitions aspire to the "higher" reaches of achievement in the professional and business world. Jewish women represent one of the highest percentages of careerists among women's groups in America. The Jewish woman marries late, if at all, and decides to have a single child, or none at all. Even career mothers with highly successful husbands will return to work after having a child, leaving its early training to surrogates. The cost of a surrogate, which often makes it mandatory for both parents to work, is no deterrent. Many mothers prefer not to consider the baleful impact of such second-hand maternal guardianship upon their child.

Since divorce rates among mixed marriage couples are from three to five times higher than among inmarried couples, mixed marrieds will delay having children until "sure" of their marital future. Delay means fewer children.

Some couples will decide not to bring children into a world plagued with crises and dangers, a world of famine, wars, and a Holocaust. Years ago I introduced my roommate at Yale to a young woman in my congregation. Eventually they decided to marry. During the pre-marital rabbinical meeting, they told me they had decided not to have children because of their fear of increasing antisemitism.

A paucity of Jewish children is sometimes the direct result of the powerful parental drive for upward social mobility. Jewish parents unflaggingly pursue the quest for financial and social success. Their goal is not only to banish such economic need and inferior status as they may have known while growing up, but also to ensure a "better" life for their offspring. It has been claimed that a primary objective for such parents is to enhance their own self-esteem by raising successful children. Obviously this is more easily achieved by the family with fewer children.

The failure of young, educated, gifted Jewish couples to have sufficient children to reproduce themselves, or the growing fashion to enter into living arrangements where children are not part of the pattern of living, directly weakens the institutions and organizations of Jewish life. Childlessness is a lethal blow to the viability of the Jewish family and to the Jewish home, the traditional centers of Judaism.

Moreover, a decline in the number of Jews, the sequel to childlessness, will undermine the political influence of American Jews. The ebbing of their influence can already be felt. In some communities the shrinking number of Jews has meant a loss of support for causes of Jewish concern. Whereas the critical mass of Jews in New York City still assures that Jewish voices will count in political decision making, in other centers like Chicago this is no longer true.

A generation ago, Jacob Arvey, chairman of the Democratic National Committee and a prominent Chicago Jew, exerted a powerful influence in Chicago and Illinois politics.[16] His political strength grew out of the densely settled Jewish wards of the west side. At that time, many Jews held positions in the city administration. Today there are virtually none. The Jewish wards are gone. The parents and grandparents have settled in the suburbs, and many of their children are members of the infertile generation. Chicago, third largest city in America, has an official, political administration in which Jews play virtually no part.

American Jews have commonly boasted of their political clout in America, claiming that their presence and influence in America did more good for Israel than their immigration to Israel ever could. With their clout diminishing, American Jews may have to moderate their boast.

With Jews producing fewer children than any other ethnic group in the country, it is not surprising that questions are being asked about the strength and continuity of the American Jewish community. Without Jews, there can be no Jewish future.

Domestic Violence

Domestic violence in the United States has reached "epidemic proportions." Fifty percent of all U.S. families have experienced family violence. What will cause astonishment is that Jews are not notably different from their Gentile neighbors, for "violence occurs in Jewish families to the same extent as in non-Jewish families."[17]

In the waning years of the twentieth century, the expected, typically peaceful Jewish home may have become a myth. But the myth endures, which only exacerbates the difficulty of dealing with family violence. Victims of spouse abuse are reluctant to come forward to testify to their plight and to take steps to stop the abuse. They feel that they are alone, thinking, "Who will believe me?" Many Jews still find it hard to believe that a Jewish husband will batter his wife and children. Abused Jewish women bear a double burden in coming forward: they thereby confess failure in their own marriage, and they undermine the myth of the idyllic Jewish family.

Because of the stigma attached to the revelation of violence, victims typically do not turn to rabbis for help. The abused will first seek out family, friends and mental health professionals. A recent study reported that only four out of 209 abused Jewish women went to the rabbi in their distress. They think of the rabbi as the chosen guardian of a tradition which sacralizes family and home, and they would be ashamed to admit of abuse by their husbands.

One of the interesting Jewish aspects of domestic violence is that Jewish women stay longer with violent partners than non-Jewish women. Gentile women will tolerate violence only for three to five years, making the break in their 30's. Jewish victims will remain with spouses from eight to ten years, terminating the relationship in their 30's and 40's.

Over the past decade, Jews have begun to display a new openness to the problem of domestic violence. Jewish women are at last bringing their complaints to sources of help, filing charges, and seeking legal redress. Jewish communities in the major cities are developing programs and opening shelters for the battered where counseling and a variety of practical help measures are available. In New York, some shelters provide kosher facilities for the growing number of Orthodox women who are abused. In bringing domestic violence out of the closet, some of the myths about spouse violence among Jews have been shattered.

Addiction

There has been a persistent belief among both Jews and non-Jews that Jews are not alcoholics or substance abusers. Yet it is now estimated that one in ten persons in the United States is addicted either to drink or to drugs, including Jews in the same ratio. We learn that Jewish college students are "over-represented" in the drug culture, heavier users than Protestants or Catholics. When we read that every day 3,000 teenagers try cocaine for the first time, that 100,000 elementary school children report getting drunk weekly, and that one-tenth are Jews, we begin to see the extent of the problem in the Jewish community.[18]

The formation in the early 70's of Jewish Alcoholics and Chemically Dependent Persons (JACOP), a Jewish counterpart of Alcoholics Anonymous, indicates that the number of Jewish addicts is growing. The organization originated in the desire of Jewish addicts to meet in a synagogue setting where a spiritual dimension might be found in the quest for healing. Most AA groups meet in churches from a similar impulse. JACOP is but another example of Jewish acculturation to a model provided by the general culture. It will surprise Jews that JACOP attracts many Orthodox and ultra-Orthodox Jews. One branch organized a retreat which was attended by 160 individuals, of whom 40 percent were observant Jews. As one commentator remarked, "*talit and tefillin* do not ward off addictive behavior."

Programs on substance abuse are regularly scheduled in synagogues and Jewish community centers. Five synagogues in the suburban enclave of a large city recently sponsored a joint gathering which all adults and children over twelve were urged to attend. A national authority on addiction addressed the packed audience, answering questions until the meeting broke up after midnight. Reflecting on addiction among Jews, Schulweis has suggested that Lenin's apothegm, "Religion is the opiate of the people," be changed to, "Opiate is the religion of the people." To Schulweis the high and increasing incidence of addiction is proof that "hedonism is the religion of our mass culture," for Jews no less than for others.[19]

Suicide

The statistics on suicide among teenagers will cause little surprise to newspaper readers. For suicide, which has trebled since the mid 1950's, is the greatest cause of death of Americans between the ages of 12 and 25. Suicide takes eighteen young lives daily and 6,000 annually. That young Jews commit suicide with disturbing frequency is attested by the volume of material circulated by Jewish sources on suicide-prevention.[20]

The Reform movement has shown a special concern about the incidence of teenage suicide. A Union of American Hebrew Congregations Task Force on Youth Suicide, organized to deal with the problem openly, has issued a kit on *Youth Suicide Prevention: Programs and Resources for Congregations*. Rabbi Joseph Glaser, late Executive Vice President of the Central Conference of American Rabbis, has warned, "We never know when .... we might be confronted by it, and we have to be prepared." In response, congregations across the country have organized meetings and seminars on the crisis of adolescent suicide. Confronting the problem so openly is a marked departure from the customary Jewish silence on the maladies of its communal life.

Cults

Some years ago Roy Larson, religious editor of the *Chicago Sun Times*, climbed into a taxi in downtown Chicago bound for O'Hare Airport, a 30-minute drive. The young driver began talking about the religious cult to which he belonged, stopping only when they pulled into the terminal. After paying the fare, Larson asked, "By the way, in what religion were you raised?" "Reform Jewish, sir," came the reply. "I guess it didn't take." In recent decades it has become apparent that the religions many young people were raised in "didn't take." Traditional religious denominations were rejected in favor of the many cults which had become part of the counter-culture and which proceeded to win the fervent loyalty of their young followers. Sometimes they abandoned every other interest or activity — school, home, family, friends — in a total commitment to the cult.

As with other socially marginal phenomena, cults have attracted a disproportionate number of Jews. A study made in California a few years ago reported that Jews made up 50 percent of San Francisco's Zen Buddhists, 30 and 15 percent respectively of Los Angeles' Sufis and Hare Krishnas. Many young Jews are also found in the Moonies, and the Scientologists. Others practice transcendental meditation and Yoga.[21]

The attraction of the cults for young Jews has been explored in some detail. It seems that individuals drawn to the cults are, for the most part, from the upper middle class, idealistic, with an I.Q. in the higher range, who have found the family religion inadequate, without meaning. This happens to be a not inaccurate sketch of many young Jews. In addition, they have become disillusioned with the values of Western society with which Judaism is now identified. The ethnic and cultural dimension of Jewishness has little meaning for them. Most of all, they find a lack of "spirituality" in Judaism. While the "spiritual" teachers of Judaism are few and not easily accessible, the gurus of the cults are on hand and readily available. The pantheistic-naturalistic cults invite the devotee to enter into God's presence directly; the way of Judaism is longer, requiring a regimen of ritual observance, the exercise of the mind, and an acquaintance with history.

Among a growing number of Jews there has for some time been an uneasy feeling that their children were joining cults because Judaism and the Jewish community were not providing for their "spiritual" needs. In all the elaborate infrastructure of the Jewish community, was too little attention, in fact, being paid to the need of the "spiritual searchers"? Young Jews, influenced by the counter-culture flourishing on the college campus, were prominent among the searchers, "turning inward" to explore exotic religions. Not a few became leaders of cult groups. I remember two anguished parents speaking to me after a Shabbat service about their son who had, some years before, joined a Hindu cult and was living in an ashram near Bombay. We commiserated with them for a while, and then the father's face suddenly brightened. "You know, Rabbi," he said, the gloom gone from his voice, "he was just made head of the ashram."

Christian missionary cults can claim far more Jews than any of the more exotic variety. Jews for Jesus is the best known, and its members, insisting that they themselves are Jews, recruit young Jews across the country. Among the youngsters distributing their leaflets on the streets of downtown Chicago, I used to meet the children of members of the congregation I served and whom I had confirmed but a few years before. Upon greeting me they would smile and speak with the imperturbable good humor of the redeemed. As I walked away, they would likely as not murmur, "Bless you, Rabbi."

In explaining the success of the cults among young Jews, Judaism has come in for a lot of blame. But there are those who say that the cause lies not so much in any failure of Judaism, but rather in the elevation of secular above spiritual values in the Jewish home. When children who have been spiritually deprived get to college, missionary cults may very well appear to them as a refuge, an oasis, a home. Their souls may indeed begin to stir in search for values beyond Gucci and St. Laurent, in search of the transcendental and mystical.

Spirituality

The lack of "spirituality" in American Jewish life has been emerging as a topic of growing concern for Jewish religious leaders. So noticeable a preoccupation has this become that one rabbi has characterized "spirituality" as a buzzword of the current religious scene. The absence of "spirituality" is apparently felt in all branches of

Judaism. "What Can We Do to Bring God Back into Our Lives?" is the question on the cover of *Reform Judaism*, house organ of the Reform movement.[22] Harold Schulweis, a leading Conservative Rabbi, admits, "We will not be able to sustain our identity without transmitting credible and compelling faith."[23] Emanuel Feldman, editor of Tradition, journal of Orthodox Jewish thought, acknowledges that, "We [the Orthodox] are still far short of being a truly spiritual community."[24]

Sensitive observers agree that across the Jewish denominational spectrum something of first importance is missing. Twenty years ago Nathan Glazer remarked that "the abstract demand to see faith, to find God, tends to find little answer among Jews.[25] Rabbi Daniel Syme, vice-president of the Union of American Hebrew congregations, noticed that in his travels around the country visiting congregations, no one spoke of God. There seemed to be an unwritten understanding that rabbis would not talk about God and congregations would ask no questions about Him. Feldman contrasts the "soulless exercise of rote" .... common in contemporary American Orthodoxy [with the] noblest internal possibilities of the Jew — *bitahon* (trust), awe, humility, courage, loyalty, *hesed* (benevolence), ahava (love).[26] Schulweis dismisses much of the current practice of Judaism as "atmospherics." "The problem is internal — it calls for inreach."[27]

The paramount importance of inwardness in Judaism has been stressed by some of the great Jewish illuminati of the past. Two hundred years ago, Israel Baal Shem Tov, the founder of Hasidism, exemplified to his followers the greater rewards of simple, direct communion with God as against scholastic immersion in Talmudic texts and codes. To the meanest life he and his disciples brought an awareness of the joy and spiritual power of finding God, a goal whose attainment did not necessarily depend upon the disciplines of ritual observance and sacred study.

Abraham Isaac Kook (1865-1935), the great scholar and mystic who became the first Ashkenazi Chief Rabbi of Palestinian Jewry, lamented the neglect of inwardness, the "domain of pure faith," in the Judaism of his time, reminding his followers of the need for a spiritual revival of its legal tradition. To his colleagues he wrote:

> My dear brothers .... We too, have sinned! We have engaged in dialectics and relished new insights into the Halacha .... but we forgot God and His might, we did not heed the admonitions of the prophets of truth, of the best of our sages .... of the saints, the scholars in the field of ethics and mysticism who insistently warned us that the study of the practical aspects of the Talmud by itself is bound to run dry unless we add to it from the vast domain of the Kabbalah, God, the domain of pure faith which stems from within the soul, and emanates from the source of life.[28]

Abraham Joshua Heschel has written of the need to recognize the mystical as well as the intellectual strand in Judaism, and that its legal tradition requires periodic spiritual renewal: "Beneath the calm surface of creed and law .... souls [are] astir. Our task .... is to go beneath the tranquillity of creed and tradition in order to hear the echoes of wrestling and to recapture the living insights."[29]

Younger Jews often say that they feel alienated from Judaism because it has no spiritual content to satisfy a need they feel. The Judaism they have known has stressed the ethnic, cultural, and social aspects of Jewishness but has said little about its spiritual dimension, the "domain of faith." In the synagogue they hear a great deal about social justice, philanthropy, and antisemitism, but not much about God, faith, and prayer. Judaism sometimes seems a religion without supernatural anchorage.

This is cited as one of the main reasons Jewish college youth are drawn to the cults. There they find the transcendental reality toward which they have been reaching and the spiritual models and guides for whom they have been searching. Parents who worry about the attraction of the cults for their children wonder why Judaism can't provide the spiritual dimension they find in the bizarre exoticisms of cults. They are asking, What can be done to bring the transcendental, the spiritual, God, back into their lives?

The challenge that this question poses yields no easy answer. It is not easy to bring God back into lives long alienated from the transcendental. God is a stranger to modern men and women, and to the society of which they are a part. If our age hasn't banished God, it has certainly shown an icy indifference to Him. As Rabbi Shlomo Riskin put it, "God is not dead. He is simply not to be found in the American synagogue."[30]

A comprehensive survey of the beliefs and attitudes of Reform rabbis and laymen published in 1972, the Lenn Report, recorded that no more than 10 percent of rabbis and 17 percent of laymen believe in God "in the more or less traditional Jewish sense."[31] We have reason to believe that the beliefs and attitudes of other Jews, affiliated and unaffiliated, may be comparable to those in the Lenn Report. Nor is it likely that in the twenty years since the publication of the Lenn Report, the gap between God and American Jews, rabbis and laity, has narrowed.

Homosexuality

It is said that eight to ten percent of the American population is homosexual. In round numbers this translates into approximately 25,000,000 gays and lesbians living in the United States. Further extrapolation leads to the conclusion that there are 60,000 Jewish gays and lesbians in America.[32]

An interesting change in the attitude of Americans toward homosexuality and homosexuals has taken place in recent years. Two decades ago the great majority of Americans looked upon gays and lesbians as perverse and degenerate, social outcasts. Today, in contrast, while it is not uncommon to consider homosexuals as being beyond the pale of normality, they are increasingly regarded with understanding and as deserving of the same rights as heterosexuals. A Gallup poll in 1989 showed that 71 per cent of the people polled favored equal job opportunities for homosexuals as against 41 per cent in 1987.[33]

The attitude of Jews and of their religious denominations toward homosexuality has also undergone significant change in recent years. Only among Orthodox Jews has there been no formal change. The Orthodox still hold with the scriptual characterization of homosexuality as an "abomination." In the Bible (*Leviticus 18,22; 20:13*) it is a sin punishable by death. Subsequent generations of rabbinic authorities have expressed an unrelenting abhorrence of homosexuality.

But the other denominations of Judaism do not share the implacable revulsion of Orthodoxy. When in the 1980's the Reconstructionists ordained a homosexual as rabbi, they became the first religious body in America to admit homosexuals as members of their clergy. Among Christian groups, the Unitarian Universalist Association now accepts homosexuals as members of the clergy. In other denominations bishops and individual churchmen will sometimes ordain gays and lesbians, often "in violation of their national church policies."[34]

Conservative Judaism has advanced slowly towards full acceptance of gays and lesbians. Homosexuals are welcomed to its synagogues and accepted as students at its rabbinical seminary. At the 1990 national convention of the Conservative Rabbinical Assembly, a prominent member declared that "from the religious eye, I see no reason [homosexuals] should not be accepted with open arms in our shuls."[35] In a letter sent to rabbis throughout the country, Rabbi Harold M. Schulweis, widely respected Conservative leader, warmly praised and recommended the book, *Twice Blessed: On Being Lesbian, Gay, and Jewish*, which regards the condition of being both homosexual and Jewish as a singular privilege. The letter was jointly signed by Rabbi Alexander M. Schindler, president of the Reform Union of American Hebrew Congregations. Another Conservative rabbi, Bradley Shavit Artson, called the book "an agent for redemptive healing that will bring us one step closer to the Messianic age."[36]

No religious movement, however, has been more supportive in the acceptance of homosexuals than Reform Judaism. Reform leaders have deployed the full authority of their institutions on behalf of gay-lesbian recognition. When the resolution to admit sexually active homosexuals into the Reform rabbinate was put to the 1990 convention of the Central Conference of American Rabbis in Seattle, it received the "overwhelming endorsement" of two-thirds of its members.[37]

Some Reform rabbis have expressed reservations about advocating and implementing a pro- gay/lesbian agenda in the Jewish community. Rabbi Eugene B. Borowitz, professor of theology at the Hebrew Union College-Jewish Institute of Religion, has declared that the implementation of the agenda would weaken the traditional family, an "already threatened institution in our society." It would undermine the sanctity of the heterosexual, procreative marriage cherished by Judaism. Homosexuals should be accorded understanding and "loving good-will," but to grant homosexuality "full equivalence with heterosexuality in the Jewish community," would be nothing less than to betray the Covenantal relationship between the Jew and his God.[38]

Borowitz believes that the pro-equivalence Reform rabbis are marching to a different drummer than their laymen. The latter, he thinks, worry about the encroachments of the pagan culture, of which they take homosexuality to be a disturbing symbol. They hold that Judaism must exercise a special concern for the procreative family. They worry lest homosexual rabbis become role models for their member's children. "For the life of me," blurted one rabbi at the Seattle convention, which endorsed acceptance of gays/lesbians in every phase of Reform polity, "I cannot see how homosexual rabbis can be the role models our people need and want."[39]

Some would question whether Borowitz is reading the mood of the Reform Jewish layman accurately. While the liberal Jew may profess a preference for heterosexual marriage, the procreative family, and a heterosexual role model for his children, he is also the perennial social activist eager to champion the victims of discrimination and to plead the cause of minorities. Gays and lesbians have become a paradigm minority on the American scene, their problems given a tragic dimension by the deadly menace of AIDS. Will a preference for heterosexual marriage distance liberal Jews from the gay/lesbian cause?

It has been suggested that a decent regard for the age-old norms of Judaism, to whom the homosexual ethos is anathema, would give American Jews pause in granting it moral equivalence with the Jewish ethos of heterosexual marriage and family. But it would be unrealistic to expect the liberal Jew, detached from the claims of *k'lal yisroel*, to help stay the advancing tide of gay/lesbian acceptance. Concern for *k'lal yisroel* plays little role in the decision making of Reform leaders, although there is no lack of polite hat tipping to the feelings and interests of Jews living in the Diaspora and in Israel. (Voltaire, that devout unbeliever, is said to have bowed and tipped his hat every time he passed a church.) The ultimate litmus test for a proposal under consideration by liberal Jews is whether it is, as Rabbi Samuel E. Karff, who presided at the 1990 Seattle convention, phrased it, "consistent with the liberal traditions of Reform Judaism."[40] There would appear to be no higher court of appeal for Reform leaders.

In all probability, an increasing number of gays and lesbians will now be choosing the rabbinate as a career. Some will no doubt serve effectively as rabbis. But questions are being asked regarding the possible nature of their influence on Jewish life, particularly upon the Jewish family. Will they continue to press for a full implementation of the gay/lesbian agenda? Will they advocate the equality of the homosexual family? Will they officiate at "affirmation" rites, or "commitment ceremonies," sanctifying "stable and loving" relationships "between people of the same sex," otherwise known as gay and lesbian marriages? Will they declare these same-sex marriages to be sanctified by God, in the spirit of one of their leaders, who confessed, "I do believe that homosexual relationships contribute to, and do not diminish, God's *kedusha*."[41]

It will be claimed that these are questions of moment only to leaders and members of the liberal Jewish community. It needs to be reiterated that this community is the largest American religious Jewish body today. Its members will be steadily augmented by the inexorable trend toward liberalism on the part of Jewish groups and movements. The deeply committed Orthodox will resolutely hold their traditional ground; other Jews will be swept along by the prevailing cultural winds.

Crime

The incidence of crime among Jews casts a shadow over the image of the Jew as exemplar of the moral and ethical way enjoined by Judaism. Gershom Scholem called the practice of criminality the "basement" of Jewish life in contrast to the "salon," consisting of its moral, religious, intellectual, and artistic levels. The occurrence of crime has been considerably lower among Jews than non-Jews, yet at different times and places Jews involved in crime have brought distress and shame to the Jewish community. In the seventeenth century there was a miniature Jewish underworld in Germany, and there were Jews among the convicts England deported to Australia in the eighteenth and nineteenth centuries. East European Jews were associated with white slavery, and American Jews were found in the ranks of Mafia gangsters and Wall Street felons.[42]

When Jews lived in poverty-stricken ghettos, crime rates were low; but with freedom from poverty and absorption into surrounding society they rose. Crime became more sophisticated with the second immigrant generation. This was the Prohibition era when bootlegging became a main engine of crime. The age of organized crime had dawned and the monetary stakes had begun to soar. Ethnic barriers were crossed as Jews became partners in crime with Italians and Irish. Gangland ventures had graduated to union and business protection, gambling, moneylending, and murder for hire. (Murder, Inc. was run by the Jewish gangster, Louis Lepke (Bucholter)). A Jew could now make it big with no capital investment. His immigrant background would be no handicap.

Jewish communal leaders were naturally unsettled and disturbed by the operations of Jewish gangsters whose criminal exploits were luridly reported in the press. Some felt that the ethnic background of Jewish gangsters received more attention than was absolutely necessary, and the time-worn question, "What will the Gentiles say?" rose to trouble Jews. It was the old Diaspora precariousness revealed in the fear that a few malefactors might jeopardize the security of all Jews. Another cause was the perception that the religious and ethical premises of Judaism were so blatantly flouted by the gangsters. Jews, after all, were summoned to be morally responsible for one another.

Within the past decade, attempts have been made to glamorize some of the Jewish mobsters of the Prohibition and post-Prohibition era. Films have depicted the mettle of Bugsy Siegal, played as a kind of Jewish Godfather by Warren Beatty, and the charisma of Dutch Schultz (Arthur Flegenheimer), played by Dustin Hoffman. The viewer is not likely to leave the theater disapproving of film icons like Beatty and Hoffman. He will succumb to their assorted charms, which was the producer's objective all along.

Albert Fried's, *The Rise and Fall of the Jewish Gangster in America,* borders on the rapturous in lauding the attributes and contribution to American culture of these murderous thugs. Gifts of mind and character, we are told, were required to be a successful gangster — tact, intelligence, command of economics. We can be proud of Bugsy Siegal for developing Las Vegas. Indeed, he deserves "a place of honor in the literature of organized crime, indeed in the history of American culture .... America is embracing Bugsy Siegal's vision; his martyrdom was not in vain."[43]

It has been suggested that celebratory tributes to Jewish gangsters in books and movies may be a proclamation of pride in Jewish "toughness." During the pre-World War II days, when antisemitic rabble-rousers were burgeoning in America, Jews took comfort in whispered assurances that Jewish mobsters had vowed that they wouldn't "let it happen here." Louis Marshall and other Jewish leaders were greatly exercised by Jewish gangsterism and mounted many podiums to denounce and explain it. But there were Jews who viewed the Jewish gangsters' militant reaction to the threat of antisemitism with a sneaking pride. The Jew need no longer be the inevitable weakling, the cowering victim. His armor might be forged in gangland, but he can emerge as a macho, the virile man who can dish it out, violently. No longer the lamb led fearfully to the slaughter, he is perhaps the defiant, self-affirming answer to Auschwitz.

Making gallant knights out of mobsters is in the English tradition of Robin Hood and the American pattern of the chivalrous outlaw. Robin Hood, a robber and occasional killer, is a legendary hero, and Jesse James and Billy the Kid, train robbers and gunslingers, folk heroes of story and ballad. Jewish racketeers have been portrayed as victims of circumstance, redeemed by pride in their Jewish identity, compassion for their Jewish kinsmen, love of family, and generosity in supporting Jewish causes. Meyer Lansky, whom Jackie Mason called the Henry Kissinger of the Mafia, was a staunch partisan of Israel who owned a penthouse in Tel Aviv and would have moved to Israel but for its refusal to give him sanctuary. In Chicago, Sam ("Greasy Thumb") Guzik was for years a financial mainstay of the Bohemian synagogue where he went to Hebrew school. In a sardonic summing up of the Brownie points of the Jewish gangsters, Sarna notes that they were "proud of their heritage, big givers to charity, and strong supporters of the state of Israel." They also respected brains, abhorred violence, and loved their children.[44]

During the eighties, unlawful practices such as insider trading, leveraged buyouts, and corporate raiding created upheaval on Wall Street and brought heavy losses to financial institutions and their thousands of investors. Jews were disproportionately involved in the skullduggery which led to the collapse of the bond market. Having broken with the violent world of gangsterism, Jews had found a quieter arena for criminal enterprise in the financial world. Indicted for fraud, the malefactors were found guilty and sentenced to prison. Some Jews, skittish as ever about Gentile stereotyping, worried about an antisemitic backlash but no overt evidence of it appeared.

In this white collar criminal world, Jews were not exactly pioneers. Spectacular feats of fraud and embezzlement had been perpetrated by the Robber Barons of the nineteenth and early twentieth centuries. Jay Gould, James Fisk, Henry Frick, Charles Yerkes, and John D. Rockefeller cut every ethical and legal corner as they built their industrial empires in the age of brass knuckles entrepreneurship. The Teapot Dome scandal of the 1920's found the unscrupulous felons Harry Sinclair and Edward Doheny bribing members of the U.S. cabinet with the possible knowledge of the President himself. The stock market crash of the 1930's saw the blue-blooded Richard Whitney engaging in the kind of fraud that landed him in prison. In the 1980's massive banking defalcations were schemed by Charles E. Keating, Jr., with the silent collusion of leading Washington legislators, and Clark Clifford, adviser to seven Presidents, was accused of "committing fraud for a crooked bank .... deliberately or unwittingly."[45] In manipulating the market, Boesky, Levine, and Milliken were treading in well-worn Wasp footsteps.

Some of the Jews who made astronomical gains in the junk bond scandal were known for their benefactions to the Jewish community. Ivan Boesky, best known of the criminals for the attention he received in the press, was a liberal contributor to a variety of Jewish charitable, cultural, and religious institutions. A board member of the Jewish Theological Seminary, he had made the largest single gift toward building a new library for the institution.[46] The rabbi of one of the convicted culprits related that whenever the congregation had a financial need, his call to the errant member made the necessary funds instantly available. Like their more violent predecessors in the criminal world, the "goniffs in Guccis" were a soft touch for Jewish philanthropy and the synagogue.

After the great immigration of the late 1890's and early 1920's, Jewish crime may be viewed as a reflex of crime in the general culture. When they moved out of the alleys of petty crime in an almost exclusively Jewish milieu, Jews entered the broad highways of organized crime pioneered and dominated by Gentiles. They became partners with non-Jewish Mafiosi in an underworld of extreme violence. Arthur Ruppin (1876-1943), pioneer Jewish sociologist, once observed that while

Christians committed crime with their hands, Jews did it with their reason. That may have been true of the Jewish world Ruppin knew — the ghetto world of Isaac Bashevis Singer, the pushcart world of Delancey Street. It was not true of the U.S. underworld. Jewish criminals of the second immigrant generation had adapted themselves to the criminal modes of America in another instance of acculturation.

In the Jewish communal view, crime is a repudiation of the values of family. "Whoever brings disrepute upon himself brings disrepute upon his whole family .... A family is like a heap of stones. Remove one, and the whole structure can collapse."[47] Nor was the religion of the Jew less stern in its condemnation of the lawbreaker. "To rob a man even of a penny is like taking his life."[48] Seen as a threat to family integrity and religious rectitude, the lawbreaker drew down the censure of law-abiding Jews.

During the pre-Emancipation centuries, these social and religious constraints kept the incidence of Jewish crime at a negligible level. But when the ghetto walls fell and Jews moved into the open societies of the west, all prior controls were dissipated. As in other aspects of his assimilated life, the Jew's criminal behavior since Emancipation has consistently mirrored the patterns of lawlessness predominant in the culture at large.

What is the trend for American Jews, considered through the prism of family and moral life? We must conclude that the old characterization of the Jews as archetype moral individuals tightly bound to their families is another victim of acculturation to American mainstream society.

Notes

1. Paula E. Hyman, "The Modern Jewish Family: Image and Reality," in *The Jewish Family: Metaphor and Memory*, ed. David Kramer (New York: Oxford University Press, 1989), p. 186
2. *Kiddushin*, 71
3. Abraham Joshua Heschel, "Warns of 'Breakdown' in Traditional Close-knit Unity of Jewish Family Causing Loss of Identity," in *Jewish Telegraphic Agency Dispatch*, 1972
4. Irving Howe, *World of Our Fathers* (New York: Harcourt Brace Jovanovich, 1976), p. 172
5. Spitzer has written trenchantly of the contemporary Jewish family: "What was the unusual has become in contemporary times a condition far more pervasive than expected. With alarming and increasing frequency one finds [in the] Jewish community and [among] Jewish families problems of alcoholism, spousal abuse, child abuse, substance abuse, breakdown in parental authority, and other tragic intrusions upon the concept of wholeness or harmony of the family" (Julia Ringold Spitzer,

"Spousal Abuse in Rabbinic and Contemporary Judaism." [New York: National Federation of Temple Sisterhoods, 1985]).

6. Yosef Goell, "Baby Talk," in *Jerusalem Post*, August 12, 1983
7. *Yebamot*, 62b
8. Jack Stern, "The President's Message," in *Central Conference of American Rabbis Yearbook* 97 (New York: CCAR, 1987), p. 8
9. Gerald B. Bubis, Saving the Jewish Family (Lanham, MD.: Jewish Center for Public Affairs/Center for Jewish Community Studies, University Press of America, 1987), p. 1. Bubis' estimate is disputed by others.
10. Bruce Phillips, "Faculty Profile," in *The Chronicle* 26 (H.U.C.-J.I.R., Oct. 1983), p. 4
11. "Divorce Inroads Among Orthodox," in *Jerusalem Post*, May 19, 1975
12. David Polish and W. Gunther Plaut, eds., *Rabbi's Manual* (New York: CCAR, 1988), pp. 97-104
13. *Yebamot* 6, 6
14. Hyman, *ibid*. p. 180
15. H.J. Roberts, "Endogenous Jewish Genocide: The Impact of the ZPG-Nonparenthood Movement," in *Reconstructionist* (November 1974), pp. 8-16
16. His influence went beyond Illinois. His sponsorship of Adlai Stevenson, first as state governor, then as presidential candidate, extended his influence throughout the nation.
17. Spitzer, *ibid*., p. 1
18. Harold M. Schulweis, "Raised in an Addictive Culture," in *Reconstructionist* (March 1989), pp. 9-12
19. *Ibid*.
20. In 1886 Nietzsche wrote, "In time of distress, Jews least of all .... try to escape by recourse to drink or suicide."
21. Steven Shaw and George E. Johnson, "Jews on an Eastern Religious Quest and the Jewish Response," Analysis 44, Institute for Jewish Policy Planning and Research of the Synagogue Council of America, 1973
22. *Reform Judaism*, Spring 1992
23. Harold Schulweis, "Are We Losing the Faith?" in *Reform Judaism*, Spring 1992, p. 4
24. Emanuel Feldman, "Observant Jews and Religious Jews," in *Tradition*, Winter 1992, p. 1
25. Nathan Glazer, *American Judaism*, second edition (Chicago: University of Chicago Press, 1972), p. 150
26. Feldman, *ibid*., p. 2
27. Schulweis, *ibid*., p. 5
28. Avraham Isaac Kook, *Orot Ha-Rav Kook* (Jerusalem: 1963), p. 101

29. Abraham Joshua Heschel, *God in Search of Man* (Philadelphia: Jewish Publication Society, 1956)
30. Shlomo Riskin, "Is the Synagogue Orthodox?" in *Moment*, April 1976, p. 16
31. Theodore I. Lenn and Associates, *Rabbi and Synagogue in Reform Judaism* (New York: CCAR, 1972), pp. 108-253
32. These estimates are based on the investigations reported in the Kinsey studies in human sexual behavior which created considerable agitation almost half a century ago. Newer studies have led to a downward revision of the number of gays and lesbians in the United States.
33. "The Future of Gay America," in *Newsweek*, March 12, 1990, p. 45
34. *Ibid.*
35. Ari L. Goldman, "Reform Judaism Votes to Accept Active Homosexuals in Rabbinate," in *New York Times*, June 26, 1990, p. 1
36. Alexander M. Schindler and Harold M. Schulweis, signatories of letter to rabbis from Beacon Press recommending book, *Twice Blessed: On Being Lesbian, Gay, and Jewish*. eds. Christie Balka and Andy Rose (Boston: Beacon Press, 1989)
37. Samuel E. Karff, "The Subtleties of Our Rabbinic Authority," in *Rabbinic Authority*, ed. Elliot L. Stevens (New York: CCAR 1990), 2: 55-62; Debra Nussbaum Cohen, "Reform Movement Torn by Gay Rabbi Issue," in *Jewish Week*, July 5-11, 1991, p. 9
38. Eugene B. Borowitz, "On Homosexuality and the Rabbinate: A Covenantal Response," in "Homosexuality, the Rabbinate, and Liberal Tradition," paper prepared for the Ad Hoc Committee on Homosexuality and the Rabbinate, CCAR, June 1989, pp. 2-13
39. Goldman, *ibid.*
40. Charles Hoffman, "Call for Judaism to Accept 'Loving' Homosexual Couples," in *Jerusalem Post*, April 15, 1988; "Report of the Ad Hoc Committee on Homosexuality and the Rabbinate," CCAR, June 15, 1990, p. 4
41. Yoel H. Kahn, "The Kedusha of Homosexual Relationships," *CCAR Yearbook* 99 (New York: CCAR, 1989, p. 138)
42. Jonathan D. Sarna, "The Jewish Way of Crime," in *Commentary*, August 1984, p. 53
43. Albert Fried, *The Rise and Fall of the Jewish Gangster in America* (New York: Holt, Rinehart and Winston, 1980)
44. Sarna, *ibid.*, p. 55
45. "Clark Clifford's Judgement," in *New York Times* (News of the Week in Review), April 11, 1993, p. 6
46. This benefaction is given an ironic twist if we recall Mordecai Kaplan's disdainful observation in 1963 that the "chief motivation of the American financial elite .... for supporting the [Jewish Theological] Seminary in the first decades of the century was to establish a training school for American-trained rabbis who might stem the proliferation of gangsterism on the Jewish east side." Cf. Abraham J. Karp, "The Conservative Rabbi — Dissatisfied but Not Unhappy," in *The American Rabbinate: A Centennial View* (Cincinnati: American Jewish Archives, 1983), p. 258

47. *Numbers R.*, 21, 3; *Genesis R.*, 100, 7
48. *Baba Kama* 119

CHAPTER 7

WALKING DOWN THE AISLE .... WHERE TO?

Then and Now

A broadside published a few years ago blazoned the warning, "If the Jewish intermarriage rate continues at 50 percent, the Jews will become an endangered species like .... " and there followed a listing of some of the more celebrated imperiled creatures of the wild — the American eagle, the snow leopard, the giant panda.

Intermarriage[1] is held to be a predominant factor in the numerical decline of Jews. Two generations ago, the rate of intermarriage was five percent. In 1989, the rate had reached 60 percent in San Francisco, Denver, and Phoenix. Four out of five non-Jewish spouses do not convert. Only 25 percent of mixed-marriage children identify as Jews when they reach adulthood. "Intermarriage on a massive scale is a fact of American Jewish life," writes Rabbi Arthur Green, former president of the Reconstructionist Rabbinical College. Egon Mayer, an authority on intermarriage, warns that because of intermarriage, the American Jewish community is "confronting a demographic revolution of unprecedented proportions."[2]

Until a generation or two ago, Jews took the Biblical ban on intermarriage with utmost seriousness. "You shall not intermarry with them; do not give your daughters to their sons, nor take their daughters for your sons. For they will turn your children from following Me to worship other gods." (*Deuteronomy 7:3,4*) When the daughter of Reb Moshe Gabriel in one of Isaac Bashevis Singer's stories married a Christian, the aunts and uncles spat at the mention of her name, the mother disowned her, and the father mourned for her as dead. In Israel Zangwill's *Children of the Ghetto,* Reb Shmuel sees his son walking with a Gentile woman. He returns home stricken and laments, "I have seen him. He is dead." In *Fiddler on the Roof,* Tevye, the father, declares his daughter dead after she marries a Christian. During my first year at the Hebrew Union College, one of the senior students, who lived in Cincinnati, announced to his family his intention of marrying a Christian. Thereupon the family renounced him, sat *shiva* (ritual period of mourning for the dead), and broke off all contact with him.

As recently as the 1970's, the issue of intermarriage could still touch a raw nerve among Jews. A popular television comedy series, *Bridget Loves Bernie,* which showed Bernie, son of a Jewish delicatessen owner, falling in love and marrying Bridget, daughter of an Irish Catholic businessman, in an ecumenical wedding, provoked a storm of protest in the Jewish community. CBS was assailed for making a mockery of sacred Jewish teaching by glamorizing intermarriage. Jewish leaders met with CBS executives and demanded that the series be dropped. One rabbi organized a boycott of the products advertised by the program's sponsors. That was in 1973.

Today such a protest would be scarcely thinkable. For marriage between Jew and non-Jew has come to be taken for granted. It would be hard to find an American Jewish family in which there has been no intermarriage. This is reflected in the numerous movies and television programs produced in the past few years featuring Jewish characters whose only loves are Gentiles. Woody Allen's loves are conspicuously Gentile. Hollywood is imitating life.

Intermarriage is still exceptional among those raised in the ultra-Orthodox community. Among Conservative Jews it is no longer uncommon, while among the Reform it is as much the rule as the exception. Sklare has pointed out that as the rate of intermarriage increases, it generates a measure of self-approval and the feeling that combating it is a losing battle. Certainly most Jewish parents today are acquiescing in what is widely held to be the inevitable wave of the future. This has been called the collapse of the "ultimate Jewish taboo," a "holocaust."[3] As James Joyce once said, Jews are being "rounded by the lathe of intermarriage."[4]

Why Jews Intermarry

Adherence by Jews to classic American liberal patterns is a leading cause of intermarriage. In a secular culture, an absolute belief in pluralism, tolerance, and egalitarianism can ultimately lead to intermarriage. Parents with a tenuous connection to Judaism, who also teach their children unquestioning acceptance of people across religious lines, should not be surprised when the children date and eventually marry non-Jews. As one observer has dryly noted, "This is one of the consequences of living in a pluralistic society."[5]

Intermarriage betrays an indifference to the continuity of Jewish life, to say nothing of the authority of Jewish teaching, or the call of Jewish tradition and sentiment. Here is a major cause for the mounting rate of intermarriage. It is a function of accommodation to the "civil religion" of the secular society. Jews move into the open society around them and without effort become almost anything they wish. It is easy to forget Jewishness, with its nagging personal, family and communal responsibilities. Egon Mayer has said that the threat to the Jewish community now comes less from external forces like antisemitism and pogroms than from the attractions of the vastly enchanting and exciting secular society. "It's a lot more fun than most of what Jewish culture has to offer."[6] Jews, like most Americans, have a resolute commitment to "fun."

Another cause for the high rate of intermarriage derives from the radically changed relationship between parents and children over the past two generations. Parents are no longer the authority figures they once were, and their values, loyalties, and sentiments are likely to be dismissed as irrelevant by children of a generation for whom self-fulfillment is often a consuming, when not an exclusive, concern. Freud and the psychiatric age loosed a flood of parental guilt when it came to exercising discipline or wielding influence in the lives of children. Parents have become intimidated by their children and uncommitted to Judaism themselves, will gloss over ancestral sanctities like inmarriage so as not to "antagonize" them. "So long as they're happy" is often the ultimate parental justification for intermarriage. As for "happiness," few parents are aware that intermarriages end in twice the number of divorces as inmarriages.

The American college campus exhibits in microcosm some of the forces at work in the erosion of traditional Jewish institutions, including inmarriage. According to Richard Joel, international director of the Hillel Foundation, seventeen out of twenty Jews who enter college have "marginal or no Jewish identity."[7] During the college years, life for the majority of Jewish students has little, if any, Jewish content. Aside from full assemblies at Rosh Hashanah and Yom Kippur services, there is little student participation in Jewish affairs. Organized Jewish activity, centered in the Hillel Foundation, engages the interest of a thin cadre of students, most of them Orthodox. How thin is apparent when one reads that only 6.1 per cent of American Jews are Orthodox and are therefore of "minimal statistical significance."[8]

Jewish studies have of recent years become part of the curriculum of many colleges, but, contrary to expectations, the response of Jewish students has been less than enthusiastic. Not a few Jewish students, ambivalent about their identity, have been caught up in the agendas of multiculturalism and political correctness, which champion the rights of all minorities (except Jews) and of Third World ethnics like the Palestinians. The campus reality is a generation of the Jewishly illiterate and indifferent, even hostile, students far more eager to explore the newly discovered intellectual, cultural, and social frontiers of the general college world than of the Jewish world. There may be random instances of Jewish commitment, such as the annual United Jewish Appeal drive on some campuses, but few cases of sustained involvement in Jewish life.

In the unconfined ambiance of the college campus there is, of course, free mixing and dating. Almost twenty years ago, a survey of the dating patterns of Jewish college students in New Orleans showed that "almost all [Jewish] college students interdate."[9] Many reports verify a demonstrated preference by Jewish fraternity and sorority members for their non-Jewish counterparts. The barriers which once created insurmountable division between Jew and non-Jew in the fraternity and sorority world, have been crumbling, and Jews and Christians have now made their way easily into each other's Greek letter lairs. And all this during the years traditionally and biologically given over to pairing off and mating. With these conditions shaping the college experience, little wonder that the American campus is a seedbed for intermarriage. "If we are committed to life in the open society .... where Jews and non-Jews mix, we have to live with intermarriage."[10] Daniel Leifer, who works with Jewish students and faculty at the University of Chicago, writes that "the campus is at the forefront of assimilation and intermarriage."[11]

Interdating

A telling example of the parents' silent complicity in the incidence of their children's intermarriages is the permissive attitude to interdating. Studies have shown that there is a strong connection between interdating and intermarriage. A poll of delegates to a biennial convention of the Union of American Hebrew Congregations, representing the leadership of the Reform movement, revealed that of the 53 percent of parents who raised no serious objection to interdating, 45 percent of their children intermarried. By contrast, inmarriage partners report a pattern of "overwhelming" indating.[12]

Such parental leniency exemplifies the cost of failure to set limits on adolescent behavior. Confused teenagers come to think there is no conflict between interdating and maintaining one's Jewish identity. Parents who hope to prevent the intermarriage of their children will oppose interdating. But setting dating limitations for children based on religious considerations will not be easy for acculturated Jews.

For a number of years at our congregation in Glencoe, the week of Confirmation included a Confirmation dance. At first I assumed that the fifteen year olds would date their Confirmation classmates or other Jewish agemates. To my surprise, some of the children and their parents approached me with the request that the children be permitted to bring non-Jews as dates. I pointed out the appropriateness of dating only Jews for a Confirmation dance. There was considerable grumbling, some indignation, some anger, during which I was classified as a ghettoized bigot. Some of the Confirmants stayed away from the dance. Not long afterwards the Confirmation dance was abolished.

Rabbis Who Officiate

A significant factor in the sanctioning of intermarriage has been the abandonment of responsibility by Reform rabbis. About half of the rabbis of this largest of Jewish denominations publicly list themselves as ready to officiate at intermarriages. Most require that assurances be given prior to the ceremony that the non-Jew will take a course in Judaism, that the couple will raise their children as Jews, and will not stage the wedding on the Sabbath, or with the co-officiation of a priest or minister. Since 1969 the list of rabbis available for intermarriage ceremonies has increased fourfold. There are others who, while not announcing their availability, will steal out of the closet to officiate. One Los Angeles rabbi explained his reluctance to list himself among his intermarrying colleagues. "The demand for mixed marriage ceremonies is so great, that I would be overrun with requests."[13]

Today the silence on intermarriage from pulpits across the country is deafening. In Glaser's 1993 communique of alarm on intermarriage to members of the Central Conference of American Rabbis, he warns his colleagues to tread gingerly. Discouraging intermarriage has its dangers. "We hear stories of people walking out on sermons (and congregations) which discuss the subject .... mildly .... cautiously .... tentatively .... apologetically." He confesses to "advising colleagues to think four times before preaching on the subject." His conclusion, born of gloom and desperation: "We .... encourage inmarriage at our peril."[14]

Some years ago a Conservative rabbi in a neighboring North Shore community told me that while his congregants had always hitherto indicated their support for his outspoken opposition to intermarriage, voiced from the pulpit, of late they had begun urging him to temper, perhaps suspend, such pronouncements. Parents had asked that when their children who were contemplating an intermarriage came to him, he refrain from discouraging the marriage. Perhaps he would try instead to persuade the non-Jew to convert. Should this prove fruitless, and if he himself would not officiate, they hoped he would recommend a rabbi who would.

No Orthodox rabbi will officiate at an intermarriage. No Conservative rabbi will, although certain rumblings indicate that change may be in the wind. The Rabbinical Assembly, the Conservative rabbinical body, is now going through the *sturm und drang* which usually precedes a decision to break with the past. Such seismic tremors preceded the decision to ordain women and are now perceptible on the issues of patrilineality and homosexuality. Meanwhile, a restless minority of Conservative rabbis is advocating a more liberal approach to conversion so as to make passage into the Jewish fold easier. Robert Gordis summarized the concern of many Conservative colleagues when he fretted, "The Jewish community simply cannot afford to lose thousands upon thousands of its sons and daughters without making a yeoman effort to reduce .... defections from its ranks."[15]

It has been charged that Reform Judaism opened the floodgates to intermarriage by flouting the age-old ban against it. And although back in 1909 the Central Conference of American Rabbis affirmed the position that mixed marriages are contrary to Jewish law, and "asked" that its members not perform them, this was, as a Reform leader observed, merely a "screen behind which one could do, and did, as one pleased."[16]

Intermarrying rabbis defend their officiating by claiming that they thereby promote Jewish survival. A former chairman of the Central Conference committee on mixed marriage, Rabbi Herman E. Schaalman, questioned this claim. Living amid the "debris of the fractured Jewish community," he commented, "with its sterility in Jewish education and rampant assimilation, [one could only question whether] performing intermarriages strengthens Jewish survival."[17]

Rabbis further justify their participation in intermarriages by the professed desire to spare couples the feeling of being "rejected." The rabbi, all sensitivity and empathy, will presumably be presiding at a drama of welcome into the religion of Abraham. But the truth may be, as Egon Mayer tells us, that it "makes no difference" whether a rabbi officiates or not. Fear of "rejection" is a remote concern for the couple, who, for the most part, couldn't care less who officiates — rabbi, judge, justice of the peace, or city clerk. Their decision has been made, and considerations of rejection or acceptance were hardly an obstacle in reaching it. It is the parents and grandparents who care, not so much for "religious" reasons as out of a need for a fig leaf of sanction for a union which may leave them less than ecstatic. The rabbi becomes the facilitator, the tool for gratifying the ritual needs of parents and grandparents, a role to which he is not unaccustomed.

When they have a pulpit vacancy, many congregations will now require that only a candidate who promises to officiate at intermarriages be considered for the position. After all, since members are calling for intermarriage services "increasingly and ever more insistently," why not hire a rabbi who will perform them without making waves? This litmus test for engaging a rabbi has been criticized by some leading rabbis on the grounds that the rabbinate must be governed by "principles," not by polls of what congregants want. "Principles must govern us. Rabbis are teachers of Judaism .... not endorsers of the positions and practices of ignorant and indifferent laymen."[18] The view of the clergy as an instrument to sanctify the heresies of laymen was famously exemplified by Henry VIII, who sacked a pesky priest for refusing to officiate at one of his marriages.

But what if a considerable component of a congregation's members consists of intermarried couples, a not unlikely possibility in the future, or even now? What if the president or some of its officers are partners in an intermarriage? In such circumstances the intermarriage issue might well become a source of tension in the congregation.

The Synagogue Confronts Intermarriage

That this is already happening is startlingly clear from reports emanating from congregations all over the country. In 1993, Rabbi Joseph Glaser, the chief executive officer of the Central Conference of American Rabbis, the largest rabbinical body in America, circulated a lengthy communique to its members sounding an alarm and issuing a warning about the "lobbies" in synagogues presently engaged in "loosening the rules of participation by non-Jews in the governance and ritual of the congregations." These lobbies, mustering their clientele of non-Jews married to Jews and their Jewish spouses, their children, and the parents, friends, and families of the mixed couples, had "taken on a life of their own" and were already a major issue in the Reform movement. Similar lobbies, according to Glaser, were at work in Conservative synagogues.[19]

This spreading phenomenon was insinuating itself into every aspect of congregational life. Non-Jews were serving as officers and board members of congregations and their auxiliaries, as well as chairs of the worship, ritual, and religious education committees. Professing Christians married to Jews, called up for the reading of the Torah, were reciting the traditional prayer praising God for "having chosen us from among all peoples." Religious school teachers who had never converted to Judaism were leading children in the declamation of the *Sh'ma*, which declares that "our God" is eternally one. In Indiana a churchgoing Catholic became co-president of a large Sisterhood, and at a Bar Mitzvah in Pennsylvania an Episcopal priest handed down the Torah to the son of a Jewish mother whom the priest had married not long before. (In some congregations the rabbis changed the prayers so as to make them theologically acceptable for a Christian reader.)

Rabbi Glaser's alarm at the "loosening" process was occasioned by the possibility that the clientele working for change in governance and ritual might become a critical mass "tipping the balance" and effectuating changes which would radically alter the Jewish character of the synagogue. The determinative question facing the movement was who are and who will comprise the critical mass in the congregations and in the movement: born and converted Jews, or the satellite clientele resulting from mixed marriage. (Glaser himself was troubled by a Reform development in recent years, when, through the Outreach programs, the focus was more upon converts than upon born Jews. He pointed out that the Outreach committees had spawned the lobbies.)

The predicaments in congregations brought about by intermarriage are viewed in conflicting perspectives by Reform leaders. Walter Jacob, president of the CCAR when Glaser circulated his warning message, feels that any attempt to adopt or temporize with proposals for the relaxation of customary norms of congregational governance and ritual must be strenuously resisted. There are fundamental theological differences between Jews and Christians, which, he holds, simply means that no Christian can be a member of a synagogue. The very idea is an absurdity, an oxymoron, which even the early Reform rabbis of radical universalist convictions dismissed as "utter folly." The synagogue is not a country club catering to the individual's social needs, but a sacred institution which demands a commitment of faith and practice. There are fixed boundaries of belief and outlook in the synagogue which cannot be crossed. We must not be afraid to say "no" to trespassers, no matter what their motivation. A synagogue cannot have a Baptist president or a Methodist religious school teacher. Judaism has often said "no" — 365 of the 613 precepts are negative mandates and five of the Ten Commandments are Thou Shalt Not's. In the twenty-first century, Judaism must not flinch from halting the slide into a syncretism of irreconcilable beliefs.

One of the leading advocates for "loosening the rules" in synagogue governance and ritual is Rabbi Alexander Schindler, recent president of the Union of American Hebrew Congregations. Schindler has always been interested in increasing the membership of the Reform movement. He had encouraged the creation of "outreach" programs in congregations, designed to draw non-Jewish spouses into the synagogue and Jewish life. In 1985, he championed the proposal for making patrilineal descent a sufficient Jewish identity warrant for Reform Jews, thus marking a historic break with the Jewish tradition which had always regarded matrilineal descent as the indispensable criterion for Jewish identity. His latest proposal, made in 1993, called for Reform Judaism to embark on a program for proselytizing unchurched non-Jews. Schindler admits that he is not on the side of the "strict constructionists," but on the side of those who tend to be "more open." To all and sundry the synagogue must be above all a warm and welcoming haven.[20]

He also seems to hold that decisions on membership eligibility should rest with the laymen of the congregation. "The authority," he has declared, "is the congregation, which, through the election of the rabbi, determines what is or is not done." Does the ambiguous "through the election of the rabbi" unveil a conception of the rabbi as merely the facilitator of the layman's will? What happened to the conception of the rabbi as leader of the congregation? It has been said that congregations no longer choose rabbis to lead; they elect them to serve. There are both laymen and rabbis who view the rabbi in today's postmodern congregation as a deputy, an agent elected to carry out the wishes of the higher lay authority.

Glaser refers to the "low level of knowledge and commitment" of the typical congregation, which in its corporate model, may demand rabbis who are willing to accept the dictum that he who pays the piper calls the tune. It is generally accepted that a shrinking number of Reform and Conservative rabbis today are able to declare with their paradigmatic forbears, Emil G. Hirsch, Stephen S. Wise, Abba Hillel Silver, Solomon Goldman, "I am the master of my fate, the captain of my soul." They are more likely to be heard bleating the bathetic ballad, "As You Desire Me."[21]

In 1973, the Central Conference of American Rabbis changed its position on mixed marriage by declaring that, while it opposed the participation of members in "any ceremony which solemnizes a mixed marriage," it would henceforth sanction such officiating if the couple undertake "a course of study of Judaism equivalent to that required for conversion." Although this resolution was intended to relax further the ban on performing intermarriages, it evoked loud and acrimonious opposition by advocates of unrestricted officiation. In a blistering diatribe, the executive dean and professor of rabbinic literature at the Hebrew Union College-Jewish Institute of Religion, Rabbi Eugene Mihaly, denounced the resolution for its attempt to impose yet another condition for intermarriage officiation, as well as to limit the freedom of the rabbi to officiate as he wished. He also assailed the resolution as "contrary to the demands of God .... of Judaism .... of true Halacha ....I plead with you .... for the sake of the Jewish people .... for the sake of Reform Judaism .... for the sake of our children .... I plead with you *l'ma'an ha-shem* (for God's sake), vote down the resolution .... God bless you."[22]

There is sometimes a commercial aspect to rabbinic participation in mixed marriages. Such rabbis may advertise their services in the press or in the Yellow Pages. Among the conditions made at first contact, usually through a secretary, there may be stipulations that no pre- or post-nuptial interviews take place, that the fee be based on the distance to the wedding site, and that the fee be paid cash on the barrelhead. Of course, most officiants claim that these marriages are performed out of principle to shield the couple from the shame of rejection and thus to reinforce the chances for Jewish survival, and some rabbis probably believe this. But one rabbi, surveying the principles at work, concluded, "If there is one principle involved here, it is the principle of the fast buck."[23]

Optimists and Realists

An objective reading of recent intermarriage statistics has raised serious questions about the viability of the American Jewish community. They suggest a cumulative erosion of commitment to Jewish institutions and a spreading secession from Jewish ranks. What, after all, is the implication of the disclosure that 72 percent of the children of intermarriages are being raised identified with a non-Jewish religion or with no religion at all? That only 24 percent of mixed marriage children identify themselves as Jews when they grow up? That in the span of one generation the percentage of Jews with Gentile spouses quintupled (seven percent in the 1950's, 35 percent in the 1980's). That 90 percent of these marriages produce children who marry non-Jews? The authors of the Brandeis Report cited as its "most striking" finding the conclusion that "many mixed marriage households are not .... likely to produce a new generation which is connected to Judaism or the Jewish people."[24]

Other analysts of American Jewish life, however, do not agree with this prognosis. On the contrary, they read the recent population studies as presaging a bright future for American Judaism and for the American Jew. Having adapted themselves to the social and cultural ethos of contemporary America, they say, Jews are developing new "modalities" of Jewishness. New norms and standards are displacing the behavior patterns of past generations. But through it all, they insist, the commitment to Jewish values and the glue of Jewish loyalty are as strong as ever. Jewish life is not being weakened but invigorated, and the Jewish community will not lose but gain in numbers. In a word, the American Jewish community is being "transformed." Those who hold this view have been dubbed "transformationists." Those who hold the opposite view, namely, that American Jews are becoming devitalized Jewishly and are declining numerically, have been called "assimilationists." The latter do not advocate assimilation but describe what they believe to be the drift toward assimilation in American Jewish life.

Typical of the optimists about the American Jewish future is Charles Silberman, who predicts a flowering of Jewish life in the transformed age that is emerging from the musty past. "We are in the early stages of a major revitalization of Jewish religious, intellectual and cultural life .... one that is likely to transform American Judaism. For when young Jews freely choose to be observant, they do so with a seriousness, vitality, imagination, and elan and, equally important, with a fund of Jewish knowledge, that are wholly new to American Jewish life.[25] Professors Fred Masserik and Steven Cohen venture that intermarriage may result in an increase rather than a decrease in Jewish population. Mordechai Rimor, an author of the Brandeis Report, noted that 50 percent of intermarriage children were "getting some kind of Jewish education. .... For me, the cup is half full, not half empty .... We haven't lost them .... They are retrievable."

This optimism is surprising. The recent intermarriage and population studies simply confirm the restrained counsel of plain sense. Professor Paula Hyman, Jewish historian at Yale, has given the name "happy sociologists" to purveyors of an unsubstantiated optimism about the future of Jewish life in America.

Conversion, Outreach, Inreach

A major finding of the Brandeis Report is that conversionary families, that is, families with one Jewish-born spouse and the other converted to Judaism, are much like inmarried families in Jewish behavior and commitment. They are likely to provide a Jewish education for their children and to contribute to Jewish philanthropy, although they are less inclined to join a congregation, affiliate with Jewish organizations, or become involved in the ethnic dimension of Jewishness. In short, conversionary families may exhibit as many Jewish "behaviors" as the inmarried, much more than the mixed married. It is, therefore, the principal recommendation of the Brandeis Report that the American Jewish community embark on an aggressive campaign of conversion targeted at the non-Jewish spouses of intermarried couples. The greater the number of conversionary families, the greater the number of Jews and the stronger the Jewish commitment, reason the researchers. Conversion must therefore become a "basic priority" of the community agenda, and "how and when to achieve the goal of conversion should constitute our focus in the coming decade."[26]

But cheerful Jewish expectations on the outcome of conversions may be unrealistic, with dubious chance for success. Perhaps advocacy of conversion is more a symptom of a community's anxiety than a solution for assimilation. Different branches of Judaism have criticized conversion, especially when it occurs just before marriage. Judaism has always frowned upon, in fact rejected, ulterior motives, including marriage, as reason for conversion. (If you wanted to convert to Judaism, you had better have a better reason than the desire to marry a Jew!) Orthodox and Conservative leaders have objected that the proposed conversion program will "make mixed marriages easier." If conversion is a cure, why discourage intermarriage or interdating? Even an official representative of Reform, which pioneered Outreach programs and has for years been sponsoring them for the rapidly increasing host of former and present non-Jews on its swelling membership rolls, doubts the efficacy of a conversion program. Lydia Keukoff, former director of the national Reform Outreach Program, and herself a convert, worries that it might not work. She has written, "How do we handle the reality that after all the outreach and welcoming, conversion is not the outcome?"

There is the stubborn reality that among younger couples now intermarrying in droves, conversion by the non-Jew is a doubtful option. In four out of five intermarriages, the non-Jewish spouse is not converting, and this may well be the wave of the future. Conversion may be urged and programmed by panicky sociologists, but there may be a paucity of takers.

The question has been asked: If intermarriage threatens the integrity and continuity of the American Jew, why not say so and openly and boldly initiate an uncompromising campaign against it? If, as the Brandeis Report predicts, outmarriage will produce a generation with no connection to Judaism or the Jewish people, why not employ the necessary, even Draconian, means to encourage inmarriage? Why not a national network of "Inreach" programs to sound the alarm and hammer home the dire message to the American Jew? Such programs — family education, child and youth indoctrination, seminars, workshops, retreats, social events, participation in the organizational structure of Jewish life, trips to Israel — are, in fact, recommended in the Brandeis Report. Nevertheless, these programs are broached as ancillary to the first priority of conversion.

It would appear that "Inreach" programs would be a far more direct and compelling instrumentality for saving Jews and Judaism. Yet it appears to be little more than an afterthought to many students of the American Jewish condition. The

Brandeis Report makes seven recommendations as an agenda for dealing with the problem of intermarriage. A renewal of the "rich and vital core of American Jewish life" is the seventh.

The truth is that a campaign against intermarriage might be sensed as futile by most American Jews. They have made their peace with intermarriage, accepted it as a given of American life. It would be fanciful to imagine acculturated Jews joining an anti-intermarriage campaign. Egon Mayer reminds us that in the past all efforts to curb intermarriage failed. The attitudes of the modern Jew and many of his spiritual leaders would seem to foredoom the idea now.

Intermarriage is a permanent and expanding feature of the American Jewish landscape. Except in the limited Orthodox world, intermarriage seems bound to increase apace. For the near future, there may not be a dramatic loss of Jewish population. Jewish identity will be undergoing continuous redefinition, so that many who never before would have been defined as Jews will now qualify. Children of a Jewish father and a non-Jewish mother will now pass muster as Jews. Individuals converted according to the minimal standards of some rabbis will be counted as Jews. So will "cultural" converts who identify with the Jewish people while still retaining their Christian faith. "Happy sociologists" will cast a net of vast width and small mesh in order to snare their questionable Jewish catch.

While discussing the dubious success of conversion as an instrumentality for becoming Jewish, we should not ignore the successful outcome of some conversions. The percentage of non-Jews who undergo conversion and become faithful followers and practitioners of Judaism is small, but there have been and are converts who are exemplary in their commitment to Judaism and the Jewish people. Every rabbi can point to some individuals and families who were converted and became part of the Temple family.

Elsie Clews Parsons, the noted anthropologist of the Southwest, once wrote, "Intermarriage is an .... obvious factor in .... cultural breakdown or cultural assimilation, which ever way you look at it."[27] With ties to the formal structure of Jewish life disintegrating for most American Jews, we should not wonder that intermarriage is a juggernaut on the loose. Perhaps here lies the deeper problem, and it is not likely to lessen in gravity, much less go away, until the Jewish community grasps the nettle and admits it. Whether honest recognition of the problem will avail, none can say.

Notes

1. Recent population studies define three patterns in their discussion of intermarriage: inmarriage, where both spouses are born Jews; conversionary marriage, where one spouse is a born Jew and one a convert to Judaism; and mixed marriage, where one

spouse is a Jew, the other an unconverted non-Jew. We shall use this nomenclature throughout our discussion.

2. Arthur Green, "Rabbis Officiating at Intermarriages," in *Jewish Post and Opinion*, May 29, 1991, p. 1; Egon Mayer, "Intermarriage: Public Issue, Private Fear," in *New York Times*, May 21, 1989, p. 2

3. Marshall Sklare, "Intermarriage and Jewish Survival," in *Commentary*, March 1970, p.13; J.J. Goldberg, "America's Vanishing Jews," in *Jerusalem Report*, November 5, 1992, pp. 29, 30

4. Richard Ellman, *James Joyce* (New York Oxford University Press, 1959), p. 354

5. Winston Pickett, "The Conversion Option," in *Jerusalem Report*, November 29, 1990, p. 36

6. Egon Mayer, "The Challenge of Intermarriage," in *Jerusalem Post* (reprinted from *Los Angeles Times*), August 20, 1991

7. Richard M. Joel, "17 of 20 Jewish Students Marginal," in *Jewish Post and Opinion*, May 29, 1991, p. 4

8. Lawrence A. Hoffman, "From Common Cold to Uncommon Healing," in *CCAR Journal: A Reform Jewish Quarterly*, Spring 1994, p. 28

9. "Almost all Students at College Interdate," in *Jewish Post and Opinion*, September 23, 1974

10. Green, *ibid.*, p. 1

11. Daniel J. Leifer, "Jewish Faculty, Reflecting the Times," in *Sh'ma*, January 11, 1991, p. 37

12. Mark Winer, response to letters on, "Mom, We're Just Dating," in *Reform Judaism*, Summer 1987, p. 32

13. John Dart, "Area Reform Rabbis Open to Mixed Marriages," in *Los Angeles Times*, January 11, 1986, p. 4

14. Joseph B. Glaser, The Gathering Crisis of Intermarriage, Central Conference of American Rabbis (New York, 1993), p. 3

15. David Singer, "Living With Intermarriage," in *Commentary*, July 1979, p. 51.

16. Report of the Ad Hoc Committee on Mixed Marriage, *CCAR Yearbook* (New York, 1973), pp. 59-64

17. *Ibid.*, p. 62.

18. *Ibid.*, p. 61.

19. Glaser, *ibid.*, passim

20. Report of the Ad Hoc Committee on Mixed Marriage, *ibid.*, p. 150

21. *As You Desire Me*. Words and music by Allie Wrubel (New York: Words and Music, Inc., 1932). A song popularized by Tony Martin in the 1940's

22. Eugene Mihaly, Response to "Report of the Ad Hoc Committee on Mixed Marriage," *CCAR Yearbook* (New York, 1973), pp. 85-87

23. Dannel Schwartz, "The Intermarriage Rip-Off," in *Moment*, August 1978, pp. 62-64
24. Gary A. Tobin, ed, *Intermarriage and American Jews Today: New Findings and Policy Implications* (Waltham, MA: 1990), passim
25. Charles E. Silberman, *A Certain People: American Jews and Their Lives Today* (New York: Summit Books, 1985), passim; "No More Mountain Overhead: Federations and the Voluntary Covenant." Address before General Assembly, Council of Jewish Federations, 1983, p. 7
26. Tobin, *ibid.*, pp. 27-29
27. Elsie Clews Parsons, *Mitla: Town of the Souls and Other Zapateco-Speaking Pueblos of Oaxaca, Mexico* (Chicago, University of Chicago, 1936), xii, 5ll-519

CHAPTER 8

INCURABLE VIRUS

Jews on Approval

Jews are acutely sensitive about the impression they make on non-Jews. It is a price they pay for living in *galut* (the Diaspora). They are perennial hostages to the question, "How am I doing?," asked while glancing furtively over the shoulder. Many Jews have a built-in applause meter working around the clock, registering not only their individual acceptance or rejection rating, but also that of all other Jews. It is a feeling characteristic of Jews, says Alan Dershowitz, to worry about what other people will say. It is the *shanda fur de goyim* [embarrassment before the gentiles] syndrome. His prescription for this anxiety is chutzpah [bold assertiveness]. Let Jews bear themselves as first-class citizens, affirming their rights without worrying about charges of dual loyalty, of being too smart, rich, or powerful.

Maurice Samuel's *Jews on Approval* clinically exposed the Jew's pathetic apprehension about not offending, passing muster, winning acceptance.[1] A current observer with a sharp eye for this nagging dybbuk imagines the Jewish community atremble each morning before opening the morning paper for fear of reading of the skullduggery of an Ivan Boesky or the criminal indictment of some stranger with a "Jewish" name.

When Professor David Mandelbaum, who taught anthropology at the University of California (Berkeley) for many years, was a graduate student at Yale, he got a job at the Jewish community center of Ansonia, Connecticut, a small mill town near New Haven. After a year at the center, he wrote a brief sketch of the Jewish community, which was in due course published in *Jewish Social Studies* under the camouflaged title "The Jews of Urbana." In it Mandelbaum mentioned that one of the main activities at the center was card playing. When a member of the center got wind of the paper and circulated it among his fellow-members, all hell broke loose. Mandelbaum was called on the carpet and threatened with dismissal. He had unveiled an activity which was seen as a communal embarrassment, a *shanda fur de goyim.* That an Ansonia mill hand would ever read an issue of *Jewish Social Studies* was remote fantasy. But what if one should? It was enough to set the Jews of Ansonia chattering with worry.

"*Sha, Sha!*" ("*Be still! Don't make waves*") is a well-worn Jewish reflex and the Sha, Sha Jew, a familiar character in Jewish humor. The story is told of two blindfolded Jews about to be shot by the Nazis. One of them complained that the blindfold was too tight. "*Sha, Sha!*" hissed the other. "you want to make trouble?"

Reading the papers to ferret out the names of Jewish miscreants, and finding some, causes clouds to gather on the Jew's horizon. On the other hand, reading of a Nobel Prize award to Isaac Bashevis Singer or of a no-hitter pitched by Sandy Koufax will make his day. He basks in their reflected glory, and like little Jack Horner preens himself, "O, what a good boy am I!"

The Jack Horner response has made it difficult for Jews to accept the reality of their humanness. Others could be rogues, scoundrels, swindlers, drunkards, adulterers, thieves. Not Jews. The truth is, of course, that Jews are like everyone else, capable both of soaring to the heights and sinking to the depths. Most of them occupy the middle latitudes. They are victims of their own creatureliness, as well as of the maladies triggered by the culture around them.

Virus at Large

The claim is sometimes made that antisemitism is no longer a problem for American Jews. A "climate of acceptance" is said to pervade American life. One writer maintains that for most Americans, "antisemitism and other forms of prejudice decline significantly from one generation to the next." Doors once closed have at last opened and Jews have ascended the upper rungs of the corporate ladder. Some have become chief executives of industrial empires. In the academic world, quotas for Jewish students and faculty have been abolished, and Jews are now presidents of Ivy League colleges. Jews have been accepted as members of social and country clubs which had never heard the footfall of a Jew, even as a guest. These transformations in the patterns of occupational and social life for Jews, it is cheerfully averred, are surely signs of the progressive breakdown of barriers between Jew and non-Jew.

But doubts cloud this sanguine view of the American intergroup scene. It is pointed out that while some Jews might occupy gilded niches in corporate America, there are still spaces in the structure which scarcely know a Jewish presence. In some strongholds of the commercial and industrial heartland — banking, insurance, petroleum — there is a conspicuous absence of Jews at the top. The presidents of Harvard, Yale, Brown, and Penn might be Jews but college campuses increasingly echo the bigotry of antisemites. Clubs in Palm Beach, Florida, and other social playgrounds are still *Judenrein* [free of Jews]. Some apartment buildings in New York City effectively bar Jews as residents, even though to do so is to break the law.

Refuting the optimistic readings on the extent of American antisemitism are the judgments of Jews themselves. Jews have gut feelings about antisemitism. These feelings have been conditioned by history, by the experience of universal antipathy and hatred, by the ghastly embrace of the Holocaust. Every age has echoed the Yiddish plaint, *Mir vollen nor laben, ober man lost nit* ("We only want to live, but they won't let us"). Jews have been schooled and tempered by antisemitism. They have been accused of cowering at phantoms, seeing antisemitism where none exists. Sometimes they do jump at shadows, but many Jews feel that in the background looms the real monster.

Twenty years ago all the surveys showed that Jewish Americans of all ages and inclinations agreed that antisemitism is a continuing problem. A 1992 Anti-Defamation League report reveals that the level of antisemitism is "worse today than any time since World War II .... Nearly 40 million adults .... one in five Americans .... hold strongly antisemitic views." In a different generation Ahad Ha'am wrote with grim delicacy, "With few exceptions [Jews] recognize that the position of a lamb among wolves is unsatisfactory."[2]

Manifestations of the growth of antisemitism in America are seen in many areas of national life. A dramatic increase in antisemitism has been taking place in the Black community. A simmering antisemitism is found on many college campuses. In 1994, the year Barnard College chose a Jew as president, 64 mezzuzot were torn from the doorposts of dormitory rooms. Television and the press are charged with waging a continuous vendetta against Israel, which some discern as the transparent mask of antisemitism. Allies in this campaign are — sometimes unwittingly — mainstream Protestant and Catholic churches. For the first time in memory, the 1992 Presidential primaries presented a candidate who was judged to be antisemitic. There are more Jewish senators and congressmen in Washington now than ever before. Yet Pat Buchanan and David Duke won the support of hundreds of thousands of voters in 1992, demonstrating that a candidate can be viable in the 1990's despite his or her antisemitism. A rabbi who was targeted in his community by a terrorist group has warned his colleagues not to list their home addresses in the phone book.[3]

In 1992 Alan Dershowitz wrote, "We are experiencing .... the most pervasive, massive, and intense proliferation of anti-Jewish propaganda since the fall of the

Third Reich. It emanates from almost every corner of the earth and it finds expression in almost every institution within our society."

There is copious evidence that in the years since Dershowitz summarized the all-encompassing range of antisemitism, neither its extent nor its virulence has diminished. Quite the contrary. Political upheavals may have wrought far-reaching change in Russia and the Communist regimes of Central and Eastern Europe, but casting off the chains of Communism seems to have reawakened old antisemitic furies. There may be more open antisemitism in Russia today than at any time during the seventy years of Soviet dictatorship. Zhirinovsky's popularity with many Russians is said to be his appeal to Jew-hatred. Robert Westrich has written that "popular antisemitism all over Eastern Europe is .... a spontaneous .... sentiment whose bottom line is that the Jews are to blame for everything that is going wrong." In some countries which have few or no Jews — China, Japan, Poland, Albania — printing presses disgorge a stream of antisemitic bile.

On the eve of the Six-Day War in 1967, when Nasser proclaimed his goal of driving Israel into the sea and the cry rang out around the Arab world, "Slaughter the Jews!", Abba Eban, then Israel's Foreign Minister, went in desperate search for support from one capital to another. Antisemitism had assumed a low profile after the Holocaust; perhaps a shadow of guilt had crept into the Christian world, and some Jews felt that antisemitism might at last be in decline. But when Eban discovered that no nation was willing to stand with Israel, he concluded that the world was divided into two camps, "those who wanted to see us destroyed and those who did not want to help."

My experience as the rabbi of a Midwest suburban congregation paralleled in miniature Eban's experience. When in 1967 I went to the Christian clergy of the community asking each to sign a petition appealing to President Johnson to try to keep the Gulf of Akaba open as a measure for preventing war, I met a series of refusals. One finally signed, not, as he told me, out of agreement with the petition but out of regard for me.

To some Jews, reading the bullish assurances of the upbeat sociologists is not much comfort. They remember that following the defilement of the ancient cemetery in Carpentras in 1990 ("obscene impalement" was performed on individual remains), 100,000 protesters marched through the streets of Paris, President Mitterrand among them. Jews were reassured. Yet Vichy France under Petain dispatched thousands of Jewish children to German death camps, and under Mitterand France was for years one of the chief arms suppliers of Saddam Hussein, who threatened to use them to destroy Israel. They may also remember that in 1921, following the assassination of Walter Rathenau, the German foreign minister, who happened to be a Jew, a million protesting demonstrators marched in Berlin. Again Jews were reassured. Eleven years later Hitler marched in triumph through the same streets. In 1992, sixty years later, Rathenau's grave in a Berlin cemetery was defiled.

Abandonment of the Jews

During World War II, the Allied powers, including the United States, showed no interest in destroying, or even disrupting, the apparatus of the Nazi death camps. Air bombardment might have achieved this, but no death camp was bombed. While raids were made on targets fifty miles from Auschwitz, Auschwitz remained unscathed. The rail lines which carried trains packed with doomed men, women, and children were never bombed. Long after the Germans knew they faced defeat, trains continued to transport their human freight to the crematoria unhindered. The historian David Wyman, a Protestant, concludes that the Allies deliberately abandoned the Jews to their fate.[4]

America's indifference to the fate of the Jews is attributed by Wyman to the "passive antisemitism" prevalent in American society at the time. Antisemitic agitators were having a field day and Jews became painfully, sometimes frighteningly, aware of the Jew-hatred spewed by native demagogues like Father Charles Coughlin, Gerald L.K. Smith, Gerald Winrod, and William Dudley Pelley. Charles Lindbergh, America's national hero, became a spokesman for America First, a movement, which, in advocating isolationism in world affairs, virtually proffered a free hand to Hitler in Europe. An opinion poll at the time reported that general atrocity reports from Europe had an impact upon Americans seven times stronger than atrocities reported against Jews.

In the 1930's, when I was rabbi of a congregation in New Haven, Connecticut, I went down to Washington, D.C. to urge our senator, Francis Maloney, to support a resolution which would have admitted to America 20,000 Jewish children from Nazi Germany. Great Britain had already taken in thousands of homeless Jewish children. At lunch in the Senate dining room, the senator told me that while he would support the measure, there was little chance for its passage. He explained that the high unemployment of the Great Depression, then at its peak, left many jobholders fearful of losing their jobs. As a consequence, immigration had been severely curtailed, and even though the Jewish children would pose no threat to the employed, so strong was the national mood against immigration, that any proposal to relax the standing restrictions would meet with defeat. The Senate rejected the measure. During the pre-war and war years, the annual immigration quota of 21,000 was never filled.

The response of the American church community to accounts of the Holocaust comprises an instructive page in the story of American interfaith relations. Virtual silence was the reaction. No major denomination spoke out in dismay or protest, and church publications tended to question the credibility of accounts describing the death camps with their deportations, starvation, and gas chambers. No moral outrage sounded in the pages of *The Christian Century*, perhaps the most influential mainstream Protestant clerical periodical. It was no different with Catholic periodicals such as *Commonwealth* and *America*, which suggested that statistics on the Jewish catastrophe were overblown.

One of Wyman's ten summary findings on the factors which contributed to the Holocaust was "the near silence of the Christian churches and almost all of their leadership."[5] Writing as a Protestant, he goes on to comment that American Christians "forgot about the Good Samaritan" or the central Christian "commitment to help the helpless."[6] In 1945, Europe's Jews were hardly mentioned in American Protestant journals. Their existence was acknowledged, however, when in 1946 the World Council of Churches called on Christians to evangelize Jews in hiding or in flight.

American Christians and Antisemitism

In 1969 Professor Jules Isaac, the French historian, published *The Teaching of Contempt*, based upon the thesis that the church, in teaching contempt for Judaism, has fomented and fostered antisemitism. The work is a classic analysis of Jew-hatred. Twenty-five years ago, in a six-volume study, *Patterns of American Prejudice*, professors Charles Y. Glock and Rodney Stark, surveying the dimensions of antisemitism in American churches, showed that 72 per cent of American Christians subscribed to "rather virulently antisemitic statements." Furthermore, those who were more religiously active harbored the more pronounced antisemitic feelings. Strong religious sentiment seemed to "[generate] intolerance toward persons of other faiths." The clergy were shown to be caught in an awkward paradox: while repudiating antisemitism, which most of them did, their traditional theology, centered in the passion (the sufferings and death of Jesus on the Cross), contributed to it. The churches, concluded the authors, stand responsible for "theologically stimulated prejudice."[7] Five years after the gloomy findings of the first survey appeared, a second survey left Glock and Stark even more pessimistic about the "change-producing potential of churches."

The editor of *The Christian Century* once declared that the "virulent disease of antisemitism [is] rooted in Christianity" and that "latent antisemitism .... pervades our Christianized culture .... The tendency to characterize the Jew as 'Christ-Killer' haunts us too deeply to be ignored as an occasional individual aberration."[8] Both Catholic and Protestant assemblies have admitted past derelictions in their teachings about Jews and their attitude toward Jews. The historic Second Vatican Council under the leadership of Pope John XXIII moved Catholic leaders to organize programs in the churches designed to redress the church's millennial antisemitism. A spirit of penitence may have informed the avowal by the 1987 General Assembly of the Presbyterian Church of "the Church's long and deep complicity in the proliferation of anti-Jewish attitudes and actions through its 'teaching of contempt' for the Jews."

Interfaith organizations, denominational commissions, and ecumenical conferences and dialogues, discuss the realities of anti-Jewish prejudice, seeking a way that leads from "the teaching of contempt" to understanding. These voices, perhaps unsettled by guilt, sound the disquiet that exists in the Christian community about the extent of the antisemitism which emanates from the churches.

Another potent factor animating antisemitism in recent years has been the support by church leaders for liberal and radical social and political causes. This liberal-leftist orientation is consistently demonstrated in the pronouncements and activities of national and international Protestant church bodies such as the National Council of Churches of Christ in America, the World Council of Churches, and the Middle East Council of Churches. The editor of *The Christian Century* has acknowledged that "the real offense of antisemitism comes from liberal Protestants."

Liberal-leftist partisans in the churches overwhelmingly identify with the Third World. They define the peoples of the Third World as the prey of predatory Western powers, victims of colonial oppression. They maintain that it is the mandate of Christianity and the obligation of the churches to help free them from the clutches of their exploitative overlords. This religious perspective, now known as "liberation theology," has become a significant component in the outlook of both the Protestant and the Catholic church. Some of the leaders of native independence movements in Third World countries, particularly in Latin America and South Africa, have been, and are today, priests and pastors who subscribe to liberation theology.

The pro-Arab cause seems to exert a hypnotic spell on liberal Christians. At a Jerusalem seminar in 1990, Professor Rosemary Ruether, tribune of liberation theology, called upon liberation theologians to "enter into solidarity with the Palestinian struggle," accusing Israel of oppressing Palestinians by expropriating their lands, terrorizing them in their homes, and driving them from their homeland. The Quakers, avatars of nonviolence, in supporting the PLO, for years architects of terror, have likened Israel to the Nazis. In 1989 the National Conference of Catholic Bishops issued a policy statement which designated the Intifada "a cry for justice." After watching a CNN television interview with Saddam Hussein in February, 1991, Jonathan Kuttab, a prominent Christian Arab, exclaimed, "For the first time I could relate to Islam. It sounded almost like liberation theology."

Anti-Zionism

Anti-Zionism has been called "one of the chief instrumentalities of contemporary Christian antisemitism," its "most fashionable contemporary guise." To Professor Seymour Martin Lipset, the anti-Zionism of the New Left is no different from the antisemitism of the Old Right. To the New Left and to the Black antisemite, "Zionism is simply a code word for Jew."

The rhetoric of anti-Zionism is often antisemitic. In a liturgy distributed in 1990 by the American National Council of Churches, Israel's government was called Herod and the coming of Jesus "the Intifada of heaven." This liturgy was called a theological exploitation of Holy Week reminiscent of its uses by the medieval church as an incitement against Jews. Professor Alan T. Davies of the University of Toronto has pointed out how easily the anti-Zionism of liberal Protestantism veers into antisemitism. "Anti-Zionism sooner or later reveals a distressing tendency to shade into antisemitism, and antisemitic convictions can be transposed without much difficulty into the .... language of anti-Zionism."

In the seventy-five years since the promulgation of the Balfour Declaration, which declared that the "British government supports the establishment of Palestine as a national home for the Jewish people," a battle cry sounded by Arabs has been *itbah al yahud*, "Death to the Jews." Not to the "Zionists" or "Revisionists" or "Israelis," but to the Jews. When Bob Simon, the CBS correspondent who was captured by the Iraqis during the Gulf war, was interrogated and beaten by an army captain, the word contemptuously hurled at him was "yehudi, yehudi," "Jew, Jew." Not "American," or "Zionist," or "Israeli," but "Jew."

Roman Catholics and Jews

On the Jews, the Roman Catholic Church has spoken with different and contradictory voices. From the Council of Nicaea in 325 C.E., when the Roman Catholic Church came into being, until the twentieth century, the voices have been predominantly harsh and unyielding. In more recent decades, they have become more moderate.

Christianity was long the chief propagator of antisemitism. Jews were accused of the full brood of antichrist blasphemies. They were demonized by a folk Christianity consisting of a farrago of myths — poisoning the wells, desecrating the Host, ritual murder. Hanging over the Christian landscape like a malignant cloud was the charge of deicide. The cry, "Christ Killer," has echoed in the ears of every generation of Jews since the days of Constantine. And always the aftermath — forced conversions, expulsions, massacres. Sometimes princes of the Church condemned these myths; more often they disseminated them. As Uri Zvi Greenberg has written, "Europe was a 'kingdom of the cross' where the hatred of Jews grew .... directly from the church and the inescapable clamor of its bells."[9]

It was in 1938 that Pius XI, in a denunciation of Nazism, astonished the world when he declared to his communicants, "Spiritually we are Semites." But his successor, Pius XII, uttered no single word of reproof of the Nazis, nor of censure for the architects of the Holocaust. In 1943, when a Vatican representative was asked if the Pope would join allied leaders in condemning the extermination of the Jews, the reply came that while the Vatican had frequently denounced atrocities, it could not publicly condemn particular atrocities. When the Vichy government began its mass deportations of French Jews, some Catholic prelates protested, but no word came from Rome.

After the fall of Mussolini, whose fascist regime had enjoyed the Pope's favor, the German military in Rome went hunting for Jews in full view of the Vatican and dispatched them to Auschwitz. At the same time, Nazi officials found sanctuary in the Vatican en route to freedom from prosecution as war criminals. As Hertzberg has remarked, the Church worried more about fleeing Nazis than dying Jews. Pius XII's successor, John XXIII, advocated and pressed for far-reaching change in the posture of the Church toward Judaism and Jews. He convened Vatican II (1962-1965), the first Church Council in a century, which acknowledged the role of Christendom in the tragic chronicle of antisemitism, and sought to expiate the sin of its Catholic perpetrators. The conclusions of Vatican II, published under the title *Nostra Aetate*, stand as the Magna Carta of a new attitude of the Church toward Judaism and Jews. It marked a break with the hatred and hostility of the past, and inspired the hope that a new era in Catholic-Jewish relations might have begun.

Pope John Paul II

John Paul II, the present pope, is a personification of the uncertain voice of the Church on the Jews. He has referred to Judaism as "our elder brother" and urged that "the task of every local church is to promote cooperation between Christians and Jews."[10] He has pointed out that "the hostility, or worse, hatred, toward Judaism are in complete contradiction with the Christian vision of the dignity of man." Yet in a homily delivered in 1989, he spoke of "Israel's infidelity to its God," and that having sinned in rejecting Jesus, the "old Israel .... wandering in search of salvation has been replaced by the new Israel," namely, the Church.

John Paul II was the first pope officially to visit the Great Synagogue of Rome. This seemed an unambiguous act of reconciliation carried out in the spirit of Vatican II, a highly visible rejection of the "teaching of contempt" which had permeated the Catholic world and brought endless anguish to the Jews. Yet in subsequent years he received at the Vatican Yasser Arafat, known to Jews as a terrorist murderer, and Kurt Waldheim, Austrian president, who lied about his Nazi past and is charged with deporting Jews to the death camps when serving in Greece as an officer of the Wehrmacht. At the Vatican the Pope hailed Waldheim as a man of peace. Not long after establishing diplomatic ties with Israel, he conferred upon him a papal knighthood.

The seeming ambivalence of John Paul II on the Jews and Judaism finds its echoes in the Catholic world at large. The action of the Carmelite Order of nuns in converting a building adjoining Auschwitz into a convent and erecting over it a twenty-three-foot cross, appeared to Jews an arrant disregard for what they sanctified as a martyr's shrine. When Jews protested, Cardinal Jozef Glemp, primate of Poland, angrily retorted, "Do not talk with us from the position of a people raised above all others, and do not dictate conditions .... Your power lies in the mass media that are easily at your disposal in many countries. Let them serve to spread anti-Polish feeling." The Mother Superior of the Carmelite Sisters of Auschwitz, in full agreement with the Cardinal, took the occasion to condemn the Israelis for their treatment of the Arabs. "Greater antisemites," she charged, "would be hard to find."

When the Vatican took the first steps toward establishing diplomatic relations with Israel in 1994, Jews hailed it as a major advance in the process of conciliation between the Church and the Jews begun in 1962 at the Vatican II Council and confirmed in 1965 with the publication of *Nostra Aetate*. For years Pope John Paul II had remained impervious to appeals for official recognition, but now, coincident with negotiations between Israel and the Palestinians, the Vatican showed its readiness to forge diplomatic ties with Israel.

German and Polish bishops were said to be preparing a declaration which, going beyond previous conciliatory statements, would acknowledge the Church's role in fostering antisemitism and in failing to prevent or impede the implementation of the Holocaust. Jewish representatives, after being shown a draft of the declaration, proclaimed it a "mind-boggling" change in its confessional candor from previous Vatican declarations. But the Vatican was quick to deny that the draft represented the official position of the Church. It had been prepared by German and Polish bishops, "not in any way by the Holy See."[11] Whatever else these puzzling twists of assertion and denial signified, they suggested that the Church was still having difficulty in coming to terms with its agenda of guilt and atonement on the Jews.

Further evidence of the Church's ambiguity is seen in some of the conclusions reached in documents issued by the Holy See since Vatican II. There seems to be no question of the desire to eradicate the teaching of contempt for Judaism, or of the Pope's personal efforts to make effective the "new spirit of cooperation, mutual understanding, and reconciliation." But it has been imputed that some sections of the new catechism for the Catholic Church (CCC) drawn up in 1992, might actually perpetuate a theological antisemitism that inspires prejudice .... [against] Jews and Judaism."[12]

Thus Jesus is portrayed as the fulfillment of God's promises to Israel. The Hebrew Scriptures are presented as "Law" in denigrated contrast to the "Love" which Christians hold predominates in Christianity. The description of Judaism in the time of Jesus is incomplete and partial, ignoring its spiritual richness and variety. These are some of the nettlesome elements which historically have resulted in the teaching of contempt.

A disturbing reflection of the Church's ambiguity on the Jews is seen in its posture on the death camps and the Holocaust. In former Nazi death camps the Church has in recent years erected Christian symbols and structures. Churches, chapels, convents, and crosses have been built and emplaced on the sites where millions of Jews were tortured, gassed, and burned. These are vast cemeteries, sacred to Jews, which now lie in the shadow of churches and crosses. What has been happening in the death camps has been called the "Christianization of the Holocaust" and has aroused apprehension and foreboding as to the Church's position on the Holocaust. In engraved memorials at the camps, Jews are scarcely mentioned. It is as though Jews were being denied the right to mourn their dead. Martin Gilbert, the historian, has pointed out that the 1917 Treaty of Lausanne ordained that the cemeteries of those who died in war must be honored and placed in the care solely of the families of the dead. "What the Catholic Church is doing," he said, "is scandalous and grotesque."

Does the Church speak on the Jews with one voice? John Paul II called Judaism "our elder brother," spoke words of goodwill and conciliation when he appeared in the Rome synagogue as the first Pope to attend a synagogue service, and wrote a moving letter of sympathy to a Jewish childhood friend in remembrance of victims of the Holocaust. Yet he also declared, "God promised His chosen people a new Covenant, one that shall be ratified with the blood of his own son Jesus, on the Cross. The Church is the new Israel."[13]

Protestants and Jews

The Reformation wrought revolutionary change in the beliefs and practices of much of the Christian world but it brought little change in its consistent hatred for the Jews. When the religious upheavals of sixteenth- century Europe began to sweep away the absolute authority of the medieval Church, hope stirred among Jews that a change in the unbroken hostility of the Christian world might be at hand. Martin Luther in his early pronouncements seemed to show understanding for their physical plight and forbearance for their faith. But when he realized that ingratiating overtures failed to win Jews to his religious banner, he turned the full flood of his anger upon them, and with his extraordinary flair for crude and violent vituperation, ventilated a hatred as fierce as any encountered from the Church. It has been said that the seeds of German Nazism were sown by Luther.

Antisemitism was so deeply embedded in the culture of medieval Europe that dissent from it was scarcely whispered even by the illustrious intellectual and religious leaders who had begun to rebel against encrusted religious prescriptions. Pico della Mirandola (1463-1494), the "ideal man" of the Renaissance, for all of his friendship with Jewish scholars, love of Hebrew, and study of Kabbala, admired King Ferdinand of Spain, who established the Inquisition and banished Jews from his kingdom. Erasmus (1467-1536), the Dutch humanist universally esteemed as a model of tolerance, in speaking of the Jews once exclaimed, "Who among us does not heartily dislike this race of men?" John Hus (1369-1415), the Czech church reformer and precursor of Protestantism, who was excommunicated by the Pope and burned at the stake, showed no sympathy for Jews.[14]

The sixteenth-century Reformation leaders, Philip Melanchthon in Germany, Ulrich Zwingli in Switzerland, and John Calvin in France displayed a deeply ingrained animus and fear of Jews. All of these religious rebels discovered a love for Hebrew, but this did not carry over to Judaism and its followers. The theology, mythology, and folklore of the Christian world would not permit even radical reformers, many of them former priests, to repudiate the most powerful of all myths — the Jew as deicide. All believed that salvation for the Jew lay only in acceptance of Jesus in the form of conversion to Christianity.

The shining exception among the religious reformers in this climate of pervasive anti-Jewish animus was Johann Reuchlin, the foremost Christian Hebraist of the fifteenth century. He championed not only the right of Jews to study their sacred books, but also for the freedom to profess their faith. "In matters relating to their faith," Reuchlin wrote, "the Jews are subject to their own judgment and no other judge; no Christian is entitled to make any decisions about it."

Although most of the leaders of the Reformation shared Christendom's endemic contempt for Jews, the religious revolt they led inaugurated changes in the social and economic fabric of Europe which in time brought far-reaching benefits to the Jews. The emphasis on the individual which developed during the Renaissance nourished defiance of ecclesiastical authority and the revolt against the monolithic power of the Church. The way was opened to religious pluralism. The princes of Protestant states who broke with Rome relished an independence which sometimes led to giving Jews a new measure of protection.

Evangelical Protestants and the Jews

American Evangelical Protestants, said to number up to 50 million, have been sharply divided from mainstream Protestant church bodies on Israel. Their theology ordains that a condition for Jesus' second coming is the restoration of the Jews to their ancient homeland. To support Israel is to hasten his coming. Hence, while the major denominations have commonly been critical or hostile toward Israel and Zionism, Evangelicals have supported the Zionist dream with an enthusiasm found in no other Christian communion.

Some American Jews are uneasy about the support of the Evangelicals. Evangelicals, whose political and social outlook is conservative, espouse views such as right-to-life and prayer in the public schools, which many Jews, persuaded by their liberal predilection, oppose. Some Jewish leaders have, therefore, urged caution in making common cause with these pro-Israel Christians.

Meanwhile, every year at the time of the *Sukkot* (Tabernacles) holiday, Evangelicals from all over the world come in their thousands on pilgrimage to Jerusalem, and in assemblies and pageants filled with deep and contagious fervor, herald their kinship and support for the State of Israel and its people. No Jewish mission approaches in numbers or zeal the annual Tabernacles pilgrimage of the Evangelicals.

It is curious that despite the strong support for Israel given by fundamentalist Protestants, prominent Jewish organizations have leveled their guns at the Evangelicals. The Anti-Defamation League and the Reform movement have warned against the extremist and anti-Jewish sentiments of the Evangelicals. No such weaponry has been deployed against the liberal-left Christians and secularists who have been among Israel's abiding enemies. For many American Jews, the rights of gays in Greenwich Village and preserving the wall of separation between church and state in Scarsdale are issues more pressing than the rights of Jewish settlers in Hebron or Efrat. The agenda of the liberal-left secularists still occupies a commanding space in the value structure of the American Jew.

Blacks and Antisemitism

Most Jews feel that Black antisemitism has reached dimensions which can no longer be minimized. Black leaders have for some time been accusing Jews of conspiracies and crimes reminiscent of the paranoid accusations of medieval Inquisitors. Echoing the falsehoods of the infamous nineteenth century forgery, *The Protocols of the Elders of Zion*, they accuse Jews of comprising a cabal bent on ruling the world. They claim that Jews were heavily involved in the slave trade, asserting that rich Jews living in Seville, Lisbon, and Newport, Rhode Island, were largely responsible in financing it. They have blamed the AIDS epidemic on Jewish doctors who, they say, inject the AIDS virus into Black babies, a throwback to the slander of the Dark Ages blaming the Jews for spreading disease by poisoning wells. They attribute the discrimination of Hollywood against Black actors and producers to the "Jewish racism of Hollywood" created by Russian Jews who control the movies.

The fear of Black antisemitism has been fueled by inflammatory rhetoric and lethal events occurring in American cities. Crown Heights in Brooklyn, where the Lubavitch Hasidim live surrounded by Blacks, has been the scene of explosive violence between Blacks and Jews. In 1991 a young Hasid was murdered after a Black boy had been accidentally killed. There followed four days of rioting during which the boy's family pastor warned that "the fire next time" would engulf other predominantly Jewish neighborhoods like Williamsburg.

During the past few years, Chicago, home base for Jesse Jackson and Louis Farrakhan, has been rife with antisemitism. When the mayor's assistant, Steve Cokely, charged Jews with being involved in a conspiracy to take over the world, and Jewish doctors with injecting Black children with AIDS, the Black director of the city's Commission on Human Relations, Rev. B. Hubert Martin, declared that he found a "ring of truth" in what Cokely said. That week, Andrew Greeley, the priest who teaches sociology at the University of Chicago, began his column in the *Chicago Sun Times* by acknowledging, "If I were Jewish, I would be terrified by the recent outburst of antisemitism in this city." He ended with, "Don't say that it can't happen here. It's already happening here." Professor Eugene Kennedy of Loyola University, Chicago, reported in the *New York Times*, "Virulent antisemitism has gripped Chicago's Black community. If I were a Jew living in Chicago today, I'd be terrified." A Chicago rabbi cautioned against complacency lest the specter of "a Lebanon or Northern Ireland" materialize in Chicago." At a Madison Square Garden rally in 1985, Louis Farrakhan, who had called Judaism a "gutter religion," shouted a warning to Jews, "You can say 'Never Again,' but when they put you in the ovens, 'Never Again' don't mean a thing."[15]

A conspicuous aspect of recent Black antisemitism has been the reluctance of Black leaders to condemn it. Abraham Foxman, director of the Anti-Defamation League, has said that the ADL no longer spends most of its time in exposing antisemitism but in pleading with "decent people" to speak out against it. These efforts have proved largely futile. Black leaders have not spoken out. In fact, they deny any responsibility for refusing to participate in what is scornfully referred to as the "disavowal syndrome." When Chicago was wracked with Black-Jewish tension in 1990, no prominent Black repudiated the venomous accusations of Steve Cokely, and days passed before he was fired by the mayor. Chicago Jewry was shocked by the silence of Black civic and religious leaders. When Jesse Jackson, Chicago's leading Black figure at the time, might have deplored the flagrant display of antisemitism, he remained silent. "Where is Jesse Jackson?" wondered Andrew Greeley in his newspaper column.

Jews find the hostility of Blacks difficult to understand. For generations, the closest ties had apparently existed between them. Jews shared with Blacks a history of oppression and the memory of slavery. Every Passover, Jews are summoned to remember the plight of slaves, "For you were slaves in the land of Egypt" (*Deuteronomy 5:15*). It was but natural for Jews to be among the strongest supporters of Blacks in their struggle for civil rights.

A hundred years ago Theodore Herzl, the founder of political Zionism, had written of the "one problem of racial misfortune unsolved .... the depths [of which] only a Jew can comprehend. I refer to the problem of the Blacks .... Once I have witnessed the redemption of Israel, my people, I wish to assist in the redemption of the black people.[16] In 1964 Martin Buber sent a cable to the South African government appealing for a suspension of the trial of Nelson Mandela and others arrested with him. "Free the accused," Buber pleaded. "Sit down with them. Negotiate with them. Give ear to their plea for self-determination."[17]

The spirit which animated Herzl and Buber has inspired a long roster of American Jews. From Julius Rosenwald, who built thousands of schools in the Black rural

South in the early decades of the century, Joel Spingarn, a founder in 1910 of the National Association for the Advancement of Colored People (NAACP), from David Einhorn, Baltimore abolitionist rabbi during the Civil War, to Abraham Joshua Heschel, rabbi and scholar, who marched at Martin Luther King's side in the South, to Andrew Goodman and Michael Schwerner, young civil rights workers murdered in Mississippi by Klansmen, Jews have been the closest social and political allies of the Blacks.

Many reasons are given for the dissipation of the apparent goodwill of the 50's and 60's and its conversion into the open antisemitism of the 80's and 90's. Blacks are said to have resented the prominence of Jews in the civil rights struggle, feeling that they were being patronized by outsiders, by "Big Brother." Perhaps resentment came from the human impulse to look upon one's benefactors with suspicion and mistrust. Jews were envied for their "success" in many spheres, hated for their image as money-grubbing merchants and fleecing slumlords. Blacks with improved vocational and professional skills were now entering the middle class and felt they were entitled to places in the economic and social order too long occupied by Jews.

Although Blacks and Jews may have formed a "grand alliance" committed to the struggle for civil rights in the post-World War II decades, in an earlier time Black antisemitism was far from unknown in America. Leonard Dinnerstein maintains that there are "continuities" between an earlier Black antisemitism and its contemporary manifestations, and that Black hostility toward Jews has, in fact, surfaced periodically since the 1920's.[18]

Many Black leaders and writers have for decades disparaged and maligned Jews. Dinnerstein has documented the anti-Jewish bias of such legendary champions of their people's rights as Booker T. Washington and W.E. Burghardt Dubois. The former often attacked Jewish country storekeepers as usurious exploiters, and when Hitler was taking control of Germany and persecuting its Jews in 1933, Dubois wrote, "Nothing has filled us with such unholy glee as Hitler and the Nordics."[19]

During the depression in the 1930's antisemitism flared in Black ghettos, and during World War II, Black journalists were indifferent to the antisemitism raging in Europe, viewing with silence the anguish of the Jews. "The truth of the matter is," editorialized a Southern Black paper, "Negroes are filled with antisemitism. In any group of Negroes, if the white people are not around, the mention of the Jew calls forth bitter tirades."

Almost fifty years ago, Ralph Bunche, Nobel Prize winner and chief United Nations negotiator in the 1949 Arab-Israel armistice conference, described the factors in the rearing of the Black child which condition him negatively toward Jews:

> In the home, the school, the church and in Negro Society at large, the Negro child is exposed to disparaging images of the Jew .... Negro parents, teachers, professors, preachers, and business men .... generalize loosely about "the Jew," his

> disagreeable "racial traits," his "sharp business practices," his "aggressiveness," "clannishness," and his prejudice against Negroes .... The Jew is not disliked by Negroes because he is "white," but because he is a Jew.[20]

In the late 1960's a new generation of writers and intellectuals arose to challenge the leadership of established figures like Roy Wilkins, Whitney Young, and even Martin Luther King, long-standing partners with Jews in mitigating the excesses of racism. Malcolm X, Stokely Carmichael, Eldridge Cleaver, Rap Brown, Harold Cruse, and Le Roi Jones, asserting a new militancy, gave full cry to anti-Jewish canards and distortions. Perhaps the strongest influence on the new leaders was Malcolm X and his classic account of what it means to be Black in America, *The Autobiography of Malcolm X*. "All I hold against Jews," admitted Malcolm X, "is that so many Jews actually were hypocrites in their claim to be friends of the American black man." The Jews played their "careful strategic" game for a simple reason. "The more prejudice in America could be focused upon the Negro, the more the white Gentile's prejudice would keep off the Jews."[21]

Dinnerstein holds that recent and current eruptions of Black antisemitism are due to the absorption by Blacks of the psychology and culture of the majority. In a word, Blacks have become acculturated to the bigotry prevalent in American society. This concurs with our analysis, which stresses the decisive role of the dominant culture in all aspects of the American Jewish experience. Conventional wisdom has it that nothing is more powerful than an idea whose time has come. Anyone familiar with the history of antisemitism would be inclined to add, or than a prejudice long implanted in the culture.

The College Campus

There is an ominous nuance in the antisemitic attitudes of Blacks: all studies indicate that young Blacks are more antisemitic than those of an older generation. Julius Lester, the Black professor who teaches at the University of Massachusetts and is a convert to Judaism, has noted that Black antisemitism is most prevalent today among the young Black students on college campuses. Nor is campus Black antisemitism without its ripple effect. "Unconcealed, virulent black antisemitism on college campuses is a growing phenomenon," asserts Arch Puddington, so that "open, poisonous anti-Jewish bigotry [is a] veritable fixture of campus political life."[22]

It is a curious irony that the American college campus of the twentieth century should have become a haven for antisemitism. We associate the college years with the free, disinterested quest for truth where the spirit of tolerance and enlightenment flourishes. A professor leaving his post in a New York university after an antisemitic attack by a colleague wrote, "Colleges and universities in this country are places where we should strive to dispel the darkness, not propagate it."

In 1990 a Midwestern university, long regarded as a Shangri-la of the liberal spirit, saw its Hillel House attacked by rock throwers and its Jewish fraternity and sorority houses vandalized and smeared with swastikas. In the same year, student newspapers at Cornell, Michigan, and Duke ran full-page broadsides questioning the authenticity of the Holocaust. On a recent Yom Kippur, the *Dartmouth Review*'s masthead bore Hitler's boast, "By warding off the Jews, I am fighting the Lord's work." Professor William Van Alstyne of the Duke Law School, praised the Duke college paper's decision to publish the Holocaust ad, chortling, "I rather admire, frankly, the policy they have tried to follow." At basketball games at a large Eastern university, Jewish women students have been regularly subjected to barracking, taunted with the epithet, "JAP" (Jewish American Princess). A West Coast student, reflecting on the campus antisemitism, ruminated, "One of the most troubling things about all of this, is that it shows that even people who are educated are capable of antisemitism." No one aware of the enthusiastic support Hitler enjoyed from German professors would be so naive as to imagine that "educated" people are less bigoted than their neighbors.

The "policy" Van Alstyne referred to is academic freedom. Under it, freedom to express, teach, or disseminate ideas is absolute. That some ideas may be rejected by history or science as worthless, or their propagation as presenting a clear and present danger to individuals and groups, does not cancel the right to advocate them. Leonard Jeffries, professor of Afro-American Studies at New York's City College, teaches that since the ancient Egyptians were Blacks, the progenitors of modern civilization were Black. Melanin, the dark skin pigment, makes Blacks intellectually and physically superior to whites, he claims.

The Holocaust, unique among the world's human tragedies, has been documented by a mass of witnesses, including survivors bearing the tattooed numbers of camp inmates on their arms. Yet a worldwide network of historical revisionists denies that the Holocaust ever happened. On many campuses, invited lecturers address student assemblies and repeat the revisionist view. All in the name of academic freedom.

Media

There is little question that the greatest influence today in shaping the attitudes and opinions of Americans is the news and entertainment media. Recent decades have seen the media, both printed and electronic, rise to a pinnacle of power. An exasperated congressman speaking not long ago from the well of the House blurted out that the people were abdicating their own thinking under the bombardment of twenty-second capsules on TV evening news. "It's about time we rejected government by sound-bite," he protested. General Giap, military leader of the North

Vietnamese, admitted that his victory was won not in the jungles of Vietnam, but on the TV screens of America. A senator told a Jewish audience after the Lebanon incursion that he had supported sanctions against Israel because television had convinced him that Israel was perpetrating a holocaust in Lebanon. Today television persuades everyone from scullery maid to senator.

The growing power of the media has aroused the apprehensions of those concerned with safeguarding the professional norms of journalism. These enshrine the principle, "to report accurately and responsibly." This simple tenet is, however, so often flouted that distrust of news reporting has become endemic. A recent survey revealed that media reporters are trusted less than politicians. A critic has described media news coverage as a stew of inaccurate reporting, cheap sensationalism, speculative analysis, and false conclusions. While it is not true of all media voices, it is true that many reporters and anchormen exhibit a hubris, an arrogance and bias, which mock the objectives of responsible journalism.

Ever since the Six-Day War in 1967, Israel has been the victim of a worldwide media onslaught. Before 1967 Israel was a fair-haired boy in the U.S. and world press. After the Holocaust, with its mass murder of six million Jews, including one and a half million children, and its virtual extirpation of Jewish life in Eastern and Central Europe, survivors had somehow made their way to Palestine to join the Jewish settlers in repulsing the armies of seven Arab states sworn to throwing them into the sea. Miraculously they established the State of Israel from whose soil Jews had been exiled for two thousand years. This phoenix risen from the ashes of annihilation, this David victorious over Goliath, was recognized as a sovereign state in the United Nations. Most of the world, including its news correspondents, perhaps feeling twinges of guilt for their silent complicity with Hitler's executioners during the Holocaust, joined in hailing the heroic saga of Jewish struggle, survival, and rebirth.

But the victory won and the new Israel launched, the world soon enough forgot, and its posture on Israel changed. The *Realpolitick* of conciliating the Arabs, lubricated by the oil of Arab sheikhs, plus a perennially residual antisemitism, transformed the attitude of the media. Now a mythologizing of the conflict between Arab and Jew supplanted objective reporting and analysis.

After the Six-Day War, Eli Wiesel summed up the world's attitude with a victim's insight. "The world begrudges Israel its victory. Its lightning campaigns against four armies and some twenty nations were won too quickly and too spectacularly .... A victorious Israel does not conform to the image and destiny certain people want to assign to it .... They love the Jew only on the cross."

Myths, Distortions, Falsehoods

One of the widely accepted myths of the Middle East is that the Palestinians are a nation. Much of the international family has been gulled by this myth. But as Joan

Kaplan and others have shown, most of the Arabs living in Israel and its contiguous territories are latecomers, poor fellaheen who wandered into the region attracted by the founding of Israel with its promise of gainful work and a better life. There had never been a people known as "Palestinians."

Another myth is that the "West Bank" (Judea and Samaria) was illegally occupied Arab territory. But as Professor Eugene V. Rostow, former Assistant Secretary of State, has argued, since Jordan attacked Israel in the Six-Day War and was thrown back across the River Jordan, Israel had the right under international law to remain and administer the occupied territory.

A third myth was that the Jewish settlements in Judea, Samaria, and Gaza were "the greatest obstacle to peace." Realistically, the primary obstacle to peace was the Arab unwillingness to accord Israel the right to exist, spelled out in the Palestinian Covenant of the Khartoum Convention of 1964 with its three Noes — No recognition, No negotiation, No peace. Although a provision of the 1992 Oslo accords called for the renunciation of the Khartoum Convention, Arafat and the PLO have never moved to carry it out. They have used every stratagem of vacillation and procrastination but have never moved forthrightly to implement it. Years after its promulgation it is still hanging in limbo.

These are some of the myths disseminated by the media and in many quarters believed as received truth. Despite their fallaciousness, to much of the media Israel remains the bullying Goliath and the Arabs the poor, persecuted David. In a deliberate inversion of Jewish historic experience, Arabs are portrayed as homeless outcasts compelled to live in exile in an Arab Diaspora.

To chronicle only a fraction of the distortions, falsehoods, and calumnies circulated by the media on the Arab-Israel conflict would be an awesome task. A sampling of some of the more bizarre misrepresentations and slanders will suggest the limits to which the media will go in assailing Israel.

When the invasion of Lebanon took place in 1982, it was everywhere reported that 600,000 Lebanese had taken flight as refugees. The total population of Lebanon was 500,000. It later transpired that much of the "news" from Lebanon consisted of PLO press handouts distributed in hotel bars frequented by the reporters. In 1990, many commentators equated Israel's policy in the territories with Saddam Hussein's invasion of Kuwait. Jeanne Kirkpatrick decried the comparison of self-defense by a democracy with unbridled aggression by a dictatorship as "intellectual chicanery."

That same year a Reuters reporter described scenes at the *simhat torah* celebration at the Western Wall, where great throngs of Jews always gather to sing and dance on the most joyous festival of the year, making it appear as though the Jews were dancing in triumph over the deaths of 21 Arabs who had died during a riot on the Temple Mount the week before. Evans and Novak regularly, almost obsessively, rehearse the sinking in 1967 of the U.S. intelligence ship, "Liberty," which happened because of the confusion which often occurs in the heat of battle, and which both the official American and Israeli investigations judged a "tragic mistake." Fifty years after the attack by Jews on the Arab village of K'far Kassem, the *Washington Post* featured a lengthy, tendentious account of the tragedy. So far as anyone could remember, the *Washington Post* has never commemorated the massacre of Israeli children at Ma'alot or the murder of Israeli athletes at the 1972 Munich Olympics.

Neither passage of time nor change of circumstance seems to have altered the anti-Israel slant of most media reporting on Israel. World conditions, regional alignments, and Israeli government policies may change. The media seems reluctant to yield its bias.

Since Israel became a party to the "peace process," the steady fusillade of anti-Israel brickbats from the media may have lost some of its intensity. After all, the Oslo accords have won the approval of much of the western world, notably of the United States. Caught up in the prevailing euphoria, the world watched as President Clinton nudged Rabin and Arafat toward a handshake on the White House lawn. Since then developments in the Middle East have resembled the fulfillment of a hype impressario's dream. Within two years the main players in the "peace process" were awarded the Nobel Peace Prize. Israel was being accepted as a respectable member in the family of nations. The Vatican had at last established diplomatic ties with Israel. Perhaps even the reporters were finding it less difficult to view Israel realistically.

But suspicious fumes still issue from the media. Try as they might to be more balanced, a good many reporters continue to sound grudging, reluctant. Ingrained habits have a long shelf life. Listening to BBC and reading Reuters reveal the difficulty of shedding bias. Few maladies are so resistant to treatment as this viral infection.

Spreading Islamic Terror

Islamic fundamentalist organizations such as Hamas and the Islamic Jihad practice terror in all its sordid modes against both Jews and such Arabs as differ from them politically. They seek to drive the Jews from the land which they have named Palestine and which they claim as uniquely sacred to them and their kinsmen. These Islamic extremists, bent on eliminating the State of Israel, have declared, "We Islamists can never accept such a state. We believe in Palestine from the river to the sea."[23] When the Israeli government deported many Hamas leaders from Israel in 1992, the world media embarked on what some called a "lynching bee of Israel." After months of facing the reproach and abuse of a world united in pleading for the Hamas leaders, many of them known plotters and killers, Israel allowed them to reenter the country. In the same year, after the Gulf War, Kuwait expelled 300,000 Palestinians and Jordanians with scarcely a whisper of protest from the United Nations or from the media.

Islam's fundamentalist leaders are at work among Muslim populations around the world rallying support for their terrorist agenda. Their ambitions go far beyond liquidating the State of Israel and undermining the regimes of the more moderate Arab states. Their bolder exploits thus far include bombing the World Trade Center in New York, blowing a Pan-Am plane out of the sky over Lockerbie, Scotland, attacking the cruise ship Achille Lauro, and bombing synagogues and Jewish communal buildings in Europe and Latin America. Iran and Syria are poles of a terrorist axis spanning the globe which plots for the day when the world will be ripe for the "only true faith of Allah."[24]

The question has been asked why in the face of these lethal threats to their security, the non-Arab nations seem to remain largely unconcerned, if not indifferent, to the growing arrogance and power of fundamentalist terrorist leaders. Certainly the media has been measured and guarded in their reporting, with none of the malign innuendo and hostility so long targeted at Israel. One senses a disinclination to cite the crimes of the imams, to protest the lifting of the arms embargo against Syria, to condemn the evils of Arab dictatorships. In several *60 Minutes* television programs, Mike Wallace virtually gave the antisemitic Syrian dictator Assad an open platform for denying the persecution of Syrian Jews, although it was universally known that nowhere was the Jew's experience of uncertainty, fear and danger greater than in Syria.

Fade-Out of Objective Truth

George Orwell, writing about the Spanish Civil War in which he fought, described the reporting of news from Spain at the time as nothing but the dissemination of lies. "This kind of thing," he said, "is frightening to me, because it often gives me the feeling that the very concept of objective truth is fading out of the world." In 1986, the head of an international news agency stationed in Jerusalem told me that with the exception of the few Jewish foreign correspondents who had become resident in Israel, most reporters were pro-Arab. Some of the latter were also Jews.

Why do so many press and television journalists favor the cause of the Arabs and show little sympathy for Israel? An important reason is the ignorance of journalists who have little knowledge of the modern history of the Middle East. They are simply not aware in any depth of the events, forces, movements, and personalities that have gone into making the intricate maze of current Middle East affairs. To hear the crisis-driven TV voices portentously declaiming news and analysis on Israel and the neighboring states, is to be exposed to the cocksure superficialities of the ill-informed. Television political commentary has been described as a "medium where encyclopedic ignorance is a job requirement."

Another reason for the pro-Arab leanings of journalists is their left-leaning ideological bias. Many grew up in the sixties when the trauma of Vietnam led to an identification with the liberal-left, thus "skewing their journalistic product." Many journalists, moreover, take for granted that Israel should be held to a higher moral standard than its adversaries. Not conspicuously religious themselves, they expect Israel to conform to Biblical models in pursuing affairs of state. Edward Alexander has called Israel a "moral playground" for sanctimonious journalists, "a gymnasium in which they do moral calisthenics to revitalize muscles grown flabby from disuse during assignments in other countries."

Jewish Troublers of Israel

Some Jews who have made their mark in the media are among Israel's most aggressive critics. There are those who seem to fire their darts with relish and who, once the target has been nailed, cling to their prey like terriers. Others aim their barbs more in sorrow than in anger, feeling themselves champions of a pure Zionist ideal which has been betrayed by Israelis. Still others plead the facile truisms of the journalists' code, "The public has a right to know," "We call'em as we see 'em." Whatever their motives and methods, these Jewish assailants of Israel are cited by non-Jewish critics as proof that Jews are divided on Israel, thus justifying their own animus. They have been compared to the "destroyers and ravishers" described by Isaiah, "Your destroyers and devastators shall go forth from you." (Isaiah 49:17). The medieval commentator, David Kimhi (1160-1235), interprets this verse as referring to "Israel's worst enemies — those who do most to tarnish Israel's fair name, [who] come from Israel's own camp."[25]

Thomas Friedman, *New York Times* correspondent and Pulitzer Prize winner, bashes Israel somewhat regretfully. His experiences in the field, he relates, particularly in Beirut, made him bury "every illusion I ever held about the Jewish state."[26] The truth is he never had too many. When a student at Brandeis, he was a leader of Bereira, the national organization which disseminated strong anti-Israel views. Daniel Pipes has said that Friedman's claim to be a neutral reporter presents "devastating implications for his integrity."

Wallace and Friedman have their imitators, Jews in the media and related areas of public discourse who miss no chance to bash Israel. Among these epigones one may count Anthony Lewis of the *New York Times*; Noam Chomsky, linguist at the Massachusetts Institute of Technology; William Navasky, editor of *The Nation*, which has published the antisemitic ranting of Gore Vidal; the late William Kunstler, perennial lawyer for leftists; and Al Vorspan, ideological guru of the Union of American Hebrew Congregations, the largest religious organization of American Jews.

One of these small-bore bombardiers is Michael Lerner, editor of *Tikkun*, a "magazine of the Jewish left." A "zealous self-promoter," according to a biographical article in the *New York Times*, who had for years "been welcomed virtually nowhere." Lerner was suddenly catapulted into the limelight when he received approving nods from President and Mrs. Clinton for his prescription for America's malaise, summarized in the catch phrase, the "politics of meaning." The "politics of meaning" urges that the "ethos of selfishness" give way to the "ethos of caring .... community .... [and] connectedness." This unexceptionable cliché persuaded the Clintons that they were "on the same wavelength" as Lerner. Hilary Clinton's nod to Lerner came in the form of an invitation to the White House.

Lerner's Judaism consists largely of social messages promoted by liberal activists. Like many progressive Jews his attitude toward Israel is strongly critical, and his following consists of a flotsam of leftists who share his negative views. Jewish leaders aware of his glaring lack of Jewish background and knowledge, dismiss him as a charlatan. That this impresario of the "politics of meaning," with his confirmed animus on Israel, might be taken seriously by the President and First Lady of the United States, puzzles many Jews.[27]

Estrangement and disengagement from their religious and ethnic roots is no novel phenomenon for Jewish journalists. In the earlier decades of the century some of America's most celebrated correspondents and columnists, such as Arthur Krock of the *New York Times* and David Lawrence of the *U.S. News and World Report*, distanced themselves from any connection with Jewish affairs. Walter Lippmann, perhaps the most eminent journalist of his time[28] was a Jew who was almost obsessive in his avoidance of reference to Jewish causes or Jews. He was admired and honored as were few men in his generation. Everybody read his syndicated daily newspaper column, Presidents consulted him, and he wielded a considerable influence on national policy and popular thought.

He wrote in praise of honesty and integrity and was looked upon as the embodiment of both. But he had a terrible time facing the world and accepting himself as a Jew. From some of his writings he emerges as the classic assimilationist Jew, a self-hater who had absorbed the ugliest antisemitic stereotypes. In 1922 he wrote, "The rich and vulgar and pretentious Jews of our big American cities .... are the real fountain of antisemitism." He echoed Goebbels when he wrote, "My sympathies are with the non-Jew. His personal manners and physical habits are, I believe, distinctly superior to the prevailing manners and habits of the Jews." During all the Hitler years, he spoke no single word of condemnation about the persecution of the Jews, about the extermination camps, about encouraging the admission of German Jews as refugees. One writer commented, "If he had spoken out as late as 1942, he might have [changed] the terrible American and British indifference to the fate of the Jews. He might have saved lives."[29] Today's hostile Jewish journalists are following a recognizable self-hating pattern.

Through a familiar psychological mechanism, a Jew will often move from despising himself to despising other Jews. Many are the ways for lashing out against the shameful fate of being a Jew, ranging all the way from reviling Jews and undermining Jewish causes, to inflicting upon oneself the ultimate form of self-hatred — suicide. Otto Weininger (1880-1903), the brilliant young Viennese Jewish intellectual, wrote scathing denunciations of the Jews. He was the self-hating Jew *in extremis*. In 1902 he was baptized. A year later he committed suicide.

English Literature on the Jews

In his summary description of antisemitism, Robert Westrich, Hebrew University historian, calls it "a measure of nightmarish paranoia, millennial fantasy, homicidal hatred, and sheer political cynicism [which] thrives on archetypal fears, anxieties and reflexes that seem to defy any rational analysis."[30] Paul Johnson, the English historian and critic, attributes the persistence of antisemitism through the centuries to the "patronage of [writers and] intellectuals." He cites the anti-Jewish writings of Seneca, Tacitus, and Juvenal, of the Church Fathers, Chrysostom, Ambrose, and Tertullian, of the French Enlightenment figures, Voltaire[31] and Diderot, down to the broad range of nineteenth and early twentieth-century pundits such as Belloc, Chesterton, Kipling, Pound, and T.S. Eliot.[32]

There is a long tradition of antisemitism in the works of some of Britain's foremost writers. Chaucer (1343-1400) based his *The Prioress' Tale* in *The Canterbury Tales* on the blood libel case of Hugh of Lincoln in the 13th century. Like so many authors of antisemitic fictions, Chaucer knew no Jews; they had been expelled from Britain in 1290. It is questionable whether Shakespeare ever met a Jew, since the England of his time still forbade Jews to reside there. This did not inhibit him from vilifying them in *The Merchant of Venice*, a prototype of poisonous antisemitic bigotry. Through Elizabethan times antisemitism seemed woven into the fabric of Britain's literary and cultural life.

The influence of the Reformation and of the readmission of the Jews to England in 1665 changed the literary appraisal of Jews. Jews are now portrayed in a dual image as both depraved and virtuous. Many writers approach the Jew with an unresolved ambiguity. Such authors as Sheridan, Scott, Shelley, Coleridge, Dickens, Kingsley, and Trollope described Jews both as objects of fear and hatred and as figures of admiration and awe.[33] The Jew as noble exemplar of moral idealism is portrayed by Robert Browning and Matthew Arnold. George Eliot's *Daniel Deronda* articulates a remarkable prevision of the Zionism of Herzl in a novel which would abolish the image of the diabolical Jew.

In recent times, antisemitism still warps the writing of prominent British literary figures. The novels of D.H. Lawrence, Raoul Dahl, and Graham Greene present characters with a sleazy Jewish aspect. T.S. Eliot, considered one of the great poets of his time, born in the U.S. but a British subject, was deeply infected with the antisemitic virus. His biographer, Michael Hastings, testifies to the poet's "seething" antisemitism. He always wrote "jew" with a small "j", and even after Auschwitz allowed his antisemitic poems to be published in a selected edition. Two of them, *Burbank with a Baedeker: Blaustein With a Cigar* and *Gerontion* contain lines which have become notorious: "The rats are underneath the piles,/ The jew is underneath the lot." "My house is a decayed house,/ And the jew squats in the window sill the owner,/ Spawned in some estaminet in Antwerp."/ "In his personal life," wrote Hastings, "[Eliot] was an antisemite and a racist. You can't take the racism out of the man."[34]

One of the greatest creative writers of modern times, James Joyce, was as favorably disposed toward Jews as any writer. Leopold Bloom, the unforgettable character in *Ulysses*, is drawn with an extraordinarily subtle and comprehensive understanding of his Jewish background and being. Joyce felt there was a kinship between the Irish and the Jews, primarily in the ambiguity both felt toward the outside world. In Zurich and Trieste he came to know a number of Jewish families, some of whom became his close friends. To a Harvard student he wrote of the "greatest sympathy he felt about the Jews." He helped a number of Jews gain freedom from countries of Nazi occupation.[35]

American Authors on Jews

Since American writers grew out of the literary and cultural tradition of English forbears, it is not surprising that the Jew as treacherous, grasping money-grubber became a stereotype in early American literature. Christian theology, old world myths and memories, economic rivalry, and mass immigration after the Civil War stoked anti-Jewish prejudice in the 19th century.

But antisemitism in the new world was less prevalent and intense than in the old. Anti-Jewish feeling was geographically determined, being more commonly encountered in the established social hierarchies of the eastern seaboard than on the open western frontier. There is a gender distinction in the view of the earlier American antisemite; while he may find the Jewish male a repellent incarnation of the diabolic, the female is often charming, intelligent, and ravishingly beautiful. Hawthorne had a revulsion for Jewish men but a fascination for Jewish women. Summarizing this not uncommon attitude, Ambrose Bierce once commented, "I hate Hebrews but adore Shebrews."

Most of the prominent early American authors approach their Jews ambiguously, some amicably, a few malevolently.[36] Longfellow saw the Jew as a sympathetic historic figure but withal as an exotic stereotype. Emerson may have admired the American Jewish poet Emma Lazarus, but he adopted the standard pejorative image of the Jew. James Russell Lowell disapproved of antisemitism but confessed to an aversion for Jews. After a visit to Palestine, Herman Melville changed the negative portrayal of his earlier writings and described the Jew in a human, spiritual dimension. He wrote a book-length poem, Clarel, in which Agar pines for the Holy Land while embroidering a cloth which bears the Hebrew words, "If I forget thee, O Jerusalem, may my right hand forget its cunning."(Psalm 137:5) Henry James' fastidious sensibilities were offended by a walk through New York's Lower East Side teeming with Jews, yet he admired Zola for his defense of Dreyfus.

Henry Adams hated Jews with a paranoid virulence, blaming them for such monumental sins as fouling the pristine pattern of New England probity and "finance capitalism." Even after recognizing Dreyfus' innocence, he remained ardently anti-Dreyfus.

Conspicuous for his rational attitude toward Jews was Mark Twain, who is noteworthy among great American writers for his sanguine and human approach to Jews. He overcame the bigotries absorbed in his early years as his feelings for human equality expanded. His famous essay on the Jews is an unequivocal tribute to an admired people. In characteristic response to a question about his feeling toward Jews, he answered, "It's enough for me if a man belongs to the human race — he can't be worse than that."

Recent years have seen a decline in the number of America's leading writers who could be considered antisemitic.[37] No taint of antisemitism is found in the pages of O. Henry, Sinclair Lewis, Edmund Wilson, John Dos Passos, James Farrell, and James Jones. On the other hand, Theodore Dreiser, one of America's foremost novelists, was strongly antisemitic. Thomas Wolfe was outspoken in his dislike of Jews. Scott Fitzgerald seems to have become more tolerant of Jews as he came to know more of them in Hollywood. Hemingway was an uncertain voice when it came to Jews. Gore Vidal, writing voluminously today, is a vicious Jew-baiter.

One of the most vituperative of all antisemites was the journalist and critic, H.L. Mencken. His antipathy for Jews was no secret during his years as an editor in Baltimore. By the time of his death in 1956 he had become something of an intellectual icon, revered not only by every ink-stained journalistic hack, but also by respectable pillars of the literary establishment. Then 25 years after his death, acting upon his prior instructions, a sealed secret diary was published in which all the sickening nuances of his race hatred were laid bare. His hatred for Jews and Blacks, pro-Nazi sympathies, bitter opposition to U.S. foreign policy in World War II were exposed to reveal a racist and antisemite of deepest dye.[38]

Some years ago in defending Ezra Pound on the charge of treason after World War II, the English post W.H. Auden admitted that "antisemitism is not only a feeling which all Gentiles at times feel, but also, and this is what matters, a feeling of which the majority are not even ashamed." In the 1930's Thomas Wolfe wrote, "I don't like Jews, and if most of the people I know would tell the truth about their feelings, I wonder how many of them could be able to say that they like Jews." A conspectus of the Anglo-American literary tradition inclines one to believe that antisemitic prejudice is one of the lingering, perhaps inescapable legacies of Anglo-American culture.

During a trip to Uruguay in 1989, Israel's President Chaim Herzog lamented, "Our bitter experience has been that the world's press and media have been the examples of our own day .... of the historic inability of the Western world to relate rationally to Jews, Judaism, and in our case, the Jewish state."[39]

Alan Dershowitz's prediction in 1982 of the proliferation of anti-Jewish propaganda is being borne out as we move into the last years of the century. Nor is it likely to diminish in scope or virulence. Evidence abounds all over the world that "hostility to minorities, formerly in the domain of the gutter or extreme right .... has begun to seep into the mainstream culture to find surprising acceptance and legitimacy."[40]

The Culture of Antisemitism

There is a social, political, and religious virus at large in the world. Its name is antisemitism. It can exist without Jewish wrongdoing. It exists without Jews. Chaim Weizmann said that the fundamental cause of antisemitism is that Jews exist. The Holocaust taught that nothing Jews do, or refrain from doing, will keep the antisemites at bay.

Salo Baron pointed out long ago that ultimately there is very little Jews can do about fighting antisemitism. Nevertheless, Jacob Katz, the distinguished contemporary historian, feels that in view of the stakes involved, every Jew is called upon to do what he can to "curb" the virus. "We are witnessing today," he has written, "various antisemitic developments all over the world. Although .... not yet of the most virulent kind, it is the duty of those capable of curbing them to do so, lest in the future they be held accountable for more terrible acts which, although still unforeseen, are in our day certainly no longer inconceivable."[41]

Culture binds people together, playing a critical role in conditioning their personality. The interrelationship of culture and personality has been studied by some of the notable anthropologists of recent decades — Ruth Benedict, Margaret Mead, Edward Sapir, Reo Fortune, Geoffrey Gorer. Their field work and writings comprise some of the important contributions to our understanding of the individual in his cultural setting.

When her celebrated *Patterns of Culture* was published in 1923, Ruth Benedict wrote a circular for the reader, which might have been written by Daniel Jonah Goldhagen for his profoundly revealing and disturbing book, *Hitler's Willing Executioners: Ordinary Germans and the Holocaust* (1996). Benedict demonstrates how the manners and morals of these tribes, and our own as well, are not piecemeal items of behavior, but consistent ways of life. They are not racial, nor the necessary consequence of human nature, but have grown up historically in the life history of the community.

The measureless inhumanity of the Holocaust was the consequence of an antisemitism rooted deeply in German culture, "an enduring hatred .... of a sort that is unrivaled by any other group hatred in western history, a hatred that has been a permanent feature of Christian civilization even into the twentieth century." "Not economic hardship, not the coercive means of a totalitarian state, not social psychological pressure, not invariable psychological propensities, but ideas about Jews that were pervasive in Germany .... induced ordinary Germans to kill unarmed, defenseless Jewish men, women, and children by the thousands, systematically and without pity." [42]

That individual temperaments tend to conform to the predominant cultural pattern is altogether relevant to our consideration of German national character. Goldhagen's work is notable among other things for its delineation of the qualities in ordinary Germans derived from the national culture, which made the Holocaust possible. Ulrich Volker in evaluating Goldhagen's book commented, "Here finally is someone who expresses what has long been a taboo: that the distinction between 'criminal Nazis' and 'normal Germans' is false; that the readiness to murder millions came from the middle of German society."[43]

Goldhagen reveals realities about the Holocaust which beggar belief. Son of a Holocaust survivor, the author discloses dimensions of Hitler's genocidal program whose credibility many individuals find it difficult if not impossible to accept. "There is a reluctance to believe," remarks Goldhagen, "that people who are core members of Western civilization would do such a thing." In Nazi Germany, it seems, there were "core members" in droves who "eagerly participated in the slaughter and killed zealously with unnecessary brutality."[44]

Eliminationist Antisemitism

The stark purpose of the antisemitic program launched by Hitler and the Germans was the extermination of the Jews — men, women, and children — wherever found, whether in the populous centers of Europe or in the remote corners of Germany's expanding empire. The goal was the elimination of the Jews from the family of man — "to the last child." Based upon extensive research in hitherto inaccessible or neglected sources and on his academic training as a sociologist teaching at Harvard, the author sets forth his findings on the etiology and actuality of what he terms Hitler's "eliminationist antisemitism."

More than 10,000 camps scattered throughout Europe held Jews captive until they were murdered. Hundreds of thousands of individuals were engaged in executing the genocide. Although special cadres were organized for murdering Jews, any able-bodied German was eligible to participate in the actual killing. Recruits aplenty filled the ranks of the uncoerced executioners. Volunteers carried out their ghastly missions with a zeal which found them wantonly brutalizing and torturing their victims, taking pride in what they did, routinely inflicting gratuitous cruelty, celebrating the murders they committed, bringing their women and children to the killing fields to watch. Churchill told the British people in 1944, "We are in the presence of a crime without a name .... There is no precedent in the human history of the world."[45]

Religious leaders from Martin Luther in the sixteenth century to Karl Barth in the twentieth fomented native antisemitism, demonized the Jews as incurably evil and dangerous, "children of the devil." Luther likened Jews to vermin who infected the society around them and were beyond the saving grace of baptism. In his *The Jews and Their Lies,* he urged his followers to burn synagogues and Jewish homes. "It is our fault," he wrote, "that we do not slay them."

The President of Germany addressing the Bundestag in 1996 acknowledged that Nazi ideology in due course permeated German public opinion, and that the antisemitic beliefs which inspired Hitler also inspired much of the German people. Hence, Goldhagen's conclusion: "The inescapable .... truth is that for the Holocaust to have occurred, an enormous number of ordinary Germans must have become Hitler's willing executioners."[46]

Hitler's Willing Executioners has been widely, even extravagantly, praised. Goldhagen's argument presented with such persuasive logic and painstaking research cannot but impress, perhaps overwhelm, the reader. Becoming a best-seller overnight in Germany, it won enthusiastic reviews in Britain and the U.S. Some reviews began on an adverse note but before the end, decibels of praise were ringing[47]. In German cities the author debated his views with panels of distinguished historians and political scientists and emerged to shouts of approval and ovations by the audience. The scenes at these meetings were said to resemble a Michael Jackson concert. In one such meeting the historian Professor Hans Mommsen began by angrily denouncing the book, only to admit later that "everything under the Nazis had been even worse than described by Goldhagen."[48]

The criticisms leveled at Goldhagen merit inquiry. The primary reproof for Goldhagen is the charge that it is grossly unjust to condemn Germans en masse for the Holocaust. Goldhagen emphasizes, however, that the historical record portrays the German Jew as a diabolized agent of evil, a constant threat and danger to the Germans, and that this together with the long train of disabilities and afflictions executed by state and church against the Jews conditioned the Germans to become instruments of genocide. Antisemitism may have thus become a component of the German national culture.

Often heard is the criticism that the "eliminationist" solution simply could not have happened, let alone succeeded. To the Holocaust revisionists this is a reflex rejoinder to the charge of murder by mass annihilation. Six million simply could not have been killed, they say, by gangs of obsessed or coerced Germans. It is not in the realm of possibility. Moreover, antisemitism was not a malaise uniquely rampant in Germany. Other countries had their wanton and brutal pogroms. The Dreyfus case exhibited the widespread antisemitism of the French. Antisemitism is not a German sin. It is part of the "nefarious capacity" within all of us called original sin. Thus the critics.

Confuting these criticisms is the striking evidence marshaled by Goldhagen showing that the eliminationist program reaped its millions of murdered victims because of the monomaniac will and the iron organization behind it. None better than the Germans at this kind of "national project." Hitler was not denied or resisted by Germans in any of his plans or ambitions. To the rest of the paradox which will astonish many who think of themselves as "core members" of Western civilization, the number of Germans who deplored Hitler far exceeded the number who deplored antisemitism. Anti-Hitlerites were often antisemites. Many members of anti-Hitler resistance were antisemitic. Germans who opposed the killing of Poles, Gypsies, and the physically and mentally handicapped did not consequentially protest the murderous extermination of Jews. Karl Barth, the renowned Swiss theologian teaching in Germany in the early 30's, became a critic of Nazism, yet remained an antisemite. We have cited the instance of Rudolf Kittel, the noted Bible authority, who made outstanding contributions to Old Testament scholarship while never relinquishing his Jew-hatred. One of the ironies of Hitler's Germany was the attitude of the plotters against Hitler's life, toward Jews. Their leaders, ranking *Wehrmacht* generals and the scions of aristocratic Prussian families, devised clandestine conspiracies against Hitler while their morbid hostility to Jews remained unchanged.

Goldhagen denies one of the principal accusations made against him, namely, that he exaggerates the intense level of involvement in antisemitism by the generality of Germans. In a letter to the *New York Times*,[49] he strongly rejected the charge that he holds the Germans responsible for "collective guilt" and "cultural genetics." He calls such notions "conceptually and morally indefensible." "There is no contradiction between explaining how the powerful antisemitism that once existed in Germany led so many ordinary Germans willingly to brutalize and kill Jews, and maintaining that the vast majority of Germans today do not share the same views. Most Germans alive today have been educated and brought up on democratic values. Everyone should recognize and applaud this."

At the same time, many leading German politicians are not so sanguine about the dawn of a new day in the attitude of Germans to Jews. Motivated perhaps by memories of the Nazi past, they are now supporters of a united Europe, and seem to be saying, "Lock us into a united Europe, otherwise we'll become too powerful and dangerous." At the time of the Gulf War, a German political leader explained his opposition to Germany's participation: "You don't give a bottle of brandy to an alcoholic." The publisher of the liberal paper *Die Zeit* warned that Goldhagen's book "might revive the more or less silenced antisemitism in Germany."[50]

Albert Einstein is recognized as the nonpareil scientific genius of the twentieth century. At the same time, he was a towering moral figure who embodied the ethical vision of man reaching for the transcendental. He was a Jew whose life and thought resonated the ideals of the Prophets of Israel. Born and educated in Germany, he came to know Germans well. While his early discoveries in physics brought eminence in the academic world and fame in the larger world beyond, in Germany his books were publicly burned.

In 1944 he spoke of the heroes of the battle of the Warsaw ghetto:

> They fought and died as members of the Jewish nation, in the struggle against organized bands of German murderers .... The Germans as an entire people are responsible for these mass murders and must be punished as a people if there is justice in the world and if the consciousness of collective responsibility in the nations is not to perish from the earth entirely. Behind the Nazi party stands the German people, who elected Hitler after he had in his book and in his speeches made his shameful intentions clear beyond the possibility of misunderstanding. The Germans are the only people who have not made any serious attempt of counter-action leading to the protection of the innocently persecuted. When they are entirely defeated and begin to lament over their fate, we must not let ourselves be deceived again, but keep in mind that they deliberately used the humanity of others to make preparation for their last and most grievous crime against humanity.[51]

As Jews become aware of the spread and virulence of antisemitism, they wonder how wide its canvas may be in the world. Daily we read and hear of the hatred for Jews fifty years after the Holocaust, and the suspicion stirs uncomfortably that the culture of antisemitism may have invaded a far wider world than Hitler's Europe. The united Arab world threatening and unleashing terror against Jews, the nations of Europe united in condemning Jews, the United Nations voting with virtual unanimity against Israel, the spotlessly moral Swiss stealing like common thieves the money and family heirlooms of hunted and tortured Holocaust victims, the world media ventilating their versions of poisonous antisemitic propaganda.

Professor Emil Fackenheim in a notable warning once declared that "authentic Jews are forbidden to give Hitler a posthumous victory." This warning, more urgent and timely than ever, is now addressed to mankind. "There is a people that dwells alone, not reckoned among the nations." (*Numbers 23,9*). As long as Israel dwells alone, severed from the world by hatred, Hitler may be winning his posthumous victory.

Notes

1. Maurice Samuel, *Jews on Approval* (New York: Liveright, 1931)
2. Ahad Ha'am, in "The Negation of the Diaspora" (1909). In *The Zionist Idea*, ed. Arthur Herzberg (Philadelphia: Jewish Publication Society, 1960), p. 270
3. *CCAR Newsletter*, August 1993

4. David S. Wyman, *The Abandonment of the Jews: America and the Holocaust 1941-1945* (New York: Pantheon, 1984), passim
5. *Ibid.*, p. 239
6. *Ibid.*, pp. x-xi
7. Charles Y. Glock and Rodney Stark, *Christian Beliefs and Anti-Semitism* (New York: Harper and Row, 1966)
8. James M. Wall, "The Virulent Disease of Anti-Semitism," in *The Christian Century*, April 24, 1974
9. David G. Roskies, *Against the Apocalypse: Resposes to Catastrophe in Modern Jewish Culture* (Cambridge: Harvard University Press, 1984)
10. Flora Lewis, "Flames from Ashes", in *New York Times*, September 3, 1989
11. "Vatican Backtracks on Reported Apology for Antisemitism," Associated Press, in *Jerusalem Post*, May 27, 1994, p. A12
12. Leon Klenecki, "A New Tissue of Interfaith Focus; Catechism of the The Church -- Catholic and Jewish Readins," in Memorandum of ADL Interfaith Affairs Committee and Participants in the Christian-Jewish Dialogue. June 6, 1994
13. Uri Dan and Dennis Eisenberg, "Biggest Lie of Them All," in *Jerusalem Post*, September 8, 1994, p. 6; Jewish Telegraphic Agency, in *Jewish Week*, October 20, 1989
14. Salo W. Baron, *A Social and Religious History of the Jews.* Second Edition (Philadelphia: Jewish Publication Society, 1952), vol. 13, pp. 174, 189
15. Walter Ruby, "Musicians Boycott Harlem", in *Jerusalem Post*, December 25, 1986
16. Amos Elon, *Herzl* (New York: Holt, Rinehart and Winston, 1975), p. 349
17. *Jerusalem Post*, March 21, 1990
18. Leonard Dinnerstein, Reply to "A Critique of Leonard Dinnerstein's 'The Origins of Black Anti-Semitism in America,'" by Stephen J. Whitfield, in *American Jewish Archives*, July 1988, pp. 99-202
19. *Ibid.*, p. 201
20. *Ibid.*
21. Murray Friedman, "Black Anti-Semitism on Rise," in *Commentary*, October 1979, p. 32
22. Arch Puddington, "Black Anti-Semitism and How it Grows," in *Commentary*, April 1994, pp. 22, 19
23. Kenneth R. Timmerman, "Interview with a Dead Bomber," in *Los Angeles Times*, reprinted in *Jerusalem Post*, November 25, 1994, p. 4
24. In the 1994 TV program, Jihad in America, the growing menace of Muslim fundamentalism in the United States was documented. The objective of the Iranian leaders is to enlist America's large Muslim population in their cause.
25. J.H. Hertz, *The Pentateuch and Haftorahs* (London., Soncino Press, 1966, second ed.), p. 794

26. Herbert Zweibon, "Thomas Friedman's Record," *Jerusalem Post*, February 16, 1993, p. 6
27. Thomas Fields-Meyer, "This Year," in *New York Times*, June 27, 1993, pp. 28-62
28. "Lippman [was] regarded as the most thoughtful, authoritative political commentator of the time." David McCullough, *Truman* (New York: Simon and Schuster, 1992), p. 525
29. Ronald Steel, *Walter Lippmann and the American Century* (New York: Random House, 1981)
30. Robert S. Westrich, *Antisemitism: The Longest Hatred* (New York: Pantheon Books, 1992)
31. Voltaire called Jews "an ignorant and barbarous people, who have long emitted the most sordid avarice with the most detestable superstition."
32. Paul Johnson, "The Oldest Poison," *Times Literary Supplement*, April 1991, pp. 5-6
33. Harold Harel Fisch, "English Literature," in *Encyclopaedia Judaica* (New York: Macmillan, 1971), vol. 6, columns 77-78
34. Michael Hastings, "Anti-Semitism Issue Slows British Fund for Eliot," in *New York Times*, August 1988; Christopher Ricks, "Eliot's Uglier Touches," in *Times Literary Supplement*, November 10, 1988
35. Richard Ellman, *James Joyce*, (New York: Oxford University Press, 1959), pp.238, 722, passim.
36. Louis Harap, *The Image of the Jew in American Literature: From Early Republic to Mass Immigration*, (Philadelphia: Jewish Publication Society, 1952)
37. Robert Michael, "American Literary Anti-Semitism," in *Midstream*, August-September 1991, pp.27-29
38. Mencken's verdict on Jews: "The most unpleasant race ever heard of."
39. David Landau, "Friendship Fills Plaza Independencia," in *Jerusalem Post*, December 13, 1989
40. Perceptive observers see much evidence that Dershowitz's 1982 summary of the "International Onslaught of Anti-Semitism" (Los Angeles; Simon Wiesenthal Center Social Action Update #10, Spring/Summer '82) is being validated as we move into the last years of the century. But in his *The Vanishing American Jew* (Boston: Little, Brown and Company, 1996) Dershowitz has moderated his sense of alarm and crisis. With non-discriminatory policies now prevailing in country clubs, colleges, and neighborhoods, he now believes that "with American Jews catapulted into the open arms of mainstream America, institutional antisemitism has virtually disappeared" from the American scene. (Jonathan Rosen, "Abraham's Drifting Children," in *New York Times Book Review*). "Antisemitism, as it affects the average American Jew, is over."
41. Jacob Katz, "Accounting for Anti-Semitism," in *Commentary*, June 1991, p. 54
42. Daniel Jonah Goldhagen, *Hitler's Willing Executioners: Ordinary Germans and the Holocaust* (New York, Knopf, 1996), p. 9

43. Amos Elon, "The Antagonist as Liberator," in *New York Times Magazine*, January 26, 1997, p. 44
44. Dinitia Smith, "A Challenging View of the Holocaust," in *New York Times*, March 17, 1996
45. William J. Vanden Heuvel, "The Holocaust Was No Secret," in *New York Times Magazine*, December 22, 1996, p. 31
46. Daniel Jonah Goldhagen, "The People's Holocaust," in *New York Times*, March 17, 1996
47. Like the Biblical Balaam, these reluctant critics were ready to curse the children of Israel but, guided by God, wound up blessing them. (*Numbers 23-24*)
48. Amos Elon, *ibid*. p.42-43
49. December 5, 1996
50. Amos Elon, *ibid*., p.42
51. Albert Einstein, *Out of My Later Years* (1956, Carol Publishing Group, New York) p.265

CHAPTER 9

AMERICAN JEWS AND ISRAEL

Since its establishment as a sovereign Jewish state a half-century ago, Israel has been at the forefront of the American Jew's interests and concerns. American Jews have thrilled to Israel's military successes, taken pride in its achievements in building a nation, grown depressed at its setbacks and alarmed at its dangers. Social commentators have emphasized the salient position of Israel on the horizon of the American Jew. Irving Howe called Israel the secular religion of Diaspora Jewry, and Nathan Glazer singled out support for Israel as the chief function of the Jewish community.

Yet despite the positive perceptions of commitment, a waning of sympathy and support for Israel seems to have manifested itself in recent years. Criticism of Israel, once muted and infrequent, is no longer uncommon. The heroic image has lost some of its luster. After Menachem Begin became prime minister in 1977, American Jews grew uneasy with the policies of his right-wing government. They were troubled by the establishment of settlements in the territories and by the military incursion into Lebanon. They were distressed by the Israeli government's position on the "Who is a Jew?" issue, on its connection with Jonathan Pollard's espionage, and with its response to the Intifada. Criticism of Israel was now in full cry, with a decibel level sometimes approaching that of Israel's sworn enemies.

During the Gulf War, practically no American Jews were to be found in Israel. The hotels were empty, the restaurants unpatronized, the sidewalk cafes deserted. Ben Yehuda Street in the center of Jerusalem heard no echo of English conversation. On Shabbat mornings on our way to the synagogue, carrying our prayer books and gas masks, we would stop to rest in the lobby of the King David Hotel, which, in its Assyrian mausoleum decor, was silent as a tomb. As we walked along the quiet streets, we recalled the scenes from former years when American Jews, community leaders on missions, paraded along these same streets wearing T-shirts imprinted with such slogans as, "We Are One," "Let My People Go," "American Jews and Israel: One Destiny." They were proclaiming their solidarity with Israel and affirming the promptings of common purpose which they probably felt. They called themselves "Federation Commandos." But in the days of need, United Jewish Appeal missions were canceled, and panicky Americans dashed in droves for departing flights out of Israel. To Israelis waiting for the Scuds to fall, the vaunted "solidarity" was as flimsy as a T-shirt with fading letters. At the time, Professor Daniel J. Elazar was constrained to write, "What many [Israelis] are now thinking about American Jews is, 'You want to tell us to make all kinds of concessions in which our security is threatened, but when it is a question of putting yourselves even remotely .... on the line for a week or ten days, you are not willing to do it.'"[1]

A year after the war, the director of Israel operations for the United Jewish Appeal reported that U.J.A. missions were not as "strong" as he had anticipated. "Even the committed people aren't coming," he said. "Now .... more non-Jews are coming to Israel, while Jews choose to go elsewhere."[2] American Jews who travel the world no longer include Israel in their itinerary. More Germans come to Israel annually than American Jews. The Gulf War saw 25 non-Orthodox Jewish tourist groups from New England canceled; every Christian tour came. The Israel Tourist Ministry is now targeting its American advertising as much at Christian groups and individuals as at Jews.

Seduction by the Liberal-Left

The waning enthusiasm for Israel may be attributed to a variety of factors, none more influential than the American Jew's enchantment with the social and political perspective of liberalism. With its espousal of the cause of universal human rights, liberalism corresponds closely with deeply cherished ideals in Jewish tradition. Born in the birthpangs of Egyptian slavery, Jews have always been enjoined to love the stranger, the underdog, the slave. No more persistent injunction in the sacred Hebrew texts exists than the command to have compassion for the stranger. "The stranger who resides with you shall be as the homeborn among you; you shall love him as yourself, for you were strangers in the land of Egypt" (*Leviticus 19:34*). In the narrative of the Passover Seder, which recounts the story of the Exodus, the heroes are victims of injustice and oppression, slaves. Later the Prophets made the ethical mandates of freedom, justice, and mercy the heart of their message.

Here we have sufficient reason for the attraction of present-day liberalism for Jews. For liberals are the reputed champions of the oppressed and persecuted, the poor and hungry, of minorities, Afro-Americans, Hispanics, Native Americans, women, gays. To the moral and ethical vision evoked by liberalism, even marginal Jews are powerfully drawn. The former passion for Judaism is transmuted into a passion for improving the world.[3]

But there is a worm in the apple. Liberalism is not impartial in deciding whose rights it will champion. Not all minorities find favor in its sight. One that often does not is Israel. Israel is the orphan in the storm left to shiver alone in the winds of adversity. Liberals extend their solicitude and support to the peoples of the Third World. Israel is not counted a part of that world. The Arabs are. Jewish liberals may not realize that being a champion of the Third World puts them in league with some of Israel's murderous enemies.

The cheek by jowl relationship between Jews and the liberal-left strikes some as an anomaly, since it would seem to contravene the Jews' own economic interests. "Jews live like Episcopalians and vote like Puerto Ricans," is an adage of election pollsters. American Jews vote the cause of the economically deprived and disadvantaged, a category far removed from their own. Since the early decades of the century, voting patterns have shown how Jews have placed their socio-ethical values above their socio-economic interests. They have thus gained the reputation of being the most liberal of all white American ethnic groups. A newspaper headline pinpointed the paradox: "U.S. Jews — More Liberal and Wealthier than Other Americans." It is a paradox which stands economic determinism on its head.

What deepens the paradox is that American Jews seem unable to realize that liberalism and the liberal-left may have abandoned the Jews. The benign liberalism of the New Deal Era has become radicalized. Liberalism now identifies with causes which in earlier decades would have been anathema. It has become increasingly tolerant of some of the guises of antisemitism, often anti-Zionism. We have already noted that some of the mainstream churches, enthralled by liberation theology, are committed backers of the Palestinians. The United Nations, cherished by liberals as the international monitor of human rights, has for years been the sounding board for vicious anti-Israel slanders and the stamping ground where a chain of anti-Israel resolutions are crafted. An ironic fillip is given to the coupling of Jews and liberalism by the disclosure that the United Nations Association is supported principally by Jews. Irving Kristol admonishes Jews to wake up to the radically biased nature of current liberalism. "Jews need to be mugged by reality," he advises.[4]

In these days leftist-liberalism with its anti-Israel bias, luxuriates on the college campus. Concern for Jews and Israel is politically incorrect. "Attending university in America," observes Wigoder, "is likely to involve alienation from the Jewish establishment, [and] as the student is attracted to [the] world of left-wing liberalism, Israel becomes a problem rather than an ideal."[5] Jews support causes championed by black bigots. The extent of such alienation becomes clear when we read that 90 per cent of Jews go to college. It should have caused little surprise, therefore, when at the 1992 assembly of the Council of Jewish Federations, it was reported that "Israel is no longer a central issue to most young Jewish Americans."[6]

The liaison between Jews and liberal-leftism is not new, and wise observers have long discerned its pitfalls and cul-de-sacs. Some years ago, in a conversation, Isaac Bashevis Singer asked me in a tone of resigned bafflement, "When will Jews stop supporting the revolutions which eventually devour them?" He was thinking of Trotsky, Kamenev, Zinoviev, Radek, and all the other revolutionaries liquidated by Stalin. All had changed their names as a gesture of rejection of their Jewish past, but to the Russian comrades they remained Jews. (To the world, Trotsky may have been a Russian revolutionary, but to the commissars he was Bronstein, the Jew.) He was thinking of Rosa Luxemburg, who, irritated by a letter asking her help for suffering Jews, growled, "Why do you pester me with your special Jewish sorrows?" and went on to speak of the suffering of African and Asian natives. The historian Jacob Talmon wondered how a Jew could show compassion for the misery of the African Bantu and only annoyance at the anguish of Jews. Someone has described universalist Jews as Jews who ache the pains of the whole world but not their own.

Anti-Israel American Jews

Jews who criticize Israel are among the catalysts of anti-Israel feeling in America. They rank with the non-Jewish media cohorts who seem never to tire of bashing Israel in the press and on television. We have already mentioned one of Israel's most truculent antagonists, Mike Wallace, who periodically has hammered Israel on *60 Minutes*, the widely watched television program. Anthony Lewis, more suave than Wallace, performs a similar function in his gray *New York Times* columns. There are Jewish community leaders and rabbis, who, while slavering moral pieties, put the knife to Israel in press conferences, letters to the editor, and pulpit cant.

Some voluble Jews, sworn to the liberal credo, have negatively influenced the attitude of American Jews toward Israel. Arthur Hertzberg, Conservative rabbi and astringent polemicist, has portrayed Israel since the Six-Day War as a country with no moral direction and a corrupting faith in power. "It would .... have been better," he believes, "had the Six-Day War ended in a draw and not in a series of stunning victories." He has called for an international conference to force Israel to make concessions to the Arabs, urged American Jews to stop supporting Israel, and rebuked Elie Wiesel for failing to sign a statement attacking Israel's policies. "He has responded to enmity against Israel," Ruth Wisse points out, "not by trying to counter it but by condemning fellow-Jews for having brought it upon themselves."[7]

Equally garrulous and acerbic a critic is Albert Vorspan, retired senior vice-president of the Reform Union of American Hebrew Congregations. Under Vorspan's leadership, the U.A.H.C. has become a prime promoter of the gamut of liberal-leftist causes, leading some wags to call it the Jewish branch of the American Civil Liberties Union. (The A.C.L.U. itself is preponderantly Jewish in its leadership and membership.) It has been suggested that devotees of Vorspan's social action program, like liberation theologians, may be seeking a spiritual cloak for their radical politics.

Vorspan is known for his barrages of denigration and contumely against Israel. Writing in the *New York Times Magazine* in 1988, he called the Lebanese War "Israel's Vietnam, Kent State, and Watts, all in one," and then proceeded to relieve himself of an avalanche of abuse against Israeli policies. Israel was the oppressor, Palestinians the victims. Israel's policy was politically and morally bankrupt, and its "continuous brutality" made him want to "crawl into a hole." With no extenuating word for Israel, the article was a prolonged screed of anger.[8] Some time later, the U.A.H.C., in a gesture that ridiculed logic, planted the Vorspan Forest and Park in a Jerusalem park in honor of "a man whose commitment and devotion to Israel is a source of inspiration for American Jewry."

A cluster of periodicals edited by Jews and fixed in the liberal-left orbit, maintains a steady drumbeat of criticism hostile to Israel. *The Nation*, edited by Victor Navasky, gained a certain odium a few years ago when it published an article by Gore Vidal widely judged to be an unrestrained disgorgement of antisemitism. Ideologically it conformed with the editor's chronic carping at Israel. The *New York Review of Books*, edited by Robert Silvers and Barbara Epstein, has for years offered sanctuary to authors antagonistic to Israel. *Village Voice* provides a smorgasbord of Israel bashing by counterculture mavens. *Tikkun*, edited by Michael Lerner, wraps its anti-Israel animus in a blanket of Jewish topical and intellectual discourse. It is a cloak not unlike the malignant cape worn by Lady Eleanore in Hawthorne's story, "Lady Eleanore's Mantle."[9]

A recent survey showed that two-thirds of American Jews are not "very attached to Israel."[10] Eighty per cent have never visited Israel. One is left to wonder to what extent, if any, this dwindling attachment may be due to the naysaying of liberal Jewish journalists and commentators. It may be naive to ask why Jews go public in attacking Israel. These adversarial critics say they can do no less than obey conscience and speak and write the truth as they see it. For such it might be well to remember Abba Eban's reminder, "It is the blood of Israelis, not of American Jews, which is shed on the field of battle." And the warning of Koheleth, "Be not righteous overmuch" (*Ecclesiastes 7:16*).

Edmund Wilson, the American critic, propounded an interesting explanation for the liberal-leftist's commitment to causes and people that ultimately betray him. The radical middle-class intellectual, he observed, lacks one essential human characteristic, the "ability to identify with his own social group. He can only identify his interests with those of an outlawed minority. His human solidarity lies only in his imagination of general human improvement."[11] This may be a not implausible profile of Jewish liberals who make common cause with Israel's enemies.

"Prophetic Judaism" has become a buzz-term in the vocabulary of Reform Judaism, a mantra often mumbled to validate whatever activist posture its spokespersons assume, from patrilineality to the rabbinical ordination of gays and lesbians to same-sex marriage. *Tikkun Olam*, "repairing the world," is a similar activist cliché, according to which man is represented as God's partner in mending the world.

Countering these excesses of hubris, Rabbi Abba Hillel Silver in a historic address before the Central Conference of American Rabbis placed Prophetic Judaism in its authentic theological and historical setting. He cautioned his colleagues against embracing the transcendental moral code of universalism as the supreme message of the Prophets while ignoring the people of Israel. They should understand that the Prophets loved the people as much as the ideals of Israel, that they must be reverent not only of prophecy but also of the people who gave birth to prophecy and to Prophets. It should be remembered above all that Prophetic Judaism was bound up with what people do, Jews, even Zionists: the upbuilding of Zion and the political restoration of Israel by and for the people.

He then went on to cite that trenchant tale from *Tanna d'bey Eliyahu*, which tells of a man who came to Elijah and questioned him in a matter of the law. "Rabbi," he said, "I have two things in my heart and I love them both dearly, the Torah and Israel, but I do not know which of the two comes first." Whereupon Elijah said to him: "Most men would say that the Torah comes first. I say to you that the holy people of Israel comes first."

Israel's American critics, at ease in their plush suburbias, look at Israel and seethe with *midat hadin* (austere moral judgment). Silver pleads for a modicum of *midat harahamim* (merciful judgment). *Nahamu, nahamu, ami* — "Comfort ye, comfort ye, my people" (*Isaiah 40,1*) — that is also Prophetic Judaism.

Jewish liberal-leftists loudly assert that their views are grounded in the "prophetic tradition," thereby, as Irving Howe suggests, "staking out a claim to Jewish legitimacy. With enough wrenching one could find 'ancestors' for almost any opinion. If one wanted a 'Jewish justification' for liberalism or radicalism, the honest course would be to provide it in terms of the present situation rather than trying to enlist prophets no longer in a position to speak for themselves."[12]

The Avoidance of Aliya

In 1892 Theodore Herzl published a novel, *Altneuland* (Old-New Land), in which he envisioned the creation and development of an independent flourishing national Jewish state. The book is now chiefly remembered for its exhortation which in time became the motto of the reborn nation, "If you will it, it is no fable." Among his visions for the future state, Herzl conjured up scenes of rabbis quitting their Diaspora communities and coming on aliya with their congregations. *Altneuland* has been called a Utopian novel, and in no particular was it more Utopian than in its author's fantasy of wholesale aliya by rabbis accompanied by their congregations. That did not happen. Herzl's heroic vision turned out to be the impossible dream. In the nearly half century of Israel's existence, it is doubtful if even one rabbi has come on aliya with his congregation, or even with a small percentage of the congregation's members.

Aliya from America has been a vortex of controversy since the earliest days of Israel's nationhood. Then Israel's greatest need was people. It was suffering from what Abba Eban called a "demographic drought." In 1948 there were no more than 600,000 Jews living in the country, many of them survivors of death camps. A country had to be built out of barren hills and parched desert. Borders adjoining hostile Arab states sworn to avenge defeat, had to be defended. Hordes of immigrants expelled from Arab lands had to be sheltered, fed, and trained for the tasks of forging a new Jewish society. There was a desperate need for immigrants whose resources of spirit, skills, and substance would qualify them to build anew the old land. These could come mainly from the Western democracies, and it was to these countries, which had contributed so much to the founding of Israel, that the call for aliya went out. It proved to be a largely fruitless summons.

In some primitive societies, there are individuals who are barred from all forms of social interaction with certain kinsmen. Any contact between them, no matter how casual, is forbidden. Prohibition commonly involves a man with women in his wife's kin group. They may not speak to each other, avert their gazes when about to meet, and should they come toward each other on a path in the forest, will disappear into the bush to forestall an encounter. The relationship between them is known as an avoidance relationship.

It may fairly be said that the attitude of the American Jew toward aliya is comparable with that of tribesmen involved in an avoidance relationship. Since the founding of the State, when Israel's greatest need was for *olim* to settle and build the land, American Jews have avoided confronting, much less attempting to meet, the need for aliya. Forty years ago when Israeli speakers came to address American Jewish assemblies about Israel, they were warned not to talk about aliya. David Ben Gurion was the recipient of such warning along with the lowly Jewish Agency *shaliah* (representative). Talk of aliya, they were told, would only alienate American Jews. Ask them to give, to exert political pressure, to hope and pray, but under no circumstances ask them to join you in Israel. Twenty years ago, a prominent Zionist journalist noted, "Among American Zionists, [there is a] psychotic dread of aliya."[13] American Jewry's faint initial response to the call for aliya has faded still further with the passing years.

Out of the aggregate American Jewish population of five and a half million, it is estimated that 71,000 have come on aliya since the founding of Israel in 1948. Of this number approximately one-third returned to the U.S. within a few years. They returned primarily not for ideological reasons but because of difficulties related to everyday living — jobs, housing, bureaucracy, family discontent, stresses of security, and military service. The single highest year for aliya was 1971 when 7,364 came; the single lowest year was 1985 when 1,915 came. The preponderant majority of those who come and of those who stay is Orthodox. Those who are more religious and have more Jewish education seem better able to overcome the quotidian problems of the new life in Israel.[14]

The aliya of Conservative and Reform Jews, who constitute 80-90 percent of the religiously affiliated, has been a meager trickle. Their rabbinical bodies no longer urge aliya; they "encourage" it. "Encourage" is one of those flaccid words that breathe ambiguity. One rabbinical pronouncement reads, "The encouragement of aliya as an option within the diverse expressions of Reform Judaism remains in the long term interest of our movement as well as of Israel." The author of this brave declaration obviously had both feet planted firmly in midair. Saperstein has remarked, "It would be revealing to investigate how many [rabbis], in looking over their sermons, could point to a single passage in which they "encouraged, let alone urged", aliya.[15] Thus is the avoidance relationship preserved.

Resolutions passed at annual Reform and Conservative rabbinic conventions enthusiastically applaud the aliya of Russian, Ethiopian, and Albanian Jews but have nothing but justification for their own immobility. "Now they can make aliya [through our support of the U.J.A. and Israel Bonds]; despite our domestic recession, we will do our utmost to make real their dream of return to Zion, and thus, do our part to sustain this modern miracle."[16] Not making aliya is thus turned into an occasion for self-congratulation.

The ambivalence of the collective American rabbinical pronouncements on aliya is an appropriate backdrop to the aliya record of individual rabbis. Herzl's expectations that rabbis would flock to the restored Jewish homeland were merely evidence of a propensity to dream euphorically. The reality bore little resemblance to the dream. Despite their pulpit rant, rabbis cling to the *golah* as tenaciously as their laymen, "lifelong Zionists" among them. Denominational differences have marked the aliya of American rabbis. Thousands of Orthodox rabbis have made aliya, although charismatic figures like Jacob Soloveichik and Menahem Mendel Schneerson never set foot on Israeli soil. Fewer Conservative rabbis have come, but these include some of their distinguished leaders — Moshe Davis, Israel Goldstein, Simon Greenberg, Avraham Halkin, Theodore Friedman. A handful of Reform rabbis have come. Many retired Orthodox and Conservative rabbis come on aliya. In the five decades since statehood, three Reform rabbis have come upon retirement. Two survive, one of whom is the author of these lines.

Yet with the grim reports on the demographic crisis now facing the American Jewish community, some Jewish leaders are articulating a degree of appreciation for Israel seldom heard in recent years. For years Jewish leaders, rabbis among them, minimized the significance of Israel in Jewish life, challenging the "centrality of Israel" in the Jewish world, belaboring Israel's moral deficiencies, mocking Israel as the Promised Land, disparaging its eminence as the world's Jewish scholastic center, lamenting the loss to America of young Jews who decide to make aliya. Now, however, American Jews are being told what benefits an Israel experience might bring for their children in strengthening their Jewish identity and in stanching the assimilationist flood gaining momentum daily.

At the 1992 convention of the Council of Jewish Federations, representing the major Jewish organizations of North America, many speakers projected Israel as the key to healing some of the identity debilities of the American Jew. They stressed the importance for every Jew of spending extended periods of time in Israel. One featured speaker recommended that the New York Federation enable each New York Jewish high school graduate to spend six months in a work or study program in Israel. Such a "practical investment," it was suggested, "could produce a committed American Jewry with a tangible connection to Israel."[17]

Yet with all these ascriptions of praise for Israel, the convention still had difficulty confronting the question of aliya. In the 112-page program, only a single one-hour session over lunch was devoted to aliya. Despite the sanguine depiction of Israel as a lifebelt for the American Jew floundering in the floodtide of intermarriage and assimilation, no serious discussion of aliya took place. The avoidance relationship was operating in full fig.

Israeli leaders have long said that the principal reason for the failure of the American aliya has been the emphasis upon fund-raising. Israelis appearing before American gatherings have for years emphasized the crucial need for money. To be sure, in the early days of national struggle and want, the period in the 50's called *tsena* (deprivation), there was a dire need for funds to provide food, clothing, and shelter for the new olim. Jews responded, many of them generously, and the act of giving undoubtedly forged a bond with the land and its people.

But the need for funds was allowed to supersede every other need, including the need for people. The consequences have been damaging both to Israel and to American Jews. It has turned Israel into a mendicant asking for handouts, and American Jews into a Lord Bountiful thinking that writing a check, while fully discharging their obligation to the Jewish people, would solve all of Israel's problems. This demeaning dependency has led Israelis to look upon Diaspora Jewry as an open credit card and Diaspora Jews upon Israel as a "distant land of needy cousins rather than a country that is theirs."[18]

In time, the period of critical need passed, but the pattern of fundraising did not. It remained the fixed symbol of Israel-Diaspora relations. The irony is that the philanthropy of all of Diaspora Jewry has never amounted to more than 2 percent of Israel's national budget.[19] Furthermore, taking into account the factor of inflation, American Jews, with all the hoopla of V.I.P. missions and "We Are One" avowals, are today giving to Israel no more than the equivalent of what they gave in the 1970's. There has also been a growing trend in Jewish communities for allocating a larger proportion of the funds raised to local needs and a smaller percentage to Israel.

Hopes and Fears

The Oslo accords of 1993 reached by Israel and the Palestinians ushered in a new, some would say revolutionary, chapter in the relationship between two long-standing adversaries. Framed in secrecy far from the world's beaten paths, the Declarations of Oslo were hailed as a herald of peace in the turbulent Middle East. On September 13, 1993, President Clinton stage-managed the signing ceremony on the White House lawn. During the ensuing year, footage of the Rabin-Arafat handshake was shown with numbing frequency on television all over the world and became the visual symbol of peace descending dove-like on the Middle East tinder box.

Jewish opinion in both Israel and America on the Declaration of Principles was divided. There were those who, agreeing with Prime Minister Rabin and Foreign Minister Peres, felt that Oslo had opened a window of hope after years of living under siege, war weariness, and rising anxiety about the future. Perhaps the promise of reconciliation and peace had dawned. Israel, for years diplomatically isolated, began to be recognized by formerly hostile nations. Even the Vatican established diplomatic ties with Israel. Peres was busy painting his "glowing vision" of the future — Israel back to its 1967 borders, a Palestinian state in Gaza and the West Bank, Syria ensconced once again on the Golan Heights. Israel, separated from a rebellious population it could no longer control but at peace with other Arab states, would at last feel secure. The "New Middle East" would emerge founded upon peace and a regional prosperity rivaling that of East Asia. Peres preened himself and Rabin as "purveyors of a new dawn," and when they along with Arafat were awarded the Nobel Peace Prize, much of the world seemed seduced by the "glowing vision."

Many Israelis have taken a different view since the handshake on the White House lawn. They are persuaded, they say, not by a "glowing vision" but by facts on the ground as they unfold from day to day — the increasing terrorist attacks on soldiers and civilians since Oslo, the failure to carry out important provisions of the Declaration of Principles such as the unwillingness or refusal to repudiate the Palestine Covenant of 1964, which pledged the Arab world to the destruction of Israel, the inability or unwillingness of the greatly expanded Arab police force in the territories to apprehend terrorists. They see the meetings with Palestinian and other Arab leaders not as a process of negotiation but as cumulative capitulation, with Israel unilaterally yielding vital rights — territory, water, security — a chain of appeasements and a repeated retreat from "red lines." So far as these Israelis can see, the Palestinians have concluded that "armed struggle" works, that since it "forced" Israel to withdraw from Gaza and Jericho, more "armed struggle" will bring about the establishment of a Palestinian state. The goal of Arafat and the PLO may therefore be not peace but the destruction of Israel. Indeed, this is apparent in the shadowy, off-camera threats of Arafat and his vengeful lieutenants, as well as in his Arabic exhortations to Arab hearers. "Believe them," say Israelis, remembering their kinsmen who in a previous generation of gathering darkness would not believe Hitler when he vowed to exterminate them.

American Jews to all appearances have supported the peace process. Pressure to do so, blatant and subtle, was applied by both the Israeli and the U.S. governments. A stream of Israeli government functionaries traveled to America to induce Jewish leaders and opinion molders to support the Rabin-Peres blueprint. President Clinton and the State Department spared no effort in working for the same goal. Clinton's 1995 State of the Union message to the nation was all but a trumpet blast for Rabin-Peres. Many of the important organizations of Jewish communal life have fallen into line — from the Council of Jewish Federations to the American Jewish Committee, from the Rabbinical Assembly to the Central Conference of American Rabbis,[20] from the President's Conference to the Anti-Defamation League, to AIPAC, from all the leftist peace organizations[21] walking in lockstep with the peace process advocates. When the U.S. government strongly supports an Israeli government policy, many American Jews, sensitive to the charge of divided loyalty, will plump for the country in which they hold citizenship.

Israelis who question the sense of the Rabin-Peres political strategy fear that the peace process, if it continues with its fatal fascination for serial appeasement, may lead not to a peaceful Middle East but to national disaster. They see Israel becoming a second Lebanon with rival Arab factions exploding in civil war. Syria will again intervene and Israel will ineluctably be drawn into the caldron. This may tempt Iran and Iraq to join forces with Syria and other Arab states now turned fundamentalist, perhaps with a post-Mubarak Egypt, a post-Hussein Jordan, all armed with their rapidly expanding arsenals of mass biological, chemical, and nuclear weapons. A Middle East *jihad* will be declared against a truncated Israel, bent at last on eliminating the hated Jewish state "in the heart of the Arab world."

Both the Israeli and United States governments have given favorable consideration to the stationing of American troops as a "monitoring" force on the Golan Heights. Many Israelis see this as a cause for future friction between the United States and Israel, the Americans wanting them withdrawn in the event of an Arab onslaught, Israel desperately needing the American armed presence as a critical deterrent against hostile military action in the Rabin-Peres "New Middle East."[22] American Jews will face an agonizing dilemma — wishing to spare Israel the consequences of an American troop withdrawal on the one hand, and on the other, dreading to counter Congressional and public opposition to maintaining a U.S. peacekeeping force on the isolated escarpments of the Golan.

Those who see the peace process as a scenario for national disaster say that one of the main reasons for the advocacy of its devotees is their failure to understand the true character of the enemy. What they fail to grasp is the extreme and uncompromising nature of Islam. Conor Cruise O'Brien has pointed out that Islam is indivisible, that Islamic fundamentalism and Islam are one. To separate Islam into graded levels of commitment to *jihad* is to miss its basic and essential extremism. Hamas, Fatah, Islamic Jihad, Democratic Front for the Liberation of Palestine, Hizbullah — there may be differences in organizational structure, membership criteria, leadership. But there is no difference in their objectives or in the expedients used in carrying them out. The actuality is that the great majority of Muslims are pledged to *jihad*. *Jihad* carried Arab armies to military glory and vast territorial expansion in medieval times and today recruits the faithful around the world under its implacable banner.

A central doctrine of Islam is *dhimma*, inferiority of non-Muslims (*dhimmis*), with an inordinate hatred reserved for Jews. Among the received myths of Jewish history are the tales of harmonious relations said to have prevailed in time past between Muslims and Jews. The authentic record, however, relates a long chronicle of calculated humiliation and persecution of Jews, during which the Golden Age in Spain was a comparatively brief respite. Maimonides, a credible witness, described the lot of the Jews under Muslim rule as one of unrelieved subjugation and contempt: "They have persecuted us severely. Never did a nation molest, degrade, debase, and hate us as much as they."[23]

Today in Middle East mosques, imams exhort their worshipers to a fanatical hatred of Jews. They rouse their congregations to join in *jihad* against Israel and condone the most violent means in pursuing it. Terrorism is such a means. Arafat has employed terrorism since the beginning of the "armed struggle." It has been the indispensable vehicle for carrying out his objectives and he shows no credible sign of relinquishing it. On the contrary, the tide of terrorism has risen dramatically since Oslo. Intermittently it may seem to recede, but the reason is more likely to be a show of Palestinian "restraint" under Arafat's control, or the yielding of another Israeli concession under the thumbscrews of "armed struggle" than to any fundamental shift in policy by the terrorists. Arafat's record of broken agreements and flouted covenants, shows that he will not, in O'Brien's view, abandon his terrorist program, nor has he any desire to do so. Those who think that he will are living in "cloud-cuckoo-land."[24]

Amos Oz, Israel's bestselling and most widely translated author, has challenged America's Jews to climb down from the press box from which they have been criticizing Israel and come onto the playing field of Israeli life to share, perhaps, determine, the action on the field. Calling their standing aside a "historic disaster," he is weary of the moral reproofs of outsiders. "Our friends .... should open their eyes and see that it is impossible to change Israel by remote control .... If it is important for them that the enlightened, humanistic, and peacekeeping Israel should prevail, *then they must be here, not there.*"[25]

There has been a miraculous migration of Jews to Israel since the dissolution of the Soviet Union and the political upheavals in Eastern and Central Europe. The new *olim* have been a unique boon for the country, constituting a critical population mass which can help solve some of its acute social and economic problems. At the same time, the need for *olim* from the Western democracies remains. It is estimated that a western aliya of 100,000 would be sufficient to effect the changes needed to allow Israel to function fully as a democratic society. *Olim* from the West could break the stranglehold of extremists on important sectors of the national life. With their strong commitment to democratic values, the only political ethos they have known, such *olim* could transform the political and social climate of the country, with resulting benefits for the great majority of Israelis.[26]

But with the past record of aliya from the West, even the modest goal of 100,000 would appear a distant prospect. For, as Abba Eban has written, Jews display a "tragic and chronic adhesiveness to the Diaspora." "Not only [do they cling] to diasporas which have their own allurements of freedom and vitality, but even to volcanic diasporas. Jews do not willingly leave the edge of the volcano."[27] They are like the Lipari Island fishermen who live under the brow of Mount Etna. When the volcano erupts, they sail away with their families, but with the eruption scarcely over, they return to stay until Etna's next upheaval, when they again take temporary flight.

To no Diaspora has the Jew adhered so steadfastly as to the American Diaspora. In all the centuries of exile, Jews have never known so much freedom, wealth, and power as in America. The contributions they have made have been balanced by their attainments in every sphere of American life. And all has been experienced in a national ethos which enshrines the ideals of liberty, equality, and justice. For Jews, America has been less Diaspora than Shangri-la, the realm in which millennial dreams have been realized. It is true that Jews have here known discrimination, prejudice, and poverty, and still do. Nor is it in dispute that many Jews worry about increasing antisemitism. It is also true that a growing number of Jews are anxious about the ability to preserve their identity and safeguard their integrity as Jews. But these seem passing vexations in the fair and pleasant land which ten Jewish generations have called home.

This attitude toward America is understandable, and to berate American Jews for embodying it, as some Israelis do, is fatuous. Not long ago, an Israeli writer condemned American Jews as fairweather friends and hypocrites, dupes and "enemies." for failing to come on aliya.[28] Such outbursts are the mark of frustration rather than of mature reflection or responsible decision making. The American Jew's transient enthusiasms for Israel, backed by his open checkbook, may strike us as naive and superficial, but there is no mean or evil purpose in them.

The inescapable truth is that most American Jews have been conditioned to be what they are and to remain where they are by the culture in which their lives are interwoven. The years in America have acculturated them to the values of the secular society. They have a spasmodic devotion to the faith of their fathers, an ephemeral attachment to its traditions, a meager knowledge of its history. Their identification with the Jewish world is shallow, their participation in it minimal. To their children and grandchildren, Judaism and Jewish tradition are more shadow than substance, echoes that become more faint with the passing years.

The broad generality of American Jews have not been cast in the mold of *Halutzim* (pioneers) inspired to help build a land where Jewish life will flourish. The vision of a Herzl, an A.D. Gordon, a Ben Gurion is associated with a world with which they may feel a sentimental bond, but no profound commitment. They have been conditioned to live in another world, in a land where, whatever its stresses and anxieties, they are at ease, at home. Not hypocrisy, cowardice, or evil have motivated American Jews in their attitude toward Israel, but the cultural imperatives of the dominant society.

Religious Conflict: Eternal Contradiction

In all history there is no more baffling irony than the sanguinary cruelties and monstrous depravities committed by the disputants in religious conflict. In every century,

> The blind avengers of religion's cause
> Forgot each precept of her peaceful laws.

Religion has brought redemption and salvation to much of humankind; it has also made "countless thousands mourn."

Nor has Judaism escaped the grim visitations of this irony. The Torah was called a Tree of Life whose "ways are ways of pleasantness, and all its paths .... peace." While never approaching the ferocity of the Crusades, or the savage conquests of the Muslims, or the holy wars of the Reformation, which dredged the depths of man's inhumanity to man, the confrontations between Sadducees and Pharisees, Karaites and Rabbanites, Marranos and Sabbateans, Hasidim and Mitnagdim over authority in Jewish law and life, could become bitter and violent, profoundly disorienting for the Jewish community. We recall that Sapir suggested that Judaism demanded that the Jew behave himself every minute of the day, else he could not come into the presence of the Almighty. With his religion imposing so oppressive a psychological burden, no wonder preoccupation with Halachic questions absorbed much of the Jew's emotional and physical energy.

Nor was internecine religious strife only a relic of older Jewish conflicts; it has been no stranger to modern times. No more than ninety years ago in Jerusalem, a conflict between rival *Haredi* disputants erupted in communal violence. A yeshiva-synagogue compound in Jerusalem was broken into and ransacked. A fierce struggle had been joined between the followers of Rabbi Samuel Salant, Chief Rabbi of Jerusalem and head of the *va'ad klali*, and the partisans of Rabbi Moses Joshua Judah Leib Diskin (the Brisker Rabbi), many of whom were members of the independent Hungarian *kollel*. Diskin strenuously opposed the more moderate positions taken by Salant, differences simmered over the disbursement of monies from abroad, and bitter conflict ensued.

The hostility was marked by proclamations, broadsides, some bearing allegedly false signatures, and polemical tracts, including one entitled, *A hutzpa fun der Brisker rebbitzin* (An impertinence from the Brisker rebbitzin). (The rebbitzin was thought to influence the decisions of her husband.)

In 1908 a climactic confrontation took place during which the followers of the *va'ad klali* demonstrated violently outside Diskin's home. When Diskin rallied his *bahurim* (disciples) for protection, the crowd, now grown into an unruly mob, burst into the Hungarian yeshiva-synagogue compound and wrecked it. History instructs us that religious strife is marked by a special virulence, and Jewish religious strife is no exception. In the resulting frenzies, even a synagogue is not immune from desecration.[29]

Orthodox and Non-Orthodox Today

In more recent years, conflict between the Orthodox and non-Orthodox has been simmering in the two principal foci of the Jewish world, Israel and the United States. The Orthodox claim that only a Judaism fixed in the matrix of Torah and its precise explication in the subsequent rabbinical codes, and in the fulfillment of the 613 ritual precepts *(mitzvot)* of the Torah can be considered authentic. Non-Orthodox Jews reject this proprietary claim. The institutions and leaders of Reform and Conservative Judaism, located predominantly in the United States and representing the overwhelming majority of non-Orthodox Jews, have taken up the cudgels in asserting their rights to legitimacy and equality in the religious framework of Jewish life. In Israel they have not infrequently petitioned the civil courts in waging the struggle for what they consider their just prerogatives. The issue is religious pluralism: the unrestricted freedom of different denominations to co-exist with full equality for their rabbis and laymen. They ask why the Orthodox establishment should be privileged to rule as unacceptable life-crisis ceremonies such as marriage, divorce, and conversion when conducted by non-Orthodox rabbis, and when their Reform and Conservative officiants are rejected as unqualified. No one, they claim, has the authority to adjudge as Jewishly illegitimate Reform/Conservative Judaism, by far the largest religious denominations in the Jewish world.

Equality, freedom of conscience, separation of church and state, restraints forbidding Congress, in the words of the First Amendment, to enact any law "respecting the establishment of religion, or prohibiting the free exercise thereof" — these are the sancta of American life, and non-Orthodox Jews, mainly thoroughly acculturated "loyal Americans," have almost instinctively held these principles to be inviolable. In sharpest contrast looms the actuality of coercion and *force majeure* which seems to control so much of Israel's religious life. American Jews perceive the religious scene in Israel through the filter of America's political and religious ideals, and are often appalled at the revelation.

An American woman raised in a Reform congregation attended Shabbat services at the Hebrew Union College in Jerusalem and was angrily annoyed because the language of the prayer book then being used was Hebrew. There wasn't even an English translation on the opposite page. Explaining to her the reason for using Hebrew as the language of prayer in Jerusalem did little to assuage her anger. She pouted and fumed as though her constitutional rights had been trampled.

An American Non-Orthodox View of Israeli Judaism

The disdain felt by non-Orthodox American Jews for Israel's traditional Jews entails more than a rejection of their religious way of life. Almost as vexatious is their strong, even mystical, commitment to Zionism. Not all Israeli traditionalists share the passion for Zion. Some indeed deplore it, believing its outcome in the creation of a political state an attempt to contravene the will of God. But to most religious Israelis, nurtured for centuries in Torah, the reality of a sovereign Jewish state is the fulfillment of God's promise.

American Jews, particularly the non-Orthodox, have derived from a tradition altogether different from the Torah-centered discipline of Orthodoxy. It grew out of the Age of Reason, of the Enlightenment, winning the enthusiastic allegiance of Jews freed from the ghetto, eager to identify with the wider world of the new Emancipation. The return to Zion held little allure. Some of their leaders condemned it out of hand. To most early Reform rabbis and leaders, nurtured by the theological postulates of the Pittsburgh Platform, Jewish nationalism was anathema, and they denounced it with unbridled fervor.

A succession of Hebrew Union College presidents vented their aversion in word and deed. Isaac Mayer Wise, founding President of H.U.C., one of the "moderate" leaders of the Reform movement, described that new Messianic movement over the ocean [as] a "momentary inebriation of morbid minds and a prostitution of Israel's holy cause to a madman's dance of unsound politicians," a creeping metaphor that mixes drunkenness, prostitution, and insanity in an indictment of Zionism which deserves a place in any anthology of invective.[30] In his first three years as Hebrew Union College president, Kaufman Kohler, more radical and militant than Wise, systematically rooted out members of the faculty suspected of Zionist leanings and abolished modern Hebrew from the curriculum. "Zionism," he fulminated, "is un-Jewish, irreligious, and un-American."[31] As late as the 1940's

Morgenstern, who followed Kohler, was comparing "the tenets of Jewish nationalism to totalitarian theory" and lamenting that "the very notion of a Jewish state was sad and tragic."[32]

A holdover of Kohler's compulsive scrutiny for Zionists was the practice of interrogating entering Hebrew Union College students for their views of Zionism. The student would meet with the admissions committee seated at a long table in the Board of Governors' room. The questioner was usually Rabbi David Philipson, the distinguished patriarchal rabbi of Rockdale Avenue Temple in Cincinnati, one of the four members of the first HUC graduating class in 1880, who shared Kohler's views. He would probe the student's sentiments on Zionism.

I was a distressingly jejune candidate for admission, whose knowledge of the political currents in the Jewish world approached the minimal, and I remember how mystified I was by Rabbi Philipson's questions, asked with a disconcertingly genial smile. Fortunately older students had forewarned us to declare ourselves non-committal on the embattled issue.

An Israeli View of American Non-Orthodox Judaism

Some Israelis are puzzled by the American Jews' loud and unrestrained strictures against the beliefs, practices, and life pattern of Israel's traditional Jews. We have noted how Reform and Conservative leaders have unleashed their armory of invective against the "fanatics .... plotting .... [their] madness" against religious pluralism. They have castigated and threatened Israelis for not ordering their life in consonance with their own American pieties such as "freedom of conscience" and "separation of church and state." But Israelis wonder how American Jews can arrogate to themselves the right to preach *musar* (moral rectitude). They may indeed constitute "80-90 percent of Diaspora Jewry .... the backbone of the Jewish community demographically, organizationally, and philanthropically." But to Israelis their Judaism seems a charade of the Judaism that has preserved Jews as Jews through the ages.

Israelis point out that the "80-90 percent" are locked in a struggle for survival as Jews. Describing the image of Reform Jews and their Judaism as pictured by Israelis, Rabbi Moses Cyrus Weiler, widely esteemed Reform rabbi long resident in Jerusalem, has written, "Most Jews of Israel associate Reform Judaism with assimilation and with unauthorized and wanton mutations of Judaism." Julius Weinberg of Cleveland State University, observed twenty years ago, "We are still haunted by the low image of Reform as a Judaism of minimalism and convenience .... " In response to the question, "What is a Reform Jew?" a Confirmation student wrote, "A Reform Jew is someone who doesn't wear a *yarmulke*, who doesn't light candles on Friday night, and who goes to the Temple when he feels like it."[33]

Seventy-two percent of the children of intermarriages are being raised in a non-Jewish religion or with no religion at all. Ninety percent will marry non-Jews. The authors of the Brandeis Report cited as its "most striking" finding the conclusion that "many mixed marriage households are not .... likely to produce a new generation which is connected to Judaism or the Jewish people." Survival and continuity have become the imperative themes of Jewish assemblages whose predominant anxiety now is not so much the minimal as the terminal Jew. Should we, ask Israelis, accept *musar* from such Jews?

Calling itself a Jewish religious movement, American Reform Judaism has nevertheless fewer than 50 percent of its families showing a mezzuzah on their doors, only 20 percent lighting Shabbat candles and chanting kiddush, less than 2 percent keeping kosher, less than 1 percent not driving on Shabbat. Most American Reform Jews ignore the ritual practices of Judaism, for as we have seen, there is nothing in their religion of guidance (<u>not</u> governance) which requires their observance. Conservative Jews are catching up, if many have not already done so, with their Reform neighbors. Secular Israelis rate much higher percentages of observance. *Musar* from non-observant American Jews? As Rabbi Waxman might respond in his own felicitous way, "You've got to be kidding!"

Not long ago a Gallup newsletter reported that the latest poll of church and synagogue attendance showed that while American Protestants and Catholics are in the 40 and 50 percentile, Jews (not including the Orthodox) are in the 11 percentile. The executive vice-president of the C.C.A.R. in describing the "hectic" activity of the typical Reform congregation, observes that "the one dead spot is the sanctuary." And the reason? "The truth is most Reform Jews do not believe that a reality exists behind the word 'God.'"[34]

Reluctant Non-Orthodox Leaders

Some of the notable Reform leaders who were outstanding personalities in the Zionist world, as well as admired figures to a generation of Israelis, apparently made no effort to organize and support a Reform movement in Israel. Three who witnessed and played a role in the nascent struggle for Israel's nationhood were Stephen S. Wise (1874-1949), Judah Leon Magnes (1877-1948, and Abba Hillel Silver (1893-1963). Each was a towering figure who exerted widespread influence throughout the Jewish world. All believed in the integration of Judaism and Zionism. Silver was committed to the "upbuilding of Jewish religious life in America and elsewhere throughout the world, including Israel .... One is no substitute for the other."[35] They were intimately involved in shaping Israel's polity, yet nothing is known of any interest or participation, let alone leadership, connected with the establishment of non-Orthodox Judaism in Israel.

One of the reasons which may account for this apparent indifference was the web of responsibilities and activities in which they were involved, ranging from world issues with their continual crises, to the more humdrum concerns of the congregational rabbinate.[36] Israel's first independent years, the post-Holocaust era, brought responsibilities of an especially onerous and exacting nature. Silver, Wise, and Magnes no doubt felt the necessity for dealing with the more urgent problems of Israel, some relating to the very viability of the State, before becoming enmeshed in the mare's nest of religious pluralism.

There may also have been an understandable reluctance to explore a modus vivendi between the Orthodox and the non-Orthodox because of the seemingly irreconcilable differences between them. Few Israelis, even the secularists, take Reform "seriously." If and when they seek or "need" religion, they go to the "real thing," the Judaism that has come down through the millennia, the Judaism of their parents. A young Israeli from an old Zichron Yaakov family, graduate of the Stanford school of business administration, told me that he saw a place for Reform in Israel but that he "would not attend," "I'm not a religious Jew, but when I go to the synagogue, I go with my father." There is wide agreement that a "new" religion in Israel must "grow" out of Israel, that it cannot be imported but must be indigenous. "Imported" religion simply won't work," as witness Reform's meager constituency after a century in Israel. These are some of the obstacles which may have given pause to charismatic American non-Orthodox rabbis in considering attempts to foster a "new" Judaism in Israel.

Stephen Wise spoke frankly of his reservations on attempts to "reform" the "synagogue of Israel." In a letter written to an Israeli friend in 1969, he wrote:

> I am more deeply interested than you can imagine by what you write of two fields in which American Jews could bring a real contribution to Israel — in American economic democracy, and in the religious life of the country. What I am afraid of is that in trying to bring order into the old-fashioned synagogue, we may achieve something as pallid and unvital as is the American Reform temple. I have, therefore, been inclined to give not the slightest interest or support to the attempt to reform or liberalize the synagogue of Israel. The Yishub must work out its own problem in its own way. I think we have not done well enough in American life to be helpful to the Yishub herein.[37]

More than a century earlier than Stephen Wise's description of Reform's anemia (1949), Isaac Mayer Wise had expressed his scorn for the kind of Jewish education imparted in the "new congregations arising everywhere in the United States." He referred to it as "a phantom affair called a Sunday School, [where] religious instruction for children is given each Sabbath or Sunday by good-hearted young women. What fruits these few hours can bring forth hardly necessitates further description." He concludes with a hopeful prediction. "But don't shudder for Judaism in our America! This snake [of inadequate Jewish education] too will have its head crushed.[38] Dr. Wise may have predicted too optimistic a prognosis for the "inadequate education" of early Reform. Objective observers still regard the Jewish education offered by the great majority of Reform religious schools as a "phantom affair." The "snake" has by no means had its head crushed. Rabbi Maurice Eisendrath, president of the U.A.H.C. a half-century ago, called religious education in the congregations a "pittance and a sham."[39]

Similar doubts about the pallor of Reform may have dissuaded Judah Leon Magnes from coming forward to organize or urge enlistment in a Reform movement. Rabbi of the Reform "Cathedral" synagogue on Fifth Avenue (1906-10), Magnes was gradually drawn to the traditional, Yiddishist Zionist East Side Jews, becoming leader of the newly formed New York Kehilla in 1908, and in 1925 founding president of Hebrew University in Jerusalem. Magnes was hardly the man to pioneer in behalf of Reform. After all, he had by his own confession "abandoned Temple Emanu-El because he judged Reform Judaism to be 'empty'"[40]

Of all the Reform leaders who might have succeeded in widening the appeal and extending the outreach of the Reform movement in Israel, perhaps none would have been so effective as Rabbi Abba Hillel Silver. With his remarkable oratorical gifts and exceptional personal magnetism, he had the power to influence masses of people. For decades throngs of admirers packed his huge Cleveland synagogue every week at religious services. He was a Pied Piper who inspired a generation of Cleveland boys to enter the rabbinate in emulation of their rabbi. For much of his life and at his death he was hailed as "Cleveland's first citizen." In Israel after World War II, he stood as a giant among world Jewish leaders. He had led the successful fight at Lake Success for Israel's sovereign recognition by the United Nations. When he arrived in Israel not long after the triumph at Lake Success, a massive throng numbering tens of thousands filled the streets of Tel Aviv to welcome him on what was nothing less than a national holiday. He took on a prophetic dimension. The people identified with him. Many Israeli cities and towns could scarcely wait to name streets after him. We can only speculate on what Reform in Israel might have become had this Reform rabbi led a campaign for recognition and expansion of the Reform movement.

But Silver did not become a Pied Piper for Reform. Returning to his community in Cleveland, he gave himself to his congregation and to the scholar's vocation, which he always cherished. To those who might wonder why no political role in the new state was proffered to this leader of immense talent and influence, the answer may lie in the formidable political adversaries who emerged in the no-holds-barred infighting and eye-gouging which marked life in the wings of Israel's political arena. It was widely believed that Ben Gurion was responsible for banishing Silver from Israel's political life.[41] Silver, however, had no intention of severing his ties with Israel. He commissioned an Israeli architect to design a home to be built on a parcel of land he owned in Jerusalem. Unfortunately, a few days after the first draft of the plans reached Cleveland, he died.[42]

Beyond the political obstacles, however, there probably remained his dissatisfaction with Reform Judaism in America. Silver was always forthright in his evaluation of men and events. Speaking and writing without fear or favor, he could confront the reality of Judaism in America without hedging. Some of his choice rebukes were reserved for the hollow, uncommitted religious charade of Reform:

> Too many of our people want an easy-going religion, one which does not interfere with their leisure, their sleep, or their television; which calls for no study and no observance; which does not challenge or disturb them; a religion without any spiritual travail; without any stab of thought or conscience; without any sacrifices; the religion of a self-pampering people. No religion has ever survived that kind of an emotional intellectual vacuum, Judaism least of all.

With equal candor he poured scorn on the spokesmen and custodians for Reform, whom he knew well, his colleagues in America: "Our Rabbinate is less informed than the average Jewish laymen .... They do not study. They do not read. They are just pompous loud speakers for stale platitudes."[43] In the final analysis Silver's doubts and reservations, shared by Wise and Magnes, may have been the safety net which protected them from being engulfed by the maelstrom of religious conflict awaiting the emissaries of an imported religion.

The wonder is that men like Abba Hillel Silver, James Heller, Felix Levy, Barnett Brickner, and Nelson Glueck, could be ordained as rabbis at the anti-Zionist Hebrew Union College of their day, with their passionate commitment to Zionism unflagging. They were joined in the 30's by some of the early graduates of the Jewish Institute of Religion — Philip Bernstein, Morton Berman, and Jacob Rudin — who, inspired by their nonpareil teacher, Stephen S. Wise, became ardent champions of the Jewish national dream. No more stirring addresses were ever heard at C.C.A.R. conventions than those delivered in the 40's and 50's by these tribunes of Zionism. We sat transfixed while the sweeping eloquence of Zion's paladins roused our fervor for Israel reborn. After the horror of war and Holocaust, we wanted to give ourselves to the people miraculously rescued, revived, redeemed. The surge of spiritual energy, optimism, and hope which coursed through the Conference made the mid-twentieth-century conventions events to treasure.

When the Hebrew Union College and the Jewish Institute of Religion merged in 1950 and Nelson Glueck became its president, it could be said that the zenith of Zionist ascendancy in the American Jewish world had been reached. For the majority of Jews, the ideals and goals of Zionism became their "religion". This was symbolically confirmed when in 1963, Glueck established a branch of HUC-JIR in Jerusalem. Here students would henceforth spend their first year of rabbinic training. Here would the bond with Israel, the Jewish past, the Jewish people, the Jewish land, be indissolubly sealed. It was anticipated that here Israel and Zion would find some of their staunchest non-Orthodox champions.

Zionist Euphoria Wanes

All that has changed. The Zionist euphoria of mid-century did not deflate suddenly. But there were disquieting echoes of dissent from the initial ecstasies of Israel's rebirth. Soon after the end of World War II the American Council for Judaism, which challenged the postulates of Zionism in a throwback to classical Reform and the Pittsburgh Platform, stirred to life in congregations founded in the nineteenth-century era of Isaac Mayer Wise.

I was the rabbi of such a congregation. No issue that I recall roused the members to such a pitch of anger as Zionism. I learned this after returning to the congregation following three years as a Marine Corps Chaplain in the Pacific. I had invited a well-known New York Rabbi, a prominent Zionist, to speak on the Zionist controversy. The Temple was packed. Aware of the classical Reform tradition of the congregation, he spoke with measured restraint. In the question period, one could feel the tension rising. After a member shouted a question, a burly town-bully type came forward and began pounding the podium with his fist. The spirit of violence was in the air. If the police, whose presence is now *de rigueur* at synagogue services, had been there, we would have called them in. Some men came forward, protectively surrounded the rabbi, and escorted him from the hall. It will come as no surprise to anyone familiar with the dynamics of contemporary congregation-rabbi relationships that for weeks after that Sabbath service, I, recently returned hero from Pacific combat, was combing brickbats out of my hair.

What disturbed American Jews about Zionism was primarily fear of the charge of divided loyalty. They were worried lest other Americans accuse them of a weakened loyalty to America because of the intrusion of a Zionist allegiance. There was the pervasive anxiety among Jews of antisemitism and the predictable readiness to blame the Jew for every fancied malfeasance. Many of the congregants were third- and fourth-generation descendants of German Jews who had come to America seeking economic opportunity and political freedom. They had prospered, given themselves to the good works of the community, contributed to its economic, intellectual and philanthropic well-being, yet they could not banish the specter of bias. They lived on approval, their psyche an amalgam of ambiguity, hesitancy, and fear. The shades of antisemitism die hard. The Zionist essayist, Ahad Ha'am, called this *ahdut b'toh herut*, "slavery in the midst of freedom." To Zionists this meant living on different levels of fear and trembling. Or as the old saw had it, "You can take the Jew out of *galut* (exile), but you can't take *galut* out of the Jew."

The attitude of the non-Orthodox American Jew toward Israel was typified by a prominent member of the HUC-JIR Board of Governors. In 1970 Nelson Glueck, the president, had just won Board approval for entering students to spend their preparatory year at the Jerusalem School of the HUC-JIR. Glueck was a charismatic, visionary planner and administrator. His handsome likeness on the cover of *Time* magazine wearing a keffiyeh evoked romantic images of Galahad and T.E. Lawrence of Arabia. No one disputed his leadership, and he routinely enjoyed the full support of his board. Yet this one layman, perhaps the most prestigious and powerful of all Board members, rose to challenge the president on the question of Zionism. In a letter which he asked Glueck to read to the Board, he wrote:

> My objection to the action adopted by the Board of Governors that the recommendation made by you for all rabbinical students to spend their freshman year in Israel is likely to create for us a much more Israeli-oriented rabbinate than we now have .... Even at the present time, without the year in Israel, the rabbinate, it seems to me, is too Israel-oriented. The year in Israel will undoubtedly increase this emphasis.

Then after some curriculum recommendations designed to make the preparatory year and rabbinical students more "American oriented," this summary caution: "You should be sure that the rabbis that we create are American-oriented rather than too strongly Israel-oriented."

In his evaluation of the curriculum, the Board member records his judgment on the value of Hebrew for Reform rabbis: "May I say that in my many experiences with different rabbis in the different temples to which I have belonged I have not found that their lack of knowledge of Hebrew or their ability to speak it faulted them and the rabbinate. There are many other causes which seem to create criticism, but not that."

In his reply Glueck tried to calm the Board member's perturbation on the danger of excessive Israel-orientation. "I really don't think it will make very much difference in the Israel-orientation of our Reform Rabbinate whether we have the year in Israel or not. Almost without exception, the candidates we accept .... are already Israel-oriented."

That may have been true of incoming students of the 70's. It may have been less true of subsequent classes. The decades which followed the 70's disclosed a gradual but distinct distancing from Israel-orientation by both laymen and rabbis among Reform Jews.

Evidence of this was the formation in the 70's of an organization designed "to assert the equality of the Diaspora with Israel and to call attention to the imbalance at present." *Bereira* ("alternative") was its name and the alternative was a policy decidedly at odds with historic Zionism. It questioned the centrality of Israel in Jewish life, assumed that the interests of the Jewish people and those of Israel might diverge, asked that a more balanced proportion of Jewish resources be divided between Israel and the Diaspora. But what created especial dismay among many Jews was not only the boldness of Bereira's challenge to the policies and actions of the Israeli government, but also the makeup of its membership, since these, it was believed, included rabbis and laymen of assured Zionist sympathy. As it was, among the one hundred members of the Bereira advisory committee were 77 rabbis, some of them prominent in the Reform, Conservative, and Reconstructionist movements.[44]

As the 70's merged into the 80's and 90's, the American Jew felt himself caught in a series of acute dilemmas. Proud witness to the miraculous re-establishment of a sovereign Israel, he still felt that his primary national identity was American. Able after all the centuries of denial to live unfettered as a Jew, he was increasingly seduced by the secular, hedonist world which left little time or opportunity for the practice of Judaism. He was becoming ineluctably the product of the surrounding pagan culture. Often in resentment for his guilt at failing to assume his role as one of the "chosen," he turned in anger upon the Jew, Judaism, and Israel. Why does the past impose demands on me? By what right does Israel intrude on my comfortable life with its daily embarrassments in the media? In a monthly newsletter to colleagues written in 1990, the president of the CCAR reported that in recent months several colleagues had "privately complained what years ago would have been unthinkable: Maybe the American Council for Judaism was right after all."[45]

When Rabbi Eric H. Yoffie assumed the presidency of the Union of American Hebrew Congregations in 1996, thereby becoming prime leader of the largest lay non-Orthodox denomination in the Diaspora (860 congregations, 1.5 million members), he quickly made it clear that the issue of religious pluralism in Israel was high, if not pre-eminent, on his agenda of concerns. In a feisty address, he laid about him with gusto, inveighing principally against Israel's *Haredi* community who are "hysterically afraid of the tiny Reform Movement," but not excepting from his criticism Jews everywhere for their increasing "secularization and desertion from Torah-true Judaism." Among these backsliders he singled out his own Reform Jews for "limitations of vision and leadership of imagination and energy, in the failure to penetrate the grass roots and gain adherents in Israel." To counter the crisis facing Jewish life in Israel and the Diaspora, Yoffie promised to launch a campaign for creating a "new Israeli Judaism" which would replace religious divisions with a meaningful liberal faith." Within a year he pledged to present "a new vision and a new plan .... to put an end to politicized, monopolistic religion in Israel."[46]

Whatever else might be said of Yoffie's declaration of faith, there is no shadow of an olive branch in or near it. Flinging down the gauntlet, he made his position vehemently clear. We have made a decision to go our own way, he is telling us, leading to .... "a new Israeli Judaism."

Some might say that his challenge to the Orthodox is not so much a declaration of faith as a declaration of war. Rabbi Yoffie appears as a militant who hangs tough. No word of conciliation, accommodation, compromise, reasoning or working together. His sentiments breathe a mood of defeatism at the possibility of a peaceful resolution of differences. He may have good reason for so feeling, recalling that no differences seem more intractable in Israel than religious differences. Almost wistfully he comments on the ease with which Prime Minister Netanyahu finds time to visit the graves of dead rabbis from Brooklyn in contrast to his adamant refusal to meet with Reform or Conservative representatives. He seems to be resigned to the conclusion that the Orthodox and non-Orthodox inhabit different worlds and that no conciliator's approach will cause the twain to meet, much less sit down together. (In due course Netanyahu did meet with non-Orthodox representatives.)

The principal problem confronting leaders of non-Orthodoxy, no matter how militant, is whether a tough, intransigent posture will avail for religious pluralism, or specifically for non-Orthodox Judaism and its devotees. The evidence furnished by knowing observers in Israel does not foster much hope. They agree in declaring that denunciations of the religious scene and its spokespersons in Israel are counterproductive.

It is increasingly conceded that in the Diaspora enthusiasm for the dream of a Jewish national home and a reborn Jewish people is abating. The fires kindled by hope for Zion reborn, for an autonomous people flourishing in freedom and dignity, are banked, and there is the chill of disappointment in the air. Few echoes of the rallying cries that once stirred the blood of *chalutzim* or kindled the visions of *olim* resonate in the Diaspora — *ahavat tsion* ("love of Zion"), *kedushat hahayim* ("sanctification of life"), *kibbutz g'luyot* ("ingathering of the exiles") — seldom are they heard today.

Non-Orthodox American Jews, having retreated from their ardent support of Israel in the post-World War II decades, threaten to become snarled in a *Religionskampf* with Israeli Orthodoxy on the question of religious pluralism. Reform leaders have thrown down the gauntlet with the promise of organizing a "new Judaism" which will bring equality to all religious streams.

There are, however, non-Orthodox voices who caution, This is not the way. If non-Orthodoxy is to grow in Israel with a larger constituency and a greater stability, it must win the understanding and support of Israelis and become constructively integrated into the life of the nation. Non-Orthodoxy will not long survive in a battleground of vendettas and pyrrhic victories. It must become normalized as part of the Israel national reality. Not in confrontation and separatism, which are the outcome of the litigious strategies vociferously pursued by the Israel Religious Action Center, but involvement in institutions and organizations with large national constituencies aiming to address the problems of Israeli and Jewish life — that is the way. It is a way far more likely to succeed than the present alienating posture.

It is equally urged that the welfare of non-Orthodoxy in the Diaspora, with a salutary reduction of indifference, bitterness, and anger, would be promoted if programs of education looking to an appreciation of Israel and Zionism were sponsored by synagogues. Synagogues and their rabbis should share the energy and resources expended on their present programs of outreach with programs centered on particularistic Jewish causes of inreach to Jews and Israelis.

Some even stress that an important element in any program for Jewish renewal should be aliya — aliya as a life option. An aliya of significant numbers from America might yet achieve the changes which would make the dreams of pioneers a reality and Israel a land of peace.

Notes

1. Daniel J. Elazar, "U.S. Jewry in the 1990's," in *Jerusalem Post*, January 29, 1991
2. Greer Fay Cashman, "Christians Set an Example," in *Jerusalem Post*, October 9, 1992
3. Irving Howe, *World of Our Fathers* (1976: Harcourt Brace Jovanovich, New York), p. 623
4. Irving Kristol, "Foreign Policy and the American Jewish Community," in *Anti-Defamation League Bulletin*, September 1980, p. 1
5. Geoffrey Wigoder, "North and South," in *Jerusalem Post*, June 5, 1990, p. 7
6. Sue Fishkoff, "North American Jewish Federations Decide to Focus on Tradition," in *Jerusalem Post*, November 15, 1992, p. 10
7. Ruth R. Wisse, "Israel Watch: The Might and the Right," in *Commentary*, September 1992, p. 48
8. Albert Vorspan, "Soul-Searching," in *New York Times Magazine*, May 8, 1988, pp. 40-55
9. Nathaniel Hawthorne, *Lady Eleanore's Mantle* (Franklin Center, Penn.: The Franklin Library, 1978), pp. 107-224
10. Barry Shrage, "Who Shall Remain Jewish and Who Not ....," in *Sh'ma*, September 18, 1992, p. 129
11. Leon Edel, ed., *Edmund Wilson: The Thirties* (New York: Farrar, Straus, and Giroux, 1980), p. 378
12. Irving Howe, *ibid*.
13. Frank, "Those U.S. Zionists Who Fear Aliyah," in *Jewish Post and Opinion*, December 22, 1973
14. Chaim I. Waxman and Michael Appel, *To Israel and Back: American Aliyah and Return Migration* (New York: American Jewish Committee Institute on American Jewish-Israeli Relations, 1986). This study cites immigration figures for the years 1948-1985, during which 69,757 olim came from the United States. During the years 1985-1992, approximately 2,500 came annually from the United States and Canada, according to the Association of Americans and Canadians in Israel (AACI).

15. Marc Saperstein, "Israel and the Reform Rabbinate," in *Tanu Rabbenu: Our Rabbis Taught*, ed. Joseph Glaser (New York: CCAR, 1990)

16. *Central Conference of American Rabbis Yearbook* (New York: CCAR, 1992).

17. Sue Fishkoff, "U.S. Orthodox, Conservatives Rap Reform Proselytization Plan," in *Jerusalem Post*, October 16, 1993

18. Hillel Halkin, "Israel-Diaspora Relations," in Address before Assembly of Jewish Agency, Jerusalem, July 1987

19. Shlomo Avineri, "A Modest Proposal," in *Jerusalem Post*, November 26, 1987

20. The Central Conference of American Rabbis meeting in Jerusalem for their annual convention in 1995 invited Feisal Husseini, Palestinian leader, to address the convention. For years on a wall at Yad V'Shem, a blown-up picture of Husseini's granduncle, the Mufti Haj Amin el-Husseini, showed him seated next to Hitler. After Oslo the government had it removed. Feisal Husseini himself had long consorted with terrorists who murdered Jews. The CCAR was not deterred from inviting him.

21. Since Israel's founding in 1948, Israelis have shown an eagerness to establish peaceful relations with neighboring states. Between *mea culpa* confessions and hopeful calls for conciliation and friendship, Israelis have appealed to Arabs to bind up the wounds of war and address the tasks of peace. Over the decades the only Arab response has been the response of silence. The poet Aharon Megged has asked, "How many Egyptians have come to Israel during all these years of peace, during all these times that our mouths have dribbled hope and trust and love?" Israelis have rushed to Cairo, Alexandria, Jaresh, Amman, "To Gaza to kiss Arafat's stubbled cheek .... Are the [Arabs] coming to Tel Aviv and Haifa to whisper sweet nothings in your ear? .... Put your ear to the door! Listen carefully! Do you hear any friendly sounds .... whisperings .... ?"

22. In an in-depth study on the stationing of U.S. forces on the Golan Heights as part of a peace agreement between Syria and Israel released in October, 1994, the Center for Security Policy in Washington, D.C. concluded that, "There is no mission or rationale for a U.S. peacekeeping force on the Golan that would justify the resulting costs and risks. Both to the U.S. and to Israel the costs would far outweigh the benefits." ("U.S. Troops on the Golan? A Special Report," in *Commentary*, December 1994, pp. 73-88)

23. American Jewish Committee. A background Memorandum. "Some of Our Best Friends ...." The Claim of Arab Tolerance. December 1975, p. 3. There are historians who see in the spreading terrorism and continuous anti-Western invective of contemporary Islam the latest chapter in the "deepening conflict between an aggressive Islam and a defensive Western civilization." Bernard Lewis, the eminent authority on Islam now teaching at Princeton, has written: "The struggle between Islam and the West has now lasted 14 centuries. It has consisted of a long series of attacks and counterattacks, jihads and crusades, conquests and reconquests. Today much of the Muslim world is again seized by an intense and violent resentment of the West. Suddenly, America had become the archenemy, the incarnation of evil, the diabolic opponent of all that is good, and specifically, for Muslims of Islam." Elaine

Sciolino, "The Red Menace Is Gone. But Here's Islam," in *New York Times Weekly Review*. January 21, 1996, p. 1

24. Conor Cruise O'Brien, "There's Only One Islam," in *Jerusalem Post*, Jan. 16, 1995, p. 6
25. Amos Oz, "To Our Friends, the Reform and Conservative," in *Davar*, Nov. 17, 1988
26. Hillel Halkin, "Israel-Diaspora Relations," Address before assembly of Jewish Agency, Jerusalem, July 1987
27. Abba Eban, "Two Cardinal Points," Special Interest Report, American Council for Judaism, July-August 1976
28. Matti Golan, *With Friends Like You – What Israelis Really Think about American Jews* (New York: Free Press, 1992)
29. Edgar E. Siskin, "Wars of the Jews," in *Jerusalem Post*, July 23, 1986, p. 10
30. CCAR Year Book, 1897-98, p. xii
31. Herbert Parzen, "The Purge of the Dissidents: Hebrew Union College and Zionism, 1903-1907," in *Jewish Social Studies*, Vol. 37, Nos. 3-4, Summer-Fall, 1975, pp. 291-322
32. Michael A. Meyer, "A Centennial History," in Samuel E. Karff, ed. *Hebrew Union College-Jewish Institute of Religion at One Hundred Years* (Cincinnati: Hebrew Union College Press, 1996) pp. 59, 67. *Ibid.*, pp. 132-33. Meyer notes that Morgenstern's original draft referred to Zionism as being "practically identical with Nazist and Fascist theory."
33. Moses Cyrus Weiler, "The Future of Progressive Judaism in Israel, in *CCAR Journal*, June 1972, pp. 13-23
34. Paul Menitoff, in *CCAR Newsletter*, Vol. 44, No. 3, p. 2.
35. Leon Feuer, "Abba Hillel Silver," in *Encyclopedia Judaica* (1971, Jerusalem, vol.14, 1543-44)
36. Leon Feuer, who was Silver's assistant at The Temple in Cleveland for fourteen years told me that Silver never missed teaching his Confirmation Class on Wednesday afternoons. After attending meetings in New York or Washington, he would board a plane which would bring him to Cleveland in time to meet with his Confirmation students, proof-read the Temple Bulletin, and attend to sundry congregational tasks.
37. Voss, ed. Stephen S. Wise, "Servant of the People," *Selected Letters*
38. Isaac Mayer Wise, (A private communication from Rabbi Dr. Wise) in *Allgemeine Zeitung des Judenthums* X1:51, Leipzig, December 13, 1847
39. Edgar E. Siskin, "A Look at Jewish Education", in *Jewish Sentinel*, Sept. 4, 1975, p. 9
40. Irving Howe, *ibid*. p. 197
41. Alexander Dushkin, the noted Hebrew educator living in Jerusalem, once told me that Ben Gurion was determined to deny any political role to Silver in Israel.
42. Personal correspondence with the late Rabbi Daniel Jeremy Silver, January 25, 1978
43. Marc Lee Raphael, *Abba Hillel Silver: A Profile in American Judaism* (New York, 1989)
44. Rabbis on Bereira Committee," in *Jewish Post*, August 9, 1974

45. Samuel E. Karff, Message from the President, November 1990, p. 1
46. Tom Tugend, "Reform Leader envisions 'new Israeli Judaism,'" in *Jerusalem Post*, December 15, 1996, p. 12

EPILOGUE

A Jewish historian writing in 1930 summed up his fears about the future of the Jewish people.

> Around us, we witness assimilation going on in a depressing degree. The losses to Judaism by intermarriage, by ignorance, by indifference, by actual conversion, are reaching proportions, which are thoroughly intimidating; if we were to go by the actual conditions and indications of the present time, there would seem to be very good ground for believing that in America and Western Europe .... Judaism and the Jews will have disappeared entirely within a century or two at the utmost.[1]

At the time, Cecil Roth's gloomy picture of the Jewish future was dismissed as the morbid fantasy of a preternatural pessimist. But now only two generations — not centuries — later a disquieting worry of Jewish leaders the world over is the prospect for Jewish continuity in the modern world. Rabbi Irving Greenberg speaks for them when he warns that "Diaspora Jewry faces a crisis of survival. Assimilation and intermarriage are swallowing it whole." Rabbi Adin Steinsaltz has termed this survival crisis a "self-inflicted holocaust," and goes on to compare the Jewish people today with the citizen of ancient Rome, who, intent on committing suicide, would climb into a warm bath, slit his veins, and quietly and peacefully bleed to death.[2]

The pessimism of Greenberg and Steinsaltz is echoed by an increasing number of perceptive observers of the American Jewish world. Some recommend measures which in their view will stay the advance of the "self-inflicted holocaust." These prescriptions have been surveyed in previous chapters. Thus there are Jewish leaders who point to Israel as the most effective answer to the malaise of identity and survival. Spending time in Israel will, they believe, provide the affirmative Jewish experiences which will serve to implant a lasting love and loyalty for Jewish life and the Jewish people. Accordingly, it is being urged that funds be set aside for enabling high school youngsters and their families to come to Israel for the "Israel Experience," which will enable them to weather the threats of intermarriage and assimilation. In addition, a communal program for intensified Jewish education is unvaryingly put forward as a remedy for the ailing Jewish condition, which now finds most Jewish children between the ages of seven and seventeen receiving no Jewish education whatsoever. The spiritual message of Judaism and the synagogue is also mentioned as a vehicle for strengthening the will of American Jews to survive.

But each of these answers is marred by unsettling flaws. While to some leaders Israel may be the linchpin of Jewish survival, to others is has become an eroded link of Jewish solidarity. Israel's standing with American Jews is far different now from that of a generation ago when sociologists called Israel and Zionism the religion of the American Jew. For the Jews of that generation Israel was pivotal to their lives as Jews. This is no longer true for their children.[3] Communities report that the "free airfares and highly subsidized trips to Israel cannot be given away." A Jewish Agency executive reported the reason: "It's a profound feeling within the Jewish family of 'I don't care. I don't need to be in Israel.'"[4] Expanded Jewish education programs are enthusiastically endorsed at national conventions but sputter like a damp squib when local communities consider the cost. More intensive programs of Jewish education, with their essential all-day schools and decent salaries for teachers, are expensive, and the American Jew may be jittery about paying the price.

There are also troubling reports that the kind of Jewish education which will inspire a devotion to Jewish particularity and survival is more often *caught* than *taught*, caught in homes and communities imbued with the values of Jewish pride and loyalty and with the disciplines of religious belief and practice.[5] As for the saving capacity of Judaism and the synagogue, the 1990 National Population Study reported that less than five percent of America's non-affiliated Jews acknowledge that "they belong to a religious group." Defining their Jewishness as ethnic or cultural, many when asked to name their religion replied, "None." With congregations apathetic, sanctuaries vacant, Jewish education programs a charade, and "Outreach" programs impotent in damming the flood tide of assimilation, the synagogue would appear a weak rampart for sustaining survival.

With the pace of assimilation accelerating, many Jews have given up the struggle for survival. But it is not easy for Jews, even the most alienated, to abdicate their historic and religious birthright, to see their children and grandchildren yield theirs as they cut the cord of Jewish continuity. Leslie Fiedler, the critic, spoke for many minimal Jews when, in reflecting upon his and his children's abandonment of Judaism, he wrote, "In any case, there is no one to say Kaddish for me when I die. I am, in short, not as I have long known, a minimal Jew — my Judaism nearly nonexistent — but as I have only recently become aware, a terminal one as well, the last of a 4000-year line." [6]

Since the appearance during the past decade of Jewish population studies, scholars have drawn conclusions on the prospects for Jewish survival which in large part agree with the demographer's findings. The doyen of Israeli sociologists, Professor Shmuel N. Eisenstadt of Hebrew University, has ventured a summary of the destiny of the American Jewish community.[7] Having for years taught at leading American universities, Eisenstadt is intimately familiar with the American Jewish scene. He believes that as a result of the shrinking number of American Jews, in addition to the forces of secularism, modernism, and assimilation, "there will be a slow shedding of many components of Jewish identity .... and the possibility of gradual, painless assimilation." Three segments of Jews will emerge from this process: the Orthodox, moving toward an increasingly exclusive sectarianism, while abandoning the universalism of the Jewish heritage; a small hard core of non-Orthodox, "who would seek to maintain a strong Jewish identity while continuing to participate in the general society;" and the "great majority, who after a few generations would drift into a painless assimilation."[8]

A study of Jewish religious denominations published in 1993 by Uri Rabhun supports Professor Eisenstadt's analysis.[9] Believing that denominational affiliation is a primary datum for determining the attitude of American Jews toward their Jewishness, Rabhun goes on to demonstrate that a conspectus of current trends in the principal denominations confirms their steady advance toward "secularization and assimilation in the surrounding general society." The largest of the American Jewish denominations now is Reform Judaism. Numerically Orthodoxy and Conservatism have declined in the last twenty years, a trend which promises to continue as Reform affiliation increases. Concurrently there has been an "enormous rise" in the percentage of non-denominational Jews.

The primary cause for the abandonment by Jews of their denominations, according to Rabbun, is intermarriage. There is a progressive "weakening" of identity in a continuum going from Orthodoxy to Conservatism to Reform to non-denominationalism, which is interpreted as the "final stage preceding assimilation."[10] The enormous rise of the non-denominationals is called the "most alarming finding" of the study. Nor is there balm for Jewish survivalists in the expected Jewish immigration to the United States "in great numbers," especially from the former Soviet Union, since such immigrants will "probably prefer not to identify themselves at all, or consider themselves as Reform Jews."[11]

Seventy years ago, Professor Robert E. Park, a leading figure among the sociologists of ethnicity at the University of Chicago, predicted the gradual assimilation of the American Jew. Writing in 1985, Nathan Glazer, Harvard sociologist known for his temperate views on the history and nature of the American Jewish community, echoed Park's forecast with reference to his own family:

> My generation looks quite different from that of my parents, as the generation of my children looks quite different from mine, and the generation of their children will be different still .... More of them will be the products of intermarriage. Less and less of the life of American Jews is derived from Jewish history, experience, culture, and religion. More and more of it is derived from the realities of American culture, American politics, and the general American religion .... Jews will survive, yes, and perhaps even continue to identify themselves as Jews, but that little by way of custom, belief or loyalty will be assured as a result of their identity as Jews. Sociologists who have persistently feared for the American Jewish future .... have been right to be fearful.[12]

In their *Jews and the New American Scene*,[13] Lipset and Raab maintain that for the large majority of Jews, "group identity and cohesiveness are severely eroding." Because Jews have zealously adopted the "American [cultural] creed," there has developed a dwindling of commitment to Jewish identity and loyalty. They foresee in two generations a reduction of the American Jewish community resulting in the loss of "at least half of the present population."

Jews have been chided for living too much in the distant past, for too literal a commitment to Moses' final exhortation to the people, "Remember the days of old, consider the years of many generations" (*Deuteronomy 32:7*). But in the closing years of this century, the time perspective of many Jews has shifted from the past to the future. Unlettered in Jewish history, alienated from the synagogue, uninterested in the institutions of Jewish corporate life, but still irked by Jewish angst and confused by questions of identity, one of the Jew's furtive anxieties has become, What does the future hold for me as a Jew? Do the faith, heritage, culture, and collective integrity of the Jew stand a chance in the modern world? Will we survive as Jews? A central question of the Diaspora Jew is no longer, "Who is a Jew?" but "Who will remain a Jew?"

To these questions there are no absolute answers. Prediction under any circumstances is precarious, and in times of swift, sudden, calamitous change, an exercise indulged by astrologers, fantasists, and fools. Anthropologists avoid prediction in the realm of social phenomena, although anthropology does hold that trends can be broadly plotted and the "social weather" forecast with some accuracy. But as

Kroeber cautions, it is "evidently unsafe to predict too sweepingly about what any culture, or aspect of culture, can or cannot do."[14]

Of more than passing interest is the example which Kroeber cites to illustrate the difficulty of venturing predictions in the cultural world. That example is the revival of Hebrew as a spoken tongue. With the rise of Zionism and the rebirth of the State of Israel, Hebrew was reborn as a language of daily use, becoming the vernacular of the people of Israel. There is no other instance in all history where a language considered dead for two thousand years was resuscitated against all conceivable odds as the living speech of a people.

After the destruction of the Temple by the Romans in 70 C.E., and the subsequent exile and dispersion of the Jews, Hebrew continued in use as a channel of communication between scholars dealing mainly with questions of Halacha, and as the language for books written by learned rabbis on sacred subjects. It was not a vernacular; it was *l'shon hakodesh*, the "holy tongue." Through the unflagging labor of a handful of pioneering Hebraists in the latter decades of the nineteenth and early decades of the twentieth century, Hebrew was forged into an everyday tongue for ordinary Jews. Prime mover and driving force of this prodigious achievement was Eliezer ben Yehudah (1858-1922), described by Shalom Spiegel as an "unshakable fanatic [with a] holy monomania [for the] ruthless tyranny of an idea." [15]

Other attempts to revive a language, notably Gaelic in Eire, Welsh in Wales, and Landsmaal in Norway, have failed despite the prolonged efforts of ardent nationalists to make them come to life among the people. In Israel today every Israeli speaks the language which is kin to the language of the Hebrew Bible. This renaissance of the storied tongue deemed sacred was a source of intense pride to the pioneers of Jewish nationalism, as it is to latter-day Zionists. It drew an exultant response from Isaac Bashevis Singer. "The Jewish people have been in exile for 2,000 years; they have lived in hundreds of countries, spoken hundreds of languages, and still have kept their old language, Hebrew." The Zionist leader, Rabbi Abba Hillel Silver, once dubbed the Jews the *hapax legomenon* among the nations, using the Greek term for a word or phrase occurring only once in a literary genre.[16] The singular cultural phenomenon of Hebrew reborn may have helped to convince him as well as others, including, perhaps, Kroeber, of the Jews' uniqueness.

Like the social scientists, historians have similarly decried their ability or warrant to foretell the future. The past is no dependable guide. Barbara Tuchman called history a "great joker likely to take an unexpected turn for which no one has planned. Its lessons cannot tell us what will happen next."[17] Recent events of momentous impact on world order have illustrated history's role as bumbling clairvoyant. No historian predicted the quick collapse of the Soviet Union and the inpouring of its Jews to Israel. No chronicler of the past previsioned the sudden toppling of the Berlin Wall. No diplomatic prestidigitator suggested that meetings between Israel and the Arabs might lead to redrawing the map of a shrunken Israel. No one foretold the possible meltdown of Diaspora Jewry or the worldwide speculation on Jewish survival.[18] The final decades of the twentieth century have brought catastrophic upheaval for the world at large and menacing existential dangers to the Jewish world, little of it foreseen. Who would now venture to foretell the future?

We are admonished by theologians, social scientists and historians not to see through a glass, darkly. No signs and portents can portray an unequivocally certain future. Jews have never made preparations for the future, for crisis. They did not anticipate the Holocaust, nor imagine, save in wildest fancy, the establishment of a sovereign Jewish state. Surveying the sweeping saga of the Jewish past, we note its unpredictability. We conclude with Glazer, "How unfinished the story is, how unclear it is what may yet happen."[19]

Notes

1. Cecil Roth, *Personalities and Events in Jewish History* (Philadelphia: Jewish Publication Society, 1953), p. 12
2. Adin Steinsaltz, "The Time is Short and the Work is Great." (Address delivered in Jerusalem, September 1933, the Aleph Club.)
3. There has been a marked decline of interest by youngsters in participating in the "Israel Experience."
4. Howard Weisband, "Can't Give a Ticket to Israel Away," in *Jerusalem Report*. July 27, 1995, p. 54
5. Geoffrey E. Block, *The Jewish Schooling of American Jews: A Study of Non-Cognitive Educational Effects*. (Harvard University, Ed. D. dissertation, 1976). A study of intermarriage by Professor Gary Tobin of Brandeis University revealed that there is "virtually no relationship between increased Jewish education and decreased intermarriage, except with unusually high levels of Jewish learning." (J.J. Goldberg, "America's Vanishing Jews," in *Jerusalem Report*, November 5, 1992, p.32.) Most of the students who complete Jewish elementary and secondary all-day schooling go off to college where the campus is a seedbed of multiculturalism, universalism, and intermarriage.
6. Kaddish (lit. "sanctification") is the mourner's prayer recited in the synagogue by members of the immediate family for eleven months following a death and thereafter on the anniversary of the death. Saying kaddish was a cherished obligation which fathers expected their sons to fulfill. A father would sometimes affectionately refer to a young son as "My kaddishel — my little kaddish sayer."

7. Shmuel N. Eisenstadt, "The American Jewish Experience and American Pluralism — A Comparative Perspective," in Seymour Martin Lipset, ed., *American Pluralism and the Jewish Community* (New Brunswick, N.J.: Transaction, 1990), pp. 43-52

8. The continuing contraction of the Jewish population is a worldwide Diaspora phenomenon. Comparative figures are revealing. In 1994 there were seventeen million more Germans than in the 1940's, nineteen million more Russians, and twenty million more Japanese. While eighteen million Jews existed in the 1930's, one-third of whom perished during World War II, it is estimated that today, there are fourteen million. In the early 30's Jews constituted one per cent of the world's population; now they comprise one-third of one percent.

9. Uzi Rabhun, "Trends in the Size of American Jewish Denominations: A Renewed Evaluation," in *CCAR Journal*: Winter 1993, pp. 1-11

10. This attenuation of Jewish identity in successive generations has been succinctly described by Barry Kosmin, executive of the Council of Jewish Federations: "There is a clear generational trend from Orthodox immigrants, to Conservative in the second generation, to Reform in the next generation, and to nothing by the fourth."

11. *Beyond Yiddishkeit: The Struggle for Jewish Identity in a Reform Synagogue* is an ethnographic study of a Reform synagogue now moving away from "ritual, tradition, and emotion" toward "universalism." Illustrative of its ideological stance is its critical attitude toward Israel and its continuous advocacy of affirmative action programs. Universalism and rationalism are seen as emptying a Jewish identity of its distinctiveness. The study concludes that "the emphasis on universalism cannot support a strong Jewish identity, rendering the Judaism taught in that synagogue little different from the ethically rooted, agnostic religions such as Unitarianism and Universalism." (Frieda Kerner Furman: *Beyond Yiddishkeit: The Struggle for Jewish Identity in a Reform Synagogue* [Albany, State University of New York Press, 1987])

12. Nathan Glazer, "On Jewish Forebodings," in *Commentary*, August 1985, pp. 34, 36

13. Seymour Martin Lipset and Earl Raab, *Jews and the New American Scene* (Cambridge: Harvard University Press, 1995)

14. Alfred L. Kroeber, *Anthropology* (New York: Harcourt Brace and Co., 1948), p.441

15. Shalom Spiegel, *Hebrew Reborn* (New York: Meridian Books, World Publishing Co., 1930) pp. 389-396

16. True of certain locutions in the Hebrew Bible.

17. Barbara W. Tuchman, "They Poisoned the Wells," in *Newsweek*, February 3, 1975, p.11

18. Jews are a diminishing population in all countries except in Israel and in Germany. Israel is experiencing the greatest Jewish population growth. Germany is the only Diaspora country where the number of Jews is increasing. The increase is substantial, a development that gives irony a bad name.

19. Nathan Glazer, "New Sociological Perspectives," in *American Jewish Yearbook* (Philadelphia: Jewish Publication Society, 1987), pp. 3-19

GLOSSARY

Acculturation. Process of interaction between two cultures resulting in varying degrees of mutual influence.

Ahava. "Love."

Aliya. "Ascent", "Going Up." Immigration to Israel. In the synagogue, going up to the reading platform to recite the blessing over the Torah.

Anti-Defamation League. Jewish civil defense organization formed by B'nai Brith to fight antisemitism.

Ashkenazim. Jews of North, Central, and Eastern Europe following a body of distinctive customs, practices and traditions.

Auto-da-fé. Public execution of heretics by burning at the stake by the Inquisition.

B'nei Brak. Town in Israel, center of religious study in ancient and modern times, occupied today preponderantly by ultra-Orthodox Jews.

Ba'al Teshuvah. "One who has returned." A penitent. A formerly non-observant Jew who returns to the practice and study of Judaism.

Balabatim. "Householders." Lay people.

Bar Mitzvah. "Son of the religious commandment." Rite of passage for a thirteen-year-old boy upon becoming a full-fledged member of the community.

Bat Mitzvah. Cognate recognition for a girl at age twelve.

Bereira. "Choice." Anti-Zionist organization of 1950's.

Bet Din. Rabbinical court of law with authority on conditions of personal status such as marriage and divorce.

Beta Israel. Ethiopian Jews.

Birkat Hagomel. "Blessing of redemption," recited after being delivered from danger or illness.

Bitahon. "Trust (in God)."

B'nai Brit. "Sons of the Covenant." Jewish fraternal order.

Brit Milah. "Covenant of Circumcision". Ritual circumcision of boy at eight days when he becomes a member of the Jewish people.

Central Conference of American Rabbis (CCAR). Principal organization of Reform rabbis founded in 1889.

Confirmation. Ceremony of modern Western Jewry, when teen-age (15-16 years) boys and girls make a group commitment to Judaism.

Conservative Judaism. Modern religious movement seeking to preserve tradition with modified Halacha.

Conversionary Marriage. Marriage between a Jew and a non-Jew converted to Judaism.

Converso. Spanish-Portuguese Jew converted to Judaism under duress.

Council of Jewish Federations (CJF). Association of Jewish philanthropic organizations.

Covenant. (Brit. Hebrew). A mutual pledge. The Covenant of Sinai, the fundamental relationship between God and the Jewish people.

Crypto-Jew. A Converso practicing Judaism in secret. Called Marrano by Christians.

D'var Torah. "Word of Torah." Oral interpretation of Torah topic or portion of the week.

Dati, Dati'im. (From "Torah Law.") Orthodox, devout.

Days of Awe. (yamim no'raim). Ten-day period from Rosh Hashana through Yom Kippur. Holiest days of the year.

Dhimmi. (Arabic). Inferior status of non-Muslim in Muslim society.

Diaspora. (Galut, golah). Dispersed Jewish communities outside the land of Israel.

Dybbuk. Soul of a sinner that enters and takes control of a living person. Kabbalistic concept.

Erev. "Evening." Eve of Shabbat or Holy Day beginning at sunset.

Exodus. Liberation of Children of Israel from Egyptian slavery. Second book of Bible.

Falashas. Ethiopians Jews. Beta Israel.

Galut, Golah. "Exile." Diaspora. Communities of Jews living outside the land of Israel.

Genizeh. "Hiding Place." Storeroom for old or damaged Hebrew books, documents, and ritual objects that may not be destroyed.

Get. "Divorce." Bill of divorcement issued by Bet Din.

Ghetto. In European cities, district in which Jews were required to live, often within walls and locked gates.

Goy(im). "Nation(s)." Colloquially, non-Jews.

Halacha (Halachot, Halachic). Jewish religious law.

Hallah. Bread baked in braided loaves for Sabbath and Holidays.

Halutz, Halutz(im). "Pioneer(s)." Early settler(s) in Israel working on the land.

Hanukah. "Dedication." Eight-day Festival of Lights commemorating the victory of the Maccabees over the Syrian Greeks, 2nd century B.C.E.

Haredi(m). "Pious," ultra-Orthodox Jew(s).

Haskalah. "Enlightenment." Movement in 19th-century Europe seeking to admit secular knowledge into Jewish life, and to apply modern scholarship to Jewish studies.

Hasidim. "Pious Ones". Members of pietist movements, especially followers of Rabbi Israel Ba'al Shem Tov, charismatic leading rabbi in Eastern Europe, c.1700-1760.

Havurah. "Fellowship." A small group of individuals formed to share Jewish study, observance, and companionship.

Hazan. "Cantor." Officient who chants the liturgy and leads the synagogue service.

Hebrew Union College (H.U.C.). Merged with Jewish Institute of Religion (J.I.R.) in 1950 (H.U.C.-J.I.R.). Reform seminary for training rabbis, cantors, educators, and communal workers, founded in 1875.

Heder. "Room." Small school for primary Jewish education.

Herem. "Ban." Excommuinication from the Jewish community.

Hesed. "Goodness," "Benevolence," "Love."

High Holidays. Rosh Hashanah (Jewish New Year) and Yom Kippur (Day of Atonement).

Hillel Foundation. Association for Jewish students on American college campuses, founded by B'nai Brit.

Hillul Ha-shem. "Desecration of the Divine Name." An act contrary to religious principle which impugns the honor of Judaism or the Jewish people.

Holocaust. Destruction of six million European Jews by the Germans in World War ll.

Humrot. "Stringencies." Strict religious practices.

Hutzpah. "Insolence." Effrontery, brazen nerve.

Inmarriage. Marriage of two Jews.

Intermarriage. Marriage of a Jew and a non-Jew.

Jewish Theological Seminary. Conservative seminary for training rabbis, cantors and educators, founded in 1886.

Jihad. (Arabic). A war of Muslims against unbelievers carried out as a religious duty.

Judenrein. "Free of Jews." (German). Goal of Nazi global assault on the Jewish people.

Kabbalah. "Receiving." Body of Jewish mysticism. Jewish mystical tradition.

Kaddish. "Sanctification." Oft-repeated prayer of praise to God in religious service. Recited also by mourners during year of mourning after death in the family and on the anniversary of death.

Kashrut. "Fit," "proper." Laws on eating and proper preparation of permissible foods.

Kedusha. "Sanctification." Liturgy of prayers in God's praise.

Kehilla. "Congregation." Of synagogue or community.

Ketuba. "Sanctification." Marriage contract.

Kiddush. "Sanctification." Prayer over sacramental wine on Sabbaths and festivals.

Kiddushin. "Sanctification." Jewish marriage and its laws.

Kippah. "Skullcap." Skullcap worn by observant Jews at all times. (Yarmulke — Yiddish).

K'lal Yisrael. "Entire community of Israel." The Jewish people collectively.

Knesset. "Assembly." Parliament of the State of Israel.

Kohen, Kohanim (pl.). "Priest(s)." Member(s) of highest hereditary religious caste who perform privileged ritual functions.

Kolel. "Comprehensive." Yeshivah for married men who receive family living stipends from the state and spend their days in study.

Liturgy. Forms of ritual prayer for public worship.

Lubavitch. Town in Belorussia which became center of influential Hasidic Habad movement (Lubavitcher Hasidim) founded by Shneour Zalman of Lyady in late 18th century. Present headquarters of international Habad movement is in Crown Heights, Brooklyn.

Matrilineal. Descent through the mother, the traditional criterion for identification as a Jew.

Mehitzah. "Partition." Partition, separation, between men's and women's sections in the traditional synagogue.

Menorah. "Lamp." Seven-branched candelabrum made for the wilderness Tabernacle and for the Jerusalem Temple. Now also the nine branched Hanukah candelabrum.

Mezzuzah. "Doorpost." Case containing small parchment scroll with verses from Torah, affixed to doorpost.

Midat hadin. "Quality of Justice," "Divine Justice," "Strictness."

Mikdash. "Holy." Sanctuary, Temple.

Mikdash Me'at. "Small sanctuary." The Jewish home.

Minyan. "Number." Quorum of ten adult Jewish males required for public worship.

Mitzvah. "Commandment." A religious duty commanded in the Torah; colloquially, a good deed.

Mixed marriage. Intermarriage between a Jew and a non-Jew.

Mohel. One who performs ritual circumcision.

Musar. Instruction, reproof.

Oleh (olim, pl.). "Ascender." Immigrant to Israel.

Orthodox. Living by beliefs and practices of traditional Judaism.

Patrilineal. Tracing descent through the father; not traditionally accepted for identification as a Jew but now accepted by Reform Jews.

Pesach. "Passover." Week-long festival commemorating the Exodus.

Pharisees. Rabbinical party, movement in Mishnaic times.

Pittsburgh Platform. 1885. Manifesto of principles of classical Reform Judaism.

Pluralism. Co-existence of various beliefs, denominations, cultures.

Pogrom. "Devastation" (Yiddish). Violent mass assault against Jews.

Posek (Poskim, pl.) "Arbiter." Rabbinic scholar who answers questions and decides in disputes over questions of Halacha.

Prophets. Biblical figures inspired to teach moral and ethical truths. Messengers to the people of the Divine Will.

Rabbi. "My master." Religious authority and teacher of Judaism. Religious leader of a congregation.

Rabbinical Alliance of America. Organization of Orthodox rabbis established in 1944.

Rabbinical Assembly of America. Association of American Conservative Rabbis. Organized in 1900.

Rebbe. Spiritual leader of a Hasidic community.

Rebbitzin. (Yiddish). Wife of rabbi.

Reconstructionism. Religious movement which regards Judaism as an evolving religious civilization, founded by Rabbi Mordecai M. Kaplan in 1934.

Religionskampf. Bitter religious conflict.

Responsa. Written answers by rabbinic authorities to questions of Jewish law.

Rosh Hashanah. "Head of the Year." Jewish New Year. One of the High Holidays.

Sadducees. Party, movement of priests and high-born in Second Temple period.

Samaritans. Dwellers in Samaria (N. Israel) who lived by Mosaic law.

Sanhedrin. Supreme court in ancient Israel.

Seder. "Order." Home ceremonial dinner on Passover eve.

Seder Pereida. "Ritual of release." Reform divorce ritual.

Sefer Torah. "Book of the Torah." Synagogue Scroll of the Law.

Sephardim. Jews of Spanish-Portuguese descent and tradition.

Seudah Sh'lishit. "Third meal." Synagogue repast following Sabbath afternoon service.

Shavuot. "Weeks," Festival of Weeks (Pentecost).

Sha'atnez. "Mixed stuff." Material of interwoven wool and linen, which Jews are forbidden to wear.

Shabbat. "Rest." The Sabbath, seventh day of week, when Jews are commanded to cease all labor; day of prayer, study, rest.

Shaliah. "Delegate." "Emissary" of Jewish Agency, who assists Jews to make aliya.

Shalom Bat. "Greeting (Peace) to a daughter." Birthday celebration for girl as observed by modern Orthodox.

Shanda. "Shame," Disrepute" (Yiddish).

Shehita. "Slaughter." Ritual slaughtering of animals as requirement for Kashrut, traditional dietary regulations.

Sheitl. "Woman's wig" (Yiddish). Wig worn by Orthodox matrons.

Shiva. "Seven." Seven days of mourning after a death in the family.

Sh'ma. "Hear." "Hear, O Israel" — Proclamation of God's unity. Central declaration of every religious service.

Shofar. "Ram's horn." Ceremonial ram's horn blown on the High Holidays and other solemn occasions.

Shtetl. "Small town" (Yiddish). Small town in Eastern Europe, (Pale of Settlement) inhabited by Jews.

Shul. "Synagogue" (Yiddish).

Shulkhan Arukh. "Prepared table." Authoritative code of Jewish law written and compiled by Joseph Caro (1564-5) in Safed.

Simhat Torah. "Rejoicing in the Law." Celebration in synagogue at conclusion of Sukkot festival when annual cycle of Torah reading is completed and begun again.

Sukkah. "Booth," Tabernacle." Flimsy, temporary structure erected for festival of Sukkot, where family eats in ritual setting.

Sukkot. "Booths." Joyous, week-long festival of the autumn harvest season.

Takkana. "Emendation," "Regulation." Supplement to laws of Torah enacted by sages or communal leaders to adapt Jewish life to changing conditions.

Tallit. "Prayer shawl." Worn by men in the synagogue for morning prayers.

Talmud. "Study," "Teach." Authoritative body of Jewish law and teaching compiled c.200 B.C.E. - 500 C.E.

Targum. "Translation." Aramaic translation of the Bible.

Tefilah. "Prayer."

Torah. "Law," "Doctrine," "Law of Moses." First five books of the Bible (Pentateuch); parchment scroll read at synagogue services; Jewish teaching.

Torah Umada. "Torah and Science." Guiding principle for Centrist Orthodox Jews.

Tefillin. "Phylacteries." Leather accessories worn on the head and arm by Orthodox men at weekly morning prayers.

Treifa. "Torn to pieces." Non-kosher, forbidden food.

Tsedaka. "Righteousness." Charity, philanthropy.

Tsena. "Austerity." Deprivation during first years of Israel's statehood, when because of lack of food and other basic commodities, Israelis found life difficult.

Union of American Hebrew Congregations (U.A.H.C.). Organization of Reform congregations, founded in 1873.

Yahadut. "Judaism," "Jewishness," Jewry.

Yeshiva. "Sitting." Institution for advanced Jewish study, especially of Talmud.

Yishuv. "Settlement." Jewish population in the Land of Israel.

Yom Kippur. "Day of Atonement." A High Holiday, holiest day of the Jewish year, given to prayer, fasting, and spiritual purification.

Yored, Yordim (pl.). "Descender." Emigrants from Israel.

Young Israel. Organization of young Orthodox Jews, founded in 1912 to advance observance and study of Orthodox Judaism.

Zemirot. "Songs." Songs sung at table during and after Sabbath and Festival meals.

Zionism. Modern political movement for re-establishment of the nation of Israel.

Zoroastrianism. Religious system taught by Zoroaster and disciples in ancient Persia, and still followed by Parsees.

Selected Publications of the Author

1983   *Washo Shamans and Peyotists: Religious Conflict in an American Indian Tribe.* University of Utah Press (Salt Lake City).

1978   *Saul Bellow in Search of Himself.* Journal of Reform Judaism. Spring 1978.

1986   *The Life and Times of Edward Sapir.* Jewish Social Studies. Vol. XLVII. Nos 3-4.

1987   *A Rabbi-Anthropologist in Israel.* Journal of Reform Judaism. Spring 1987.

   Transcendental and Folk Aspects of Judaism. Judaism: A Quarterly Journal of Jewish Life and Thought. Vol. 36, No. 3. Summer 1987.

1989   *George Herzog: A Peerless Musicologist Remembered.* American Jewish Archives. Vol. 41, No. 1.

1991   *Edward Sapir: Linguist, Anthropologist, Humanist.* By Regna Darnell. A Review. Language. Vol. 67, No. 3.

   Portrait of an Unsung Genius. Review Essay. American Jewish Archives. Vol. XLIII, No. 2.